INSIDE ACT

To Steven:
Thanks for all your
wonderful plays + for
making UNC proud!
All best,
[signature]

INSIDE ACT

How Ten Actors Made It—
and How You Can Too

Ken Womble

HANSEN PUBLISHING GROUP

Inside Act: How Ten Actors Made It and How You Can Too
Copyright © 2014 by Hansen Publishing Group, LLC

ISBN: (PAPER) 978-1-60182-059-4

ISBN: (EBOOK) 978-1-60182-060-0

Cover design by Matt Hansen.

Book interior design by Jon Hansen.

Hansen Publishing Group, LLC
302 Ryders Lane
East Brunswick, NJ 08816

http://hansenpublishing.com

For my wonderful wife Sandy who is always there for me,

For the passionate and brave souls who make acting their life

and

For all those who aspire to

Contents

Foreword

How? The three letters that define our early work as actors. How did those actors get in that film? How did they get that Broadway role? How did they get onstage at the Tyrone Guthrie Theatre?

How???

It seems to us as miraculous as if the goddess Athena had taken the golden stairway down from Olympus and was suddenly making us tea in our kitchen. And about as likely that it would ever happen to us.

Yes, we can read the ubiquitous business books for the actor about getting an agent and a manager and taking courses in voice, acting, and nailing the beer commercial, but they lack the truly human dimension that makes us understand.

So, read this book.

Two things become immediately clear: first, successful actors truly have remarkable talents. Second, they actually weren't sure they had them. What is also apparent is that whatever their appraisal of their own talents may be, they would walk through barbed wire in their skivvies to act. They move forward through good luck, ill fortune, unpleasant humans, and economic deprivation.

Will. The answer to how is *will*. Now there are out there, a very, very few golden creatures on whom the sky showers rubies and who scoot up the mountain as if they stood on an escalator. These unicorn-actors are so rare that they wouldn't make a book and would barely cover a postage stamp. Besides, they are unbelievably irritating to us. They are, frankly, not how it works.

The people and their careers in this book are exactly how it works, God bless them. They earn what they get in the face of adversity and a basically uncaring universe. They move forward and eventually luck just gives in to them—it has no other choice. And this forward movement over a career's rocky ground produces the best damn stories you can imagine (and some of the fiercest as well) and is, dare I say, inspiring and sustaining to the reader at the same time that it is brutally realistic.

Oh, there is one other thing. Just when they can't go another step, they meet the right person. Funny how that works. And this person magically knows where the right door is, and, with very little flourish, opens it and the iron will of our heroes begins to pay off.

Moral: keep slogging through the mud because the person who will open the door is definitely out there.

Now before you decide the foreword has been written by the rainbow-faerie, let me point out that for many their will or their talent, or both, is not sufficient.

But to find out which you are, you have to have the will to find out. I've seen many first rate talents who lacked the cojones to make the slog.

Will.

Have it or forget it.

JON JORY

Acknowledgments

This book is the result of a huge team effort. I couldn't have written it without the support of so many great friends and colleagues. From the bottom of my heart, I would like to thank:

The talented actors who shared your inspiring stories of struggle and ultimate success in the toughest business in the world—I admire you all.

The agents, managers, directors, coaches, composers, casting directors and producers who generously related your experiences about these actors.

Sandy Womble, my wife and toughest and best critic, who not only reworked chapter after chapter with me, but offered support and humor when my fears arose.

Jon Hansen, my publisher at Hansen Publishing Group, for liking what I wrote and for skillfully guiding me through my first book; Jody Hansen, at Hansen Publishing Group, for your valuable help in the editing process.

Victoria Morris, president of Lexikat Entertainment for all the actor introductions and for your guidance and advice since the beginning.

David Grapes, Chair of Theatre Arts and Dance at the University of Northern Colorado, for all the actor intros and for helping whenever I asked.

David Larson, television director and children's book author, for your literary skill that made my book proposal sing and for your ongoing support.

Jon Jory, iconic director, playwright and teacher, for writing such a marvelous foreword.

Stephen J. May, author of *Michener: A Writer's Journey*, for all the meetings at Starbucks to share your expertise on writing.

Dave Lefkowitz, co-publisher of *Performing Arts Insider*, for your advice and for reminding me of the value of brevity.

Danny Whitman, Director of Communications and Development at Broadway Cares / Equity Fights AIDS, for introducing me to so many wonderful actors.

Alicia Ruskin, Vice President at KMR Talent, for also introducing me to so many wonderful actors.

Dr. Andrew Svedlow of the University of Northern Colorado, for your strong support in securing my book grant. Annie Epperson, Michele Athanasiou and Lory Clukey of UNC's Faculty Research and Publication Board for approving—and then extending—my book grant.

Dan Satriana, UNC general counsel, for your expert legal advice. Tom McNally, UNC theatre head of performance, for your help in securing a key success team member. Nate Haas, of UNC public relations, for your assistance with marketing. My students at UNC, for your creative ideas.

Michael Larsen, literary agent and author of *How to Write a Book Proposal*, for teaching me how to do just that.

Vicki Duncan, of Duncan Business Services, for being the best transcriber I could hope for.

Shelly Munholland, Sherry May, Dr. Michele Schwietz, Dr. Mark Montemayor, Maria Lahman, Dr. Robbyn Wacker, Zachariah Tkachyk, Connie Willis, Georgia Buchanan and Bill Bowers, for your advice and assistance.

Greg Womble, my little brother, for your marketing expertise.

Mom, Jeana, Cornelia, Nancy and N.F. for your love and support.

The writers of the many acting business books from whom I've learned so much.

Introduction

The inspiration for this book arose from my work with aspiring professional actors.

I teach acting at the University of Northern Colorado, a midsized university in Greeley on the plains of northeastern Colorado. One of my courses is called Audition Techniques. In it, we explore various methods of auditioning and dig deep into the acting business. My students are passionate about acting and want to know everything they can about the business before taking the plunge into it. And I want to help them.

One of their biggest questions is always, "Why do some actors make it and others don't?"

That question has also fascinated and tormented me ever since I gave up my own pursuit of acting as a profession.

I had worked quite a bit as an actor—two Off Broadway plays, four recurring roles on soaps, night time TV and independent films—and had studied with two of the finest acting teachers in the country. I had an agent, good audition skills, great headshots and had been told I was talented with "a good look."

Yet I hadn't fulfilled my definition of "making it" by consistently earning a living as an actor. I still loved acting, but after sixteen years in New York and Los Angeles, I felt it was time to let go and try something else.

When I started teaching and directing, acting took a backseat. As time passed teaching became my new passion. Yet, I still hadn't found the answer to my question, "Why do some actors make it and others don't?"

So, I set out to find it.

After a good deal of research and consideration I decided to write a book, a book that would feature the people who would probably know the answer—working actors.

I wanted to interview a variety of successful actors, listening to each one's story and focusing on critical moments and turning points.

Good, but I wanted to take things a step further. I would also speak with the people who knew the actors and their work because they could see the actors from the outside, they could be more objective, so I decided to interview their agents, managers, directors and coaches.

Then from all these interviews, I would identify the most frequently used actions, skills, and beliefs—the keys to these actors' success.

Aspiring actors would learn, once and for all, the answer to the question: "Why do some actors make it and others don't?" And they would be able to use that answer to create acting careers themselves.

This book is about what sets successful actors apart. It's about the inner choices, the inside acts of working actors, acts that have propelled them to thriving careers in one of the most competitive professions on the planet.

I hope their journeys will inspire you to take your own unique journey as an actor, to also experience the profound passion, and joy that being a successful, working actor can bring.

INSIDE ACT

DEBRA MONK

CHAPTER 1

Whatever is Necessary

DEBRA MONK

Emmy and Tony Award-winner Debra Monk has appeared on film in: *This Is Where I Leave You* (Fall 2014), *Reaching Home, One For the Money, Ass Backwards, The Great Buck Howard, The Savages, Palindromes, Center Stage, Devil's Advocate, In & Out, Extreme Measures, The Bridges of Madison County, Jeffrey,* and *Fearless.*

She has starred on Broadway in *Cat on a Hot Tin Roof, Curtains* (Drama Desk Award, Tony nomination), *Chicago, Reckless, Thou Shalt Not; Ah, Wilderness!, Steel Pier* (Tony nomination), *Company; Picnic* (Tony nomination), *Redwood Curtain* (Tony Award), *Nick and Nora,* and *Pump Boys and Dinettes* (Coauthor, Tony Nomination).

On television, she has appeared as George's mother on *Grey's Anatomy,* Ellen's mother on *Damages,* Will Schuester's mother on *Glee,* and Elizabeth Burke's mother on *White Collar.* She has also guest-starred on: *Reckless, Girls, Brothers and Sisters, Ghost Whisperer, The Closer, Notes from the Underbelly, Desperate Housewives, Law and Order, Frasier* and appeared in the TV movies: *Good Luck, Charlie: It's Christmas!, The Music Man, Eloise at the Plaza, Eloise at Christmastime, Ellen Foster,* and *Redwood Curtain* (reviving her Tony-winning performance).

She won the Emmy Award for Outstanding Guest Actress in a Drama Series for her portrayal of Katie Sipowicz on *NYPD Blue.*

Ken Womble: *Debra, what caused the first spark of interest that you had in becoming a performer?*

Debra Monk: I had never seen a play. We were lower middle class—to go to a movie was a big deal, so I was really a television kid, and I thought all I was going to do was marry my high school sweetheart and have kids and be a housewife. And lo and behold, he didn't ask me to marry him, and I was lost. So I became a secretary.

At the time they needed teachers really bad, and if you said you would teach, your education was free. So all I had to pay for was my expenses. In college everybody had to take speech class, and the guy who taught the class was also one of the theatre folk; his name was Dr. Press. And I did a speech, and afterwards he pulled me aside and said, "Would you like to audition for my play?" And I said, "I've never seen a play. I don't know what plays are." And he said, "Well audition," and it was *The Birthday Party* and to this day I don't know what the hell it's about. But I auditioned for it, and I got the part of Lu Lu.

And Dr. Press said "You're just not ready to go to New York, you need to study. You probably won't work, and you need to have your graduate degree so you can teach." I said, "Okay."

That's when I applied to SMU and Yale; I got into SMU and was really well-trained.

I came to New York and basically for four years couldn't get a job, couldn't get an agent. But I worked as a waitress, and I kept a little diary. I'd never written anything in my life, and I met this great gal named Cass Morgan, and she was trained as a singer. I was trained as an actress. She wanted to learn more about acting; I wanted to learn more about singing. So we decided let's write a little something for ourselves.

And we started to write this story about these two gals who were waitresses. Her husband was working on a thing about these gas station attendants, so we combined forces and it became *Pump Boys and Dinettes.*

When we first did it, we put the money into it ourselves because we didn't have any producers. We started it Off Off Broadway, and a year later we were on Broadway.

And, by the way, we did a year on Broadway, and I could not get an agent. Nobody would take me seriously because I was singing country western.

I couldn't get another job and got offered to do yet another production of *Pump Boys* in a mall in Minnesota or Milwaukee or someplace, I can't remember. I thought, "Oh my God, I'm going to be doing this show for the rest of my life, and I don't have an agent."

One of the gals in the show had an agent, and she kept flying back and forth to New York on her day off and auditioning for all these things and I was so jealous.

One of the places I always wanted to work was the Actors Theatre of Louisville. So on my day off I flew myself there. They sent me up to Cory Madden, the assistant to Jon Jory, the artistic director, and I said "I want to audition." And she said, "Well you can't do that, we only go through agents." I said "I don't have an agent. I flew myself in from—" wherever the hell I was—"Can I just do my audition for you?"

So I did my audition for her. And she said, "I can't do anything for you." I said "I understand, but just listen to me. If there's anything, I'll fly myself back. I don't have an agent but this is what I want to do."

So cut to a couple months later. Jon was coming in to New York to replace, sadly, a wonderful actress who was killed in a car accident, and as he was leaving his assistant said, "Well, you might want to see this woman, Debra Monk."

So I got a call to come to audition and I got the part.

KW: *What was the show?*

DM: *The Undoing*, a new play. And I ended up going to Louisville for the Humana Festival and then to the short festival, and I was there five or six months out of the year working, doing lead roles. And during my first show the agents I ended up signing with came, saw me in that show, and signed me. So that's how I found an agent.

KW: *Was that the Gage Group?*

DM: Yeah. I couldn't get an agent when I was on Broadway, but when I was in Kentucky, I got an agent.

KW: *It sounds like the Actors' Theatre of Louisville really created some breakthroughs for you?*

DM: Totally. I met Jon Jory, who's an incredible director, and a great mentor of mine, and a great teacher. He was the first one to really believe in me as an actress and kept casting me in these parts that I would never get in New York at that time because I wasn't known at all. So it was a great place to meet other actors, other directors, other great playwrights, and people who were just starting out. I remember John Turturro was just starting out. Oh, my God! Kathy Bates was there.

KW: *Has it also been your training ground?*

DM: I have to say I was really well trained when I left SMU. What they gave me at Louisville was a chance to use that training, a chance to do it. I was a brand new actor, so I needed to fail, to learn how to have courage, to learn how to try a scene and for it not to work—you know what I mean? I think it takes years and years and years of doing it, over and over and over until you start to really start to feel confident about what you can do.

KW: *I don't think a lot of actors would've done what you did by spending your own money and going down to Louisville to audition.*

Was that a big act of faith?

DM: It was an act of desperation. I didn't know what else to do. I couldn't get an agent. I was on Broadway for a year! I just decided to take a chance and to go there. It really was just not knowing what to do and going "Well, how am I going to do this?"

What I've learned about this business is never to have unrealistic expectations about what will happen next. You just have to do your best work and be open to what you might have to do to get that next job, meaning you might have to audition even though you don't want to audition, or you might have to go meet somebody.

I mean the expectation is if I do this enough they will know what I can do, and they will just offer me a job.

Well that isn't always true, you know? It's certainly not true in television and movies where the producers get younger and younger, so they don't really know who you are.

Nothing has ever come that easy. I've had to work really hard for everything, and I've had to bide my time for everything. But not like, bam, because I did that show, it equaled all this stuff. It never was like that for me.

KW: *Why do you think that has been the case?*

DM: I have no idea. I mean I've won Emmys, I've won a Tony, I've done all these things, and it still doesn't necessarily equate that you are going to get the next part.

I was at the Actors Theatre of Louisville for three seasons and I thought, I can stay in Actors Theatre of Louisville heaven for the rest of my life and just do all these wonderful plays. But if I really want to do New York, I've got to go back and face New York.

So I decided to go back.

And one of the first weeks I was back, a wonderful guy named Mark Hardwick, who was a cocreator of *Pump Boys*, called me up and was working on this music from Lawrence Welk, which we loved by the way. And I play the drums, so he said, "Deb, can we come over and play some of this funny Lawrence Welk music?"

And meanwhile I got a call, because of *Pump Boys,* to come and sing at a benefit. And I thought, "Oh God, I don't want to sing by myself." And I called back and said, "You know, we're working on some of this really funny music, can we bring the group with us, there's four of us?" And we were working on this rendition of *Exodus,* and we did it at this benefit and people laughed hysterically. And so we thought "Oh, my God, we're on to something."

So, immediately we started working on this. And we decided they were four kind of band nerds from high school who everybody thought were going to be really successful and then, cut to after high school, and none of them made it. One became a mailman, one became a housewife, one became a secretary, and they are getting together for a ten-year reunion, and they're going to honor their music teacher.

And that was the basis of *Oil City Symphony*. It was a really sweet, lovely, funny show and it ran for a year Off Broadway [winning a Drama Desk and an Outer Critic's Circle Award for best Off Broadway musical].

And now I'm back doing another musical and I thought, "I'll never be able to be an actress here. I'm just going to be doing these shows that I write, that's all I can do."

And while I was doing *Oil City Symphony*, I auditioned for Playwrights Horizons and I got cast in this play which Don Scardino directed, and because of that, from then on I started doing plays.

KW: *You appeared in Lanford Wilson's* Redwood Curtain *on Broadway in 1993. Tell me about that.*
DM: There was a repertory theatre in New York, Circle Rep Company, and I always wanted to work rep, but I could not get an audition because they had their company. And I found out

from someone that they had a lab, the Circle Rep Lab, another group of actors who could do readings.

So I auditioned for the Lab, and I got into it and was asked to do a reading of *Prelude to a Kiss;* I played Mary-Louise Parker's mom. And they said to me, "You're just too young to play that part" [in a full production].

And I said, "Oh, that's too bad, but you know I could wear a wig." And I got cast in it.

And we did it Off Broadway at Circle Rep and then we moved to Broadway and that became my first Broadway play. But the only way I got that was to audition for the Lab.

Lanford Wilson saw me in *Prelude to a Kiss,* and afterwards I got sent a copy of *Redwood Curtain* with a letter from Lanford saying, "I wrote this play with you in mind; read it, and let me know what you think." He wrote a play for me! And I won a Tony for it.

And like I said, I just auditioned for the Lab! If I hadn't, he would never have written a play for me. So it was a very, very, very, very special experience.

KW: *Do you still audition for plays and musicals?*
DM: For the most part I don't audition for plays and musicals. I mean, I do and will if it's a director that I don't know, who's never seen me.

KW: *When you do audition for plays and musicals how did you prepare for them?*
DM: Well, first I read the play to see if it's a part that I feel I'm right for that I really want to do. I like to memorize the scene, but I hold the script. If I have questions, I will call my agent and he will then call the casting people with my questions like "Where is she from? Is there an accent?"

I think it's really important for actors to only audition for things that they're right for. Although, when you're a young actor you want to audition for almost everything, even if you're not right for it. So I think it's really important to read it and say, "Can I really do this?"

You want to find out where this is going to be playing? How long is your commitment? All those things. Otherwise you're just wasting everybody's time and your own.

The only acting class I ever took besides SMU was an improv class, and it was one of the great, great classes I'd ever taken because in improv you have to make a bold choice. And it really taught me to go into an audition, make a choice that is truthful and right for the piece, but a bold choice.

Before that I always was trying to figure out what they might want. You cannot act when you're sitting there thinking, "What do they want, what do they want?"

And my little trick, which always works, is I go in and say, "I've worked on this, so I'll show you what I have and then if you want me to try something else, I will." That always lets them know right away, one, you've worked on it; two, you're ready to have them direct you.

I try to be really well prepared. If it's a play that is performing in New York and you're going in as a replacement, I think it's really important to go see the play. I can't tell you, from being on the other side of the table when we did *Pump Boys and Dinettes,* how many people came in and didn't know what the play was about. Hadn't seen it. Hadn't read it. The more knowledge you have about it, the better.

KW: *Do you come in with a performance for an audition?*
DM: Well I don't think you *can* come in with a performance. I come in really well prepared with the scene. If it's a secretary or a businesswoman, I dress in a suit. If it's a mom, I try to dress in something a little more casual. You're reading with a reader, so

it's hard to do it like what you would in the play. But I try to do as realistic and as full as I can.

KW: *Could you briefly describe an audition where you felt like everything was working perfectly and you just nailed it?*
DM: When I auditioned for a recurring part on *White Collar* to play Tiffani Thiessen's mother, it was described as a wholesome, yet elegant mom. The scene was very sweet, about a mother and father coming to visit, and they were bringing her a birthday present. I've played this kind of a part a lot. I recur on *Damages, Grey's Anatomy,* and *Glee.* I've done a lot of moms.

So I went in knowing that this was something I could do. I walked in to the audition, I sat down, and they said, "Oh, my God! You look just like Tiffani Thiessen; you could totally be her mother." So I knew I had one thing going for me.

In the scene my son-in-law is an FBI guy, and they had this running joke that every time he would see her he'd say, "Put your hands up," kind of as a joke, and then I would sing that song "Bad boys, bad boys, what ya' gonna do" from *Cops.* So I looked it up online to see how the whole song went and at the audition I sang more of it, which was much funnier.

I decided to make a bold choice and go in and really do her. So when I finished it, they were laughing; they really loved it. They asked me to come back and make an adjustment at the end. So I made the adjustment; instead of being really sweet and nice, I got a little bit weary of him.

So I thought the audition went well because, one, they said "Boy, you look like her;" two, they seemed to be really happy to see me and knew of my work; three, I prepared really well and made a bold choice; and four, I was able to take a direction and do what they wanted.

For me, that was a good audition and I got the part!

KW: *It's amazing to me that you've done over a dozen Broadway shows, half of them musicals and half of them straight plays. I think that really speaks to your versatility as a performer and it's very unusual today.*

DM: It's incredibly unusual. I'm very, very, very lucky. That's all I can say. I have so many friends who are incredible actors who got cast in musicals and really had a hard time ever getting in a play. And I've had friends who were in plays who can't get into musicals.

KW: *Why do you think other very talented actors don't work nearly as much as you? What do you think you're doing right in that way?*

DM: I don't know. I don't understand that. I don't know if it's the timing, I really don't know what makes some people be able to work more than others. Every part that I audition for, I could name at least ten other actresses who could do it.

Part of it is your talent, part of it is the timing, part of it is what you look like, and part of it is totally random. I don't know! It's crazy.

KW: *How important has type been for you? And if it has played a role, has it been more positive or negative?*

DM: Type to me is about what you're capable of doing. Some people are only known for doing dramas. Some people can only do comedy or feel more comfortable in a comedy.

What I have found is the casting people and the directors don't always have the imagination that—if they're looking for a blonde and you're a brunette—they don't really think "Oh my God I could put a blonde wig on that person and make her a blonde."

I've been cast a lot as the big ballsy singer, and yet I also play kind of sweet moms. So I think you have to know what your range can be, and if you want to go against it. I've done big belty songs, and if I want to go in and be thought of as a soprano in something, then I'd better come in with an audition that shows that I can really sing that.

If you want to go against type, you then have to prove that you can do something you've never done.

KW: *Do you feel that in theatre you've been cast in a wider range of roles than in film and TV?*
DM: Well, I don't know. I've done everything in film and television from jail wardens to sweet moms. I've gotten to play a lot of different parts.

I might want to play a British aristocrat, and my agent will submit me to the casting people and they'll say, "Well, no, we don't think of Deb as that." And then I will say, "Please, please, please, I'd like to audition, get me an audition." And I will come in trying to prove that I can play that.

But the casting people want to cover their asses too because their job is to bring in people that their director is going to love. So they don't want to necessarily bring in somebody who may not be what they're supposed to be, and then they look bad in front of the directors. See how it works? It's all tricky.

For theatre there's probably a little more leeway in trying to see if you can do something. But a lot of times they have such specifics. They want to do everything that's going to make it easier for them.

And if they know you fit into that slot it's so much easier if you just come in and fit into that slot. So, for the most part people know what I can do and I get calls for those parts.

KW: *What's your best quality as an actor?*
DM: I'm fearless. It's something that I didn't always have as a young actress. I was so scared, "Will they like me? Will I be doing it right?" You can't do anything when you're in a state of fear. This took me years to get to. That does not mean that I'm not afraid opening nights or I don't get nervous and, you know, you have these doubts about yourself.

But I will go to an audition, I will go to rehearsal, I will go to the TV set, I will go to the movie set, and I will go out there and try, and not be afraid. "Oh my God, are they going to like me? Why was that cameraman looking away? Why aren't they laughing?" All those things that can make you kind of crazy, I worked really hard to let them go and just go in and do my job.

KW: *It seems like that would be more enjoyable, too.*

DM: Totally! I mean you're having fun. It's not like trying to find a cure for cancer. And you're right. I think if you can go in with no fear, you will have fun and you will learn and you will grow. You can go beyond what you think you might have been able to go beyond.

KW: *How do you think you got past that fear?*

DM: It didn't just happen in a show. I've worked and worked and worked and worked, and the more you work, you start to have more confidence. You're less fearful because you have more confidence.

I was never a big, huge singer and all of a sudden I just let go of the fear, and I had this big old belting thing that happened. And part of that was because I got cast in *Steel Pier,* and I was with the incredible John Kander and Fred Ebb who are the nicest people in show business and were great coaches. They really helped me learn and gave me the support and confidence that I could do this.

And then I had that incredible song, "Everybody's Girl." I never knew I could sing a song like that. And then I did.

Part of it is just the opportunities I've had and accepting that I'm going to work. Most likely I will get a job. So, you start to have confidence and then you can say, "I can do this."

KW: *How important is your belief in yourself as a performer?*

DM: It's crucial. I think part of the belief in yourself comes from the knowledge of what you really can do. If you need a sweet, funny mom, I'm your gal. If you need a ball busting, tough gal or a southern gal, I'm your gal. There are certain things that I know I can do.

So when you have an audition, or you're asked to do a part, you go in with a sense of confidence because you know you can do that kind of a part.

So I think confidence comes from the knowledge and the experience of what you know you can do and what you can't do, combined with an acceptance from other people.

KW: *You're also exceedingly talented. How important has that been for you?*
DM: Well, I think it's important for everybody. You have to have talent and you have to have luck. I think those things go hand in hand.

My wonderful professor, Dr. Press, who by the way has seen every show I've done since college, said to me, "You have passion for this! But you need training." What I knew as a kid was that I was funny. So I think talent is really important; I just wasn't aware that I had it! [*Laughs*]

I think somebody could be incredibly talented, but you never see it because they don't come off well in the audition, or they need the environment for their talent to be nurtured. I've heard people say, "Oh God, she doesn't audition well." So she doesn't get the job. It's interesting what gives one person a chance to do this and another person not.

KW: *It seems to me you just have to keep going through the fear.*
DM: Yeah. I think so too.

KW: *What are perhaps one or two of the smartest things you've done for your career, and if you could go back and change one or two things, what would they be?*

DM: The smartest thing I've ever done was go to graduate school to be trained. I wasn't ready to come to New York. And it was good for me to be in that environment in Texas. All I had to do was study. I think if I'd come here and tried to work I don't know if I could've done it.

I don't have anything I'd change. There is nothing that I've ever accepted or turned down that I wish I had done. I really believe that things happen when they're supposed to happen.

KW: *I've heard it said about the acting profession that if you have a fallback plan, you'll fall back. Do you believe that?*
DM: I don't know if I agree with that. Friends of mine have taught and have kept working. Marian Seldes is one of the great actresses of all time, and she taught for years at Julliard.

But I never thought of a fallback plan. I tried to save my money to live in a way that's good. I've never spent a lot of money on things because I wanted to save that money so that if I didn't get a job I could hold out until I got something. I don't have children; I don't have big expenses.

I have always been driven by the fact that I love acting, and the minute I don't love this anymore I'm not going to do it.

When I wrote *Pump Boys*, it was because I just wanted to work. I never wrote it thinking, "Okay, now my fallback plan is I'm going to write something for myself." I never think of it as a fallback plan. I just think of it as a forward-thinking plan, and if it doesn't work out for me or I don't like it anymore, then I'll figure out something else to do.

KW: *All the statistics tell us that acting is an incredibly difficult profession. At any given time there are far more actors out of work than are working. However, you've defied these odds, enjoying quite a bit of success. How have you done it?*

DM: I don't know what makes one person able to succeed in this and another person not, especially if they have the same training, the same talent.

I think I wasn't willing to give up. Like I said, I was fearless. For example, I don't know what made me, at that audition for Dr. Hobgood [at Southern Methodist University] get on my knees and say, "You've got to take me. You've got to put me into graduate school."

What made me fly myself to Actors Theatre of Louisville and audition when nobody else would do that? You know? What made me audition for Circle Rep?

Sometimes actors say, "Well they *should* be asking me to do this. Why should I audition?" Or, "I'm not going to fly there. I've never done that." I've said, "You know what? They're not asking me. My phone's not ringing. So I either have the choice to sit here and wait for somebody to call, or get off my ass and fly myself to the Actors Theatre of Louisville and audition myself."

I will go the extra mile. I will be really prepared. I'm always on time for my auditions. I'm really nice to everybody.

My job is to show up, do my work and try not to cause a problem. So I think that I have a sense of how to fit in, what to do. But at the same time, I'm not afraid to go for it and do things that some of my friends might say they're not going to do.

There are certain things I will not do as well. I don't want to work with a director who is a mean person. I have no desire—I don't care how famous they are—to be in a situation where I feel like people are being hurt with some type of psychodrama thing. Life's too short. I'd rather not do the show.

KW: *I think that's great.*

DM: What I'm most proud of is I had willingness, I had passion, and I had desire to do this, and I was able to humble myself and do things a lot of other people weren't.

To be on Broadway, in *Pump Boys and Dinettes* and not get an agent, that could have driven many people out of the business. I was upset about it, but I thought, "Okay, I have to keep going." Because I wasn't willing to give it up. So then you either leave the business, or you sit around angry and bitter, or you say, "What else can I do?" You know, those are the questions you have to ask.

KW: *That sounds very healthy, physically and emotionally.*

DM: Well it is, because what you can say at the end of the day is, "I tried."

When I was first starting to get movies and my agent, Phil Adelman, was negotiating things I said, "Well, do you think we could ask?" He said, "Yes. Hey Deb, it never hurts to ask." And it was a great thing because you just have to be prepared to hear a no. That's all.

I know the worst thing is to never ask, to never try and then to always regret. And if it didn't happen, okay. So what's next?

Debra Monk Success Team Member

JON JORY

Ken Womble: *Jon, you were a pioneer in the early days of the American Regional Theatre Movement and then artistic director of the Actor's Theatre of Louisville, and you're a widely published playwright as well. It's an honor to speak with someone who has contributed so much to the American theatre.*

Jon Jory: Oh that's very kind of you, Ken. Thank you.

KW: *Debra told me the story of auditioning at Actor's Theatre of Louisville. What do you think the story says about her?*
JJ: I don't really remember the history. What I do know is that when I finally did see her I hired her on the spot.

KW: *Really?*
JJ: Yeah. I think this was the first time I employed her. A member of our company, a very fine actress named Susan Kingsley, was about to appear in the Humana Festival playing the lead in the play and Ms. Kingsley went away on a vacation and driving back from that vacation was killed in a car accident.

KW: *That's tragic.*
JJ: Yes. This was a very difficult actress to replace. She had a very strong country personality, rural personality; she was extremely sharp and had tremendous presence. And so I was very worried.

And when I saw Debra it was literally like the clouds had opened and she had descended. Because she had this odd combination of qualities which Ms. Kingsley had. And I believe Debra had to replace her immediately. I think we were going into rehearsal in a couple of days.

And it was ironically, given the circumstances, a play about a man who had committed a hit and run accident killing another man and had sought out his wife without telling her what had happened to try to make amends to her.

KW: *That's kind of scary.*
JJ: Yeah it was a little scary.

KW: *It sounds like she was perfect for the role.*
JJ: She was not only perfect for the role, but this woman had been in our company for some time. She was dearly beloved. And I think it was a very difficult human situation—not only acting

situation—for Debra to walk into. And her immense warmth and concern for other human beings, her delicacy in understanding, her ability to create ensemble in the most difficult of situations was as important as her obvious talent.

KW: *What was your first impression of her?*
JJ: My first impression of her was a combination of toughness and warmth, a very hard combination to find in actors. You can find one or the other, but you don't often find them put together.

We were a southern theatre, and we did quite a number of southern plays. And because of the way the south is made up, there are a lot of plays dealing with rural lives. And there are very few first-rate American actors who can do that. There are a lot of them who can imitate it, but there are very few people who can embody it, and Debra is one of them.

KW: *Do you think if she hadn't been right for the role but had done a good audition that you would have remembered her?*
JJ: Oh sure. I mean Debra's work was extremely striking. You know, I think of acting as a decathlon event. It's not just that you have to excel in the hurdles; you also have to do the shot put and the pole vault. And what is apparent about Debra is not simply her talent, but the range of skills that make up her talent.

I think the pool of A+ actors is actually quite small. I would say probably well under 500. So if you waltz into a regional theatre somewhere, you work with A+ talents, but you certainly don't work with a bunch of them at once. And I think it's apparent about Debra almost immediately, in auditions or even having a meal with her, that she is an A+ talent.

KW: *She told me her work at Actors Theatre was a real breakthrough for her as an actress, I think both artistically and professionally, because she got to do all these wonderful plays.*

JJ: Debra did a lot of work with us and was sort of a de facto member of our ensemble.

KW: *She said you were first person to really believe in her as an actress.*
JJ: Well, listen, that is complimentary beyond my wildest dreams. I don't, you know, wander around with a t-shirt that says "mentor." I just went about my work and she was a wonderful part of that work, and I probably learned as much from her as she learned from me.

KW: *As you know, Debra doesn't audition often for theatre now, but she always auditions for film and television.*
JJ: Right.

KW: *And I asked her what are some of the things that she does—or she thinks are necessary in auditions—and she said she makes bold choices.*
JJ: That's interesting. Making bold choices is, of course, crucial. What is crucial to the bold choice is your ability to back that up psychologically.

KW: *Ah.*
JJ: There are a lot of people who make bold choices and then you wish they would go home.

KW: *[Laughs]*
JJ: The point is that she's capable of making the bold choice that reveals the psychology of the role. And I'm sure that's one of the reasons she gets cast in film as often as she does.

KW: *That's very interesting. I had never thought of it like that because you do have to back it up, it can't just be a randomly bold choice.*

JJ: Oh, you have to back it up inside the context of the play. That's why I say she has good dramaturgical sense. I mean that word can be off-putting, but on a much simpler level she just knows what it's about and she makes a bold choice within that context.

KW: *Do you think that's instinctual with her?*
JJ: Yes, yes. You know, there's another reason. Actors get hired, but a lot of actors don't get re-hired. And really a career in this business, as sort of multifarious as it is, is based on getting re-hired. And Debra is re-hired because it is a pleasure to go through the creative process with her.

She makes you feel good about your contribution. She is entirely open to ideas from others. She appreciates other talents. Not only does she deliver what you need of the role, but she makes it much easier for everybody else to do good work.

KW: *It seems like a lot of actors, one way or another, shoot themselves in the foot.*
JJ: Oh absolutely. The theatre is almost precisely like a small town. And word gets around. You know?

When I do auditions, I often have a sense that there's something a little odd about this person's social skills in the audition. And the first thing I do is pick up their résumé and call the last three places they have worked. So, you know, once you hit the postman with the frying pan the word is out.

I'm not privy to most of the places Deb works, but I can't imagine she gets anything but good press: (a) she can do the job and (b) she does the job so that others can do their job.

KW: *Wow, great quality, and in my experience rare as well.*
JJ: Yes.

KW: *Debra has been a working actor for over thirty years and she continues to work at a high level: over a dozen Broadway plays, many regional theatre plays, and lots of film and television. What else do you see in her as a person and a performer that's kept her going for long?*

JJ: Well, she obviously has star quality which has been most visible at the highest level on the Broadway musical stage. It's a quality that, when demanded, takes over and says ,"this is mine now." And that's necessary to playing large roles in highly visible situations.

And the second thing about that quality is it doesn't seem forced. She just takes over. We read about this in many professions, particularly in moments of crisis, and I think nothing is more a moment of crisis than a big number on the musical stage.

She doesn't demand more than what would be her share of the time in a rehearsal process. I work with a lot of actors who take waaaay more than the amount of time I can give them. Some actors will be pulling me aside; they have one scene in the play and you would think that they were playing *King Lear*. Debra doesn't do that. When she needs help she asks for it—but she asks for help, she doesn't ask for attention.

KW: *So it sounds like it's all in service of the work.*
JJ: That is correct.

KW: *How important a role do you believe that type, that sometimes dirty word, has played for Debra?*
JJ: I don't really know the answer to that question. I'm tenuous about this because I don't really have a clue what Deb's type is.

KW: *I think it's hard to pin down because she's played so many things.*
JJ: That's correct. I think, by now, she has way transcended any type she used to be.

KW: *I think in television and film she's typed a bit more than on stage.*

JJ: And what would you say that type is?

KW: *She told me she plays moms with sort of an attitude and also very sweet moms, both extremes.*

JJ: Well now you hit on an interesting point. Debra can make extremes seem dimensional. And a lot of people when they play extremes they're playing only one or two qualities. She humanizes the extreme while allowing it to exist.

KW: *What are some of her best qualities?*

JJ: She has a completely unforced charm. That has enormous impact because she isn't working at it. Debra just *has* it. Very often in musical work there is a falloff in terms of your perception of the talent once the song is over. And with Debra there's no falloff.

She also has an innate sense of what the important part is. Whether it's the important part of a speech or the important part of a scene or the important part of the play, do you know? And she can sense what the moments are that have to be in place to make the role work. Now there are other actors who know where their moments are, but they can't necessarily deliver them. She has both qualities.

KW: *How important a role has talent and belief in herself played for Debra?*

JJ: I think Debra's interested in the problem in front of her. Is she understanding the problem? But I don't think she internalizes that in terms of belief in herself. I think Debra basically believes that if she can understand the problem, she can solve the problem.

So I don't know what part in that belief in yourself plays. I would assume her ability to put herself in highly visible circumstances in the theatre and film implies belief in herself.

KW: *All of the statistics tell us that acting is an incredibly difficult profession. At any given time there are far more actors out of work than are working. However, Debra has defied these odds, enjoying quite a bit of success in her career. How has she done it?*
JJ: Well, I don't mean to satirize the question, but she's done it by being so good at it that people have to hire her!

KW: *Ah. That's a perfect answer. Because it seems to me that sometimes actors who are successful are not always necessarily the best at it.*
JJ: No, that's true. But that usually impairs their longevity.

And also Debra is no snob. You know, Deb is playing with her name above the title on Broadway one month and she's playing a one scene part on television the next month. And I don't think she sees any difference. I think one of the crucial things that this brings up is she has a healthy ego. People who don't have healthy egos can be very easily destroyed or stretched out of shape by the profession.

KW: *Well it seems like it would be constant. She would constantly be out of shape.*
JJ: Yes, exactly, because some people don't like that. If they have the star dressing room one week, they don't like it when nobody's paying attention to them on the set the next week.

I don't think Deb thinks about that. She thinks about herself as an actor. She does things that interest her. And she does them all well.

Debra Monk Success Team Member

STEVEN UNGER

Ken Womble: *Steven you're an agent at the Gage Group, a bicoastal talent agency. Could you tell me a bit about your company and the mediums you work in?*
Steven Unger: Sure. We work in theatre, film, and television. Martin Gage started the company here in New York in 1973. He moved to LA and opened up an LA office in 1975. I have been here since 1981. We have people starring on Broadway, on sitcoms, in movies; we have series regulars. We work in all mediums.

KW: *When you first met Debra what was your impression of her?*
SU: Oh, very funny, very personable. And I think with actors the first time they go into an audition or meeting with an agent or a producer or a director, that audition or meeting begins the minute they walk in the room. And Debra's personality has made her one of the most liked people in the business.

Here in New York, on Broadway, everybody loves Deb. When she goes out to LA and she's on a set of a movie or of a TV show, people always call back and go, "Oh my God, she's so great." I think that she is just so real, and that's part of the charm of Debra Monk.

KW: Pump Boys and Dinettes, *I think you would agree, was her first break as an actor.*
SU: Oh, absolutely.

KW: *Would you say* Redwood Curtain *was also a turning point for Debra since she won the Tony Award for Best Featured Actress in a Play?*
SU: Absolutely, because from then on in she was "Tony Award winner, Debra Monk," and not just "great actress Debra Monk."

KW: *She's also won an Emmy Award, a couple of Drama Desks—just about every major award except for an Oscar. However, she told me that she's had to work hard for everything's she's gotten. Why do you think that's the case?*
SU: I think this is not an easy business. Everybody has to work hard.

I think working hard is also choosing the right properties. And I will tell you that we have taken jobs that may not have been the money job, but they might have been the right career job. And I think that's something that a lot of people get blindsided with also: "I could do this play and I could make all this money," or "I could do this great role in a movie and make, for a week, less money." But that movie will lead to better opportunities.

KW: *When I asked her about auditioning, Debra said you can't act when you're trying to figure out what they, meaning the auditors, want. You have to make bold choices.*
SU: Right.

KW: *Would you say that Debra's bold choices as an actor have paid off for her?*
SU: Oh absolutely! Most of the time it's in the hands of the actor to go, "Okay, can I make this work? How do I make this work?" And sometimes Deb can walk in there and they go, "Wow, we never thought of it being played that way, that's perfect! Hire her!" Or, "That's great, but we want it played a little more solemnly," or "a little more crazy," or whatever the case may be.

Sometimes a director will work with you, sometimes they'll just love your choice right from the beginning, sometimes they give you no information at all. So it is always up to the actor to go in with something because you don't know what they want.

KW: *How important a role has type played for Debra, and has that been more of a positive or a negative would you say?*

SU: Well, you know what it is? When you play a role that you get defined with, that's what they think you can do. I think it's an easy slam dunk for a producer or a casting director when they know somebody has played something so specific to say, "Okay, get Debra Monk, she just did something like that in *Curtains*." So sometimes it happens. And it happens to every actor.

The character Carmen, in *Curtains* was a loud, abrasive Broadway producer. And it's interesting because a lot of people have called for roles that are very similar to that and unless they're really well written, Debra's turned them down.

With Debra, every role has been different. I mean what she did in *Curtains* is very different than what she did in *Pump Boys* or in *Picnic* or in *Redwood Curtain*. That's the beauty of someone like Debra Monk who can just be a chameleon and go from one extreme to the other.

KW: *Do you think that's easier to do in theatre, than in film and television?*

SU: It's probably easier in theatre. In television and film sometimes you have to remind them that, "Oh, no, she can play the serious person. You saw her as the wild, crazy woman on *Desperate Housewives,* but she can also be the tender, loving mother on *Grey's Anatomy."*

KW: *When Debra auditions, what kind of feedback do you get from casting directors and directors? Are there one or two things that she consistently does right?*

SU: There's never anything less than they love her and she gets it, or they love her but they've decided to change the role because they're going a whole different way physically or age-wise.

KW: *How important is it for an actor to be personable in relation-ships in the show business community?*
SU: Oh my God, I mean we've all heard stories about certain people who haven't gotten jobs because they're just too difficult to work with or they're just unreliable. There are people in this business that are so talented, but there are things that come along with the package and some of it is attitude, some of it is lateness, or absenteeism or being unprepared. And I think Debra takes her work so seriously, yet in a sort of matter-of-fact way. And she has fun. There's always that light in her eyes.

KW: *Steven, what are some of her best qualities as a performer?*
SU: I think her dedication, her commitment. In *Curtains* which ran a year on Broadway she was a great coleader. She and David Hyde Pierce were the two stars above the title and Debra was there to help the show, to promote the show and people in the cast turned to her for things. I think that's a tribute to her personality, to her commitment to the show.

Debra goes into every job two hundred percent. She does her homework and she comes prepared and there's no diva attitude. Debra's just there to do the work, to have fun, and to entertain.

She's approachable. I've watched her sit and sign autographs. I've watched her on the 104 bus going uptown talking to people who just saw her in a show or a movie. I think that we all know there are stars out there who are very unapproachable, who close their doors, who just jump in their car, and Deb is not that way at all.

KW: *How important a role has talent and belief in herself played for Debra?*
SU: Debra knows what she can do, and I think when an actor knows that they're capable of something, and they can take these words from a page and bring them to life, it's exquisite. I think talent is a big part of it, and I think confidence is a big part of it.

I respect an actor who sometimes says, "I don't think this is something that I can do justice to." And Debra has said on a number of occasions, when we've read scripts, especially for some TV pilots, "This is *not* the role for me. I can do it, and be fine, but this is not for me."

It has to be something that she believes in. I think she has felt strong about her decisions and said, "Okay, I'm going to take this part and I'm going to run with it." And I think that's the excitement a producer or a director gets from Debra too. Its like, "Okay, I know how to do this. I'll make this work." And that's the beauty of Debra Monk.

KW: *She sounds very workman-like, in a good way.*
SU: Yes. Very much.

KW: *All the statistics tell us that acting is an incredibly difficult profession. At any given time there are far more actors out of work than are working. However, Debra has defied these odds, enjoying quite a bit of success. How has she done it?*
SU: When you work with Debra Monk once, you're going to want to work with her again. And I think that's really what it comes down to. If you hire Debra Monk, you're going to have a good old time, and she's going to get the job done and it's not about, "My trailer is twelve feet shorter than that next person's trailer," or, "Why is my costume green and her's red?"

Debra's on the top of everybody's list because they know she'll deliver.

What are the keys that have led Debra Monk to a successful acting career?

She creates her own work

Debra created something out of nothing with *Pump Boys and Dinettes* and *Oil City Symphony*. The shows led to Tony Award nominations and years of acting work.

She takes risks

Frustrated with her inability to land straight roles, Debra took a risk that few actors would take when she flew to Kentucky at her own expense to audition for Actors Theatre of Louisville. She hadn't been invited and the chances of a payoff were slim, yet her action paid off quickly and powerfully with one leading role after another at ATL.

She has tenacity

When Debra was on the cusp of a dramatic acting breakthrough with the move of *Prelude to a Kiss* to Broadway, she was thought too young for the role. Then her will and *tenacity* took over. Debra suggested to the director, Norman René, she wear a wig. It worked, and when the show opened on Broadway, Debra had arrived as a serious dramatic actor.

She is fearless as an actor

Inspiration can sometimes come from unexpected places. Debra found hers in an improvisation class where she learned to work spontaneously and take emotional risks, to be *fearless*.

Fearlessness won her recurring roles on television and freed her up as a performer. Coached in *Steel Pier* by the legendary John Kander and Fred Ebb, she let go of the fear of singing in a big voice and was, once again, rewarded with a Tony Award nomination.

She has talent

Success team members, theatre critics, and Tony Award voters all agree that Debra is enormously talented. And it seems clear that talent has played a huge role in Debra's successful acting career.

She believes in herself and knows her skills as an actor

Debra said that believing in herself as a performer has been "crucial." And both she and Steven Unger agree that confidence stems partly from knowing what she can—and can't—do as a performer. "If you need a sweet, funny mom, I'm your gal. If you need a ball busting, tough gal or a southern gal, I'm your gal."

She doesn't have a fallback plan

Driven by her passion for acting Debra has designed her lifestyle to support that passion. Having never thought of a fallback plan, Debra relies on her "forward-thinking" plan and knows that "if it doesn't work out for me or I don't like it anymore then I'll figure out something else to do."

People want to work with her—over and over

Working actors comprise a small community of artists, with most employed for only short periods at a time—a week on an episodic TV show, a month on a feature film, three months on a play. An actor's behavior on a set or a stage is crucial to being re-hired. Yet, not all actors live by these rules.

Debra always does. Both Jon Jory and Steven Unger agree that Debra is a pleasure, and people want to work with her again and again.

She does whatever is necessary to succeed

Debra has one quality that seems to override all others—*a willingness to do whatever is necessary to succeed.*

From begging a professor to get into graduate school, to spending her own money for a general audition, to being willing to audition even after achieving Broadway stardom, no matter the cost, Debra takes actions that get results.

It hasn't been easy, but through her talent, her perseverance and her will to succeed Debra Monk has overcome the odds and created a distinguished acting career.

ERIC LADIN

CHAPTER 2

I'm Going To Go For This

ERIC LADIN

Eric Ladin is recently known from the hit HBO original series *Boardwalk Empire* on which he plays J. Edgar Hoover. He has just signed with HBO again in their new original series *The Brink* where he will join Jack Black and Tim Robbins. Often recognized for his work on *The Killing*, the award winning drama from AMC, Eric played political advisor Jamie Wright. He started his career in HBO's hard-hitting miniseries *Generation Kill*, and recurred as January Jones' brother in AMC's award winning series *Mad Men*, and as Chloë Sevigny's diabolical doctor/brother in HBO's *Big Love*. He has guest starred on *Justified, Dexter, Grey's Anatomy, Criminal Minds, Suits, The Mentalist* and *CSI*, and can be seen in the independent film *Highland Park*.

Eric stars as Cole McGrath in the video game *Infamous 2* and, in a complete change of pace, voices History Channel's reality series, *Mudcats*.

A proud native of Houston, Texas, Eric attended The Kinkaid School where he was honored with the 2012 Distinguished Young Alumnus Award. He resides in Los Angeles with his wife, Katy, their son Maxfield and dog Chance. He is also a proud member of UNICEF's Next Generation Los Angeles Steering Committee and welcomes the opportunity to help UNICEF achieve the goal of ZERO!

....

Ken Womble: *You were born in Houston, Texas. How did you become interested in acting?*

Eric Ladin: I guess it stemmed from the fact that I just loved to be the center of attention. I was always trying to make my family laugh and putting on some sort of performance in my living room. And that kind of translated into school.

And it was probably sixth or seventh grade that my drama teacher—we were extremely lucky to have a fantastic drama program—said, "You know, you should really think about this." And then in high school it became a real priority. I played sports a little bit, but I was always doing whatever show we were working on. So I knew it was something I wanted to pursue.

KW: *Then you became a theatre major at USC. Was it a competitive audition to get into their program?*
EL: It was. I auditioned for the BFA program, which has eighteen students from across the country, and I ended up being accepted into that. And then a little bit into school, I actually transferred over into a BA program. I was still able to work on BFA shows, but I was also able to write and produce and perform a one-man show and I directed three different shows.

KW: *Do you think being in Los Angeles helped you start to make connections in the industry?*
EL: I do. After my sophomore year, I got a job as a waiter and started to take some acting classes outside of USC and meet people. And then I did what we used to do in the olden days—get a book of agents and managers and send out two hundred headshots and résumés blindly, which, you know, 97% would get thrown away by the assistant. And I ended up finding an agent through that. And I booked a couple of national commercials.

So once I graduated I had my SAG card, I had gotten a little work and I had a manager and an agent.

KW: *What a great jump-start into the business.*

EL: Yeah. I really wanted to try to make that a priority. That's what made me decide, "Okay, I'll go to USC; I'll be in LA and that'll be the advantage of having gone there," as opposed to a Carnegie Mellon or something.

KW: *Would you consider your training at USC important, or were you doing it on your own?*

EL: I think that it was extremely important in the sense that I became a much better actor while I was there. Working with great professors, I met a bunch of great people, utilized the world renowned TV and film school and did student films and a student television show and started to learn how to be in front of a camera.

But, you know, much like any school environment, theatre in particular is what you make of it. If you're going to go to college for theatre, I think it's important to really go in with the attitude of, "I'm going to do absolutely everything that I can and take advantage of all these resources while I'm here."

KW: *A lot of actors just focus on performance, but it seems like you were also thinking in other ways.*

EL: Well, if you're [only] thinking about performance that's a quick way to a really short career, especially in TV and film.

We all perform. That's why we do what we do, we love it. But that's not the hard part. I mean once you get the job, to go on set and go through hair and makeup and put on a wardrobe and act with other great people…that's the easiest part of the whole gig.

The hard part is busting your ass and trying to get the gig. And so many young, aspiring actors come out to LA and they just wait for that manager or agent to show up. And then once they get a manager or an agent, they just wait for them to call and have auditions for them. And in the meantime they go out and party and do whatever they do.

I've been here for fifteen years, and I've watched countless people go right back to Colorado and Indiana, and say, "This is not for me." I mean you have to be willing to just pound the pavement. You have to be disciplined. You have to wake up every morning and say, "What am I going to do for *my* career today? What am *I* going to do?" Not, "What am I going to wait for an agent or somebody to do for me." You know, it's not a 9 to 5. You don't have a place to go. You don't have an office. You don't have anybody to answer to. It's all self-discipline.

KW: *In the video game* Infamous 2, *you play superhero Cole McGrath. You said in an interview that in your audition you were relatable as a person and that's why you may have gotten the role. Do you think being relatable has been significant for you in getting work?*
EL: Yeah, I do. I think it's also extremely circumstantial for the job.

KW: *Just how you connect with the director or the casting director?*
EL: Absolutely. You know, at this point in my career, I see a lot of the same guys when I go into an audition. So, that might be the difference maker. You know, I'm a USC guy and the director's a USC guy, and we start talking about USC football and it's a toss-up between two actors—then maybe that was the difference—or the fact that we both like to play golf.

So, I think that's what people call "being great in the room." When you spend two years on a television show, or six months in the middle of Detroit shooting a movie, they want somebody that they can hang out with and relate to. I think that's a huge component.

KW: *On HBO's* Generation Kill *you played a marine corporal in Iraq. Would you say that was your first major break?*
EL: It was an extremely reputable network, HBO, doing a mini-series on a topic that is controversial and extremely prevalent at the time, by two writers, David Simon and Ed Burns who created *The Wire* which many think is the best TV show ever. So, yeah, that was huge for me.

I didn't have the biggest part in the world, but I came home from doing that and all of a sudden a lot of doors started to open for me. I started to get some other cable shows like *Mad Men* and *Big Love*. It kind of put me on a path towards doing some really high quality cable television.

KW: *By doors starting to open, do you mean you started getting better auditions?*
EL: Yeah. It was the first time where my manager said, "Okay, we're getting calls from agents now who are interested in meeting with you," as opposed to her having to call agents.

And then I ended up actually signing with a new agent after that, and now people were becoming more and more excited about me. And as an actor you need representation to be excited about you and see that you're marketable. I mean there's a bottom line, and that's getting paid. They've got to know that you can make money for them.

I mean casting directors only have a certain amount of time in their day. And what you learn as you go through this is that they're going to see the people that they know and that are on the producer's list, first and foremost. And then after that they might open the door to some new people that they haven't heard of. So that becomes difficult if you don't have anything for your agent or manager to try to sell.

When they call and say, "Hey, I've got this guy Eric and he's really great and you've got to see him," they hear that all day long.

When they say, "Hey, I've got this guy Eric, just came off HBO's mini-series *Generation Kill*, the thing's going to premier this summer, it's going to be ridiculous, it's HBO, he's great, they love him over there," then all of a sudden their ears perk up and they become, "Okay, if he's done an HBO show he must have something, let's see him." You know? And so it becomes easier for you to start to be considered for higher caliber stuff.

KW: *Soon after* Generation Kill *you were cast in another recurring role in* Mad Men *as William Hoffstadt. Was that a breakthrough role as well?*
EL: Well, *Mad Men* was a little bit different. By the end of Season 2, when I was introduced, and then throughout Season 3 *Mad Men* had really started to become a huge hit. It was the first time in my career that, any room I walked into, industry people knew who I was. And it was the first time that people on the street might say, "Hey, wait, are you the guy on *Mad Men*?"

KW: *So, you'd been on an HBO show and now you were on* Mad Men *which had won all these Emmys. Were you getting a reputation as a young character actor who does quality shows?*
EL: Yeah, I think at that point it became, "Oh, okay, this is a great stepping stone." And then when I did *Big Love*, the third show in a row that I was on that had critics' acclaim. I think that was the point where it dawned on me, "Okay, now I should really focus on making this a career trajectory for myself."

I hate saying high quality because *CSI* is extremely high quality. I wasn't ready to say, "Oh, I'm going to turn my nose up or I'm too good for this other show," but I started to say, "I'm having the opportunity to work on shows that I like to watch and I want to try to maintain that."

I think that as an actor you have to listen. One of the major powers that you have, when the time comes in your career, is to say no to certain work and try to specifically choose the projects that you want to work on.

And that comes at a price, you know. HBO and AMC and Showtime don't pay as well as CBS and NBC and ABC. And they don't work as long. They're typically ten or twelve episode seasons, as opposed to twenty-three episode seasons. So, I mean, you're sacrificing that for doing work that might be more important to you.

You have to work hard to be able to be choosy. You have to have guts to be choosy because it might mean turning down things when you need the money. I mean, it's a very difficult, delicate thing to try to balance, but I think you've just got to go with your gut.

KW: *It's great that you've had these opportunities, and I've got to say you're a very good actor. I'm sure that has a lot to do with it as well.*
EL: Thank you very much. I think at this point if you're a good actor you're going to continue to work, you know? Everybody might be given opportunities at the beginning of their career, but you have to be good to stay in the game.

You know, at thirty-four, thirty-five years old the reason that I see all the same people is because all the other ones went home. They're not doing this anymore. And so the people that I see are all working actors and they're all good actors.

So, you know, it's not really about who's going to go in there and do the best; it's who's going to go in there and make the strongest choices for that particular role.

KW: *You said something in another interview that really struck me. You were talking about* Mad Men *and how Matt Weiner, the show runner, keeps stories fresh and moving. It seems as though you clearly understand how episodic television works. Was it conscious on your part to learn that, or has it just come from working so much?*

EL: No, that was a conscious thing. You know I had an acting teacher that [gave] homework to watch hours upon hours of television. And I know a lot of actors, some working actors, who snobbishly will say, "I don't own a TV."

KW: *That's not smart.*

EL: I think that's the most absurd thing in the world. I mean that's like a furniture salesman saying, "I don't have sofas, why would I even have sofas in my house?" I don't know; you're selling them.

I watch a ton of TV. You know, there's a huge difference between a single-camera comedy like *Modern Family* and a multi-camera comedy like *Friends.* There's a different tempo.

And when my agent called and said, "Hey I've got an audition for you," I was going to be damned not to know exactly what kind of show that was. And I think that it's irresponsible for an actor to do that. You know, *CSI* and *Law and Order* and procedurals like that are different than *Breaking Bad* and *Mad Men* and *Damages.* They just are.

I mean there are choices that I would make in auditions for certain shows that I would say, "This isn't really how I'd play it, but I know exactly how they want it in this scene." Like the end of Act II, you know it's going to go right into a commercial and you know that's how they want it to end.

KW: *Can you give me an example of an audition where your gut said do one thing, but you knew the show needed something else?*

EL: In a comedy if you're reading for a guest star chances are they're not writing for you to get the laughs. They're writing for you to set up laughs for the series regular. Now, can you get laughs? Sure. But really and truly you're there to set up for the series regular.

If you're reading for a procedural like *Law and Order* and you're at the beginning of the show know that, chances are, they want the audience to think you're guilty. So play that. That's why they've written you. They want the audience at the end of the first commercial to say, "Oh man, it's that guy," but in the end we find out you're not. If you watch enough procedural television, you know that that's just how it works. There is a formula.

So, I think it's incredibly important to be knowledgeable about television and who the audience for the show is.

KW: *On AMC's* The Killing *you played Jamie Wright, the campaign manager for Darren Richmond. How big a break was that?*
EL: It was a huge break. Other pilots that I've booked have never ended up going to series, so this was the first time that [happened] and it was a really critically acclaimed, smart show. And it was great because it kept me on the path of high-caliber cable drama television.

And it probably put me on a different playing field. I'm finding now that I'm on producers' lists and I'm getting more offers and not having to audition for shows—they're just offering me stuff. And so that's been big for me. You know, it's always great when people in the industry can turn on every single week and see your face on television.

KW: *You mentioned that your character, Jamie, was great at what he did and was extremely smart and successful at a young age. It seems like those traits may apply to you. Do they? And do you think they have anything to do with you getting the role?*

43

EL: I mean in all honesty, yes. There are things in performances that an actor embodies. You know. Do I think that Anthony Hopkins really eats people? No. But do I think that there are parts of Hannibal Lecter that are truly Anthony Hopkins? Yes.

There are inevitably parts of me in that character. And I think you have to find those things because that will help you make it grounded and real. So, yeah, there are definitely aspects of him that are very Eric Ladin.

KW: *It seems you've been cast as kind of morally compromised characters. Has that been more positive or negative for you?*
EL: You know, I enjoy it. I always think it's more fun to play people that are conflicted and morally compromised and tortured. You don't get to go kill people in your real life, but you can do it on TV and that's kind of fun. You know what I mean? And I know that might sound sick, but you get to experience things that you wouldn't normally get to experience. It's scary. It's dangerous, but that's why I love what I do.

Whenever I play someone "bad" it's tough for me because I don't look at it like that. I make a point not to judge the characters that I play. I think the moment that you start to judge you're not going to be grounded.

And I always try to justify their actions. I make sure that I find things in their life that I can truly, truly say, "I understand why you did this." And that's the very difficult part of doing it, but I think that's maybe why I've been successful in playing those kinds of characters.

KW: *Ideally an actor brings more to a character than is written, and it seems that actors who work a lot do that.*
EL: Yeah. Listen, there are fantastic writers out there, and I've been fortunate to work with a lot of them. But the fun part of what we do

is finding new things, and once you start to embody that character, things just happen spontaneously. When you're in the middle of a scene, things tend to happen if you're completely grounded in your character and allowing yourself to kind of go places.

KW: *How important has type been for you? Because it seems like most actors who work a lot, whether they like it or not, are somewhat typed.*

EL: Well, I'm always extremely grateful for the opportunities that I'm given. And I've played several different kinds of...you might want to call them "bad" or antagonists. All were extremely different.

And I've had conversations with my people about moving forward, what the next steps are going to be and roles that I would like to try to find.

I love comedy. I used to do stand-up and I think I'm a pretty funny person in my regular life, but I don't have a ton of comedy on my résumé. I've booked a couple of comedy pilots that never went anywhere...maybe that's supposed to tell me something. But I'm hoping to do some comedy going forward and find other things.

But really, it's extremely circumstantial. If something came along and he was a "bad guy" and I loved the material, it would be tough to turn it down just saying, "No I don't want to get typecast as that." The fact of the matter is, if you're getting typecast you're obviously good at what you're doing. So why not do it? It's hard enough to get work.

KW: *Absolutely. When you were just starting to get work, did you think playing bad guys was a positive thing?*

EL: Yeah, I think probably. I mean early on I played mostly rednecks, and there was a time where I was basically like, "God, should I not play a southern guy anymore? I'm playing so many."

And I had an acting teacher say, "Why don't you play southern guys until you are afforded the opportunity to play something else, until you can get to be the most famous redneck?" And I went straight to *Generation Kill* where I played a redneck, so to speak, and then when I got home I played a 1962 waspy, stuck up brat on *Mad Men*, which is as far from redneck as you get.

KW: *How important would you say it is for an actor to come to the point where he or she stops worrying about paying the bills and starts being selective about the jobs they choose?*
EL: I guess it depends on how important that is for you and how many bills you have. I mean there are probably fantastic actors that live in little studio apartments and don't really require [anything] other than eggs and peanut butter, so I guess for them it really isn't that important.

I think that really and truly everybody has their own thing. I mean I have friends who have three kids that they're trying to put through school. So for them being on a show that pays a lot of money where maybe they don't necessarily get to do the highest caliber of work, but they're putting their kids through school and being able to do something that they love, that's important. You know what I mean?

KW: *Yeah, absolutely. Was it important for you to get to that point?*
EL: Well, of course! I mean any actor wants to be able to do it and not wait tables. But I'm also constantly thinking about conserving because that next job might not come for a little while.

You know, could I essentially tell my agent or manager to go find me a job, I don't really care what it is, I have no money—yes. Do I want to do that—no. Because I want to try to be picky and I think that in the long run it'll end up helping me in my career.

KW: *You seem to be very clear-eyed about the business.*

EL: Yeah, you have to be clear-eyed. You know, at the end of the day we're artists, so we're not getting that paycheck every two weeks.

KW: *Let's switch to auditions for a second. Could you describe an audition where you absolutely nailed it? What did you feel that you were doing right in that audition?*

EL: Well, it starts with homework. Usually the auditions that I don't feel great about are the ones that I haven't prepared correctly for, so when I got into the room I wasn't able to really trust myself and my homework and let go. But if I'm prepared, then usually I go in and do exactly what I want to do.

Now, there are differences in terms of "nailed it." A lot of people will go into a room, do exactly what they prepared and then the producers or casting directors will say, "That was great, thanks so much for coming in," and they'll all of a sudden go, "Oh God, I didn't nail it," because they didn't say, "cool," or, "Are you definitely available for this date?" Well, now you're letting the reaction of the people in the room dictate what you believe your performance was.

You have to be very confident and say, "Look, I did everything I wanted to do. Now if they're not buying it, that's a whole different thing."

KW: *It sounds like you're saying if you do what you want to do, and what you've prepared, that's a successful audition because that's all you can do.*

EL: Yes. And I think that's really important for young actors to remember; you can only do so much.

I left an audition three weeks ago and my agent said, "How did that go?" And I said, "I did what I wanted to do, but the director and I weren't on the same page." And then my agent called me back two days later and said, "By the way you're in the mix for that role. The director is just not a very responsive guy."

That is why you can't judge how your audition went based on the feedback in the room. Maybe the producer broke up with a blonde boyfriend and you walk in and you're blonde and they're like, "I'm not having it. He looks like my ex-boyfriend." You know what I mean? So there's *nothing* I can do about that.

I've become more and more okay with going into an audition and if it doesn't go my way, being okay with it. Because I know that that's the way I want to portray this character. And if that's not what you're buying then please, by all means, give it to someone else. And that way it won't be a headache for everybody.

KW: *I've heard it said about the acting profession if you have a fallback plan you'll fall back. Do you believe that?*
EL: Well, I believe that it's such a difficult industry that if you're like, "God, I really love acting, I think it'd be fun, but I also really love the law," you know, go to law school. Because I think in your head you'll doubt whether what you're doing is the right decision.

I always knew that I wanted to do this and I knew that I was going to do this and I was going to be successful at this. But I also know that if for some reason I'm, God forbid, hit by a bus tomorrow and I have no legs and I've got to do something else, there are other things I'm capable of doing.

KW: *Was there a moment when you decided to be an actor and nothing else?*
EL: Yeah. When I was in college was the first time I actually said, "I'm going to go for this."

KW: *What brought you to that decision?*
EL: I think I saw I was having success and I felt I was good at it and so I said, "You know, I can make a living doing this."

KW: *How do you think a director who has cast you multiple times would describe working with you?*
EL: Well, I would hope they would say, "He's extremely prepared, diligent, professional, open to direction, but sticks by his guns."

I'm always open to direction, but I'm also very confident and secure in my choices. Not to the point of hardheadedness or stubbornness, but definitely to the point of fighting for what I believe is right.

And a lot of that comes from experience because, as an actor, you learn very quickly that you're not the last line of defense. On camera even if it's a take that they say, "Would you just do this once for me, just to try it," well, lo and behold that's the one that's on television.

KW: *Right, the one you didn't want to do.*
EL: Exactly. And listen, there's a lot of other political stuff that goes on in editing. So, I've become very secure in being able to stick by my guns when I feel like I need to.

KW: *Would you say most actors do that?*
EL: Yeah, the ones that have worked a lot. You know, when you're young and you go on set, you just want to please everybody, so no matter what they say you do it.

KW: *Right.*
EL: And then all of a sudden you cringe when it's on television.

KW: *What would you say is your best quality as an actor?*
EL: I never want to be the guy that's not prepared. You know, I've been on set with actors who don't know their lines or they're not ready and willing. And they have lost sight of what it is they're actually there to do, and I don't want to be that guy.

KW: *What part would you say momentum and timing have played in your career?*
EL: Everything. Because there have been times in my career where I didn't get a job and I was crushed. And then six weeks later *Generation Kill* came along. And I wouldn't have been able to do that had I gotten the other job, a pilot that never even got picked up.

And I don't think it's strictly up to the actor. I think it has probably even more to do with the actor's representation. I mean there are certain times in your career where you have heat and that's up to your representation to capitalize on that.

And then for the actor to be able to choose correctly. I probably have more opportunity now than ever in my career, but I also have more responsibility because I have to choose correctly and if I don't it could damage my career. So, you know, there comes a lot of responsibility in terms of momentum.

KW: *How important to your success is your belief in yourself as a performer?*
EL: Everything. I mean you have to. If you don't have confidence, you're toast. Work begets work and the reason is because you walk into rooms confident.

I mean, I'm walking into a room and in the back of my mind if I don't get the job I'm okay with it. And that's a really powerful weapon. As opposed to the guy that just walked in before me and needs this job, will do anything to get this job so that he doesn't have to go back and wait tables. I mean they can smell that from a mile away.

I help people with auditions, and I often use this analogy with actors, especially girls: when you go to a bar and there's the guy that all he wants to do is get laid, he's repulsive to you. And then there's the guy—you go up and you all start chatting, but he literally could care less; he's just a nice guy and you can tell. And that's the guy that you're attracted to, you know? Not the guy that wants it, needs it, and will do anything for it.

It's one of the reasons people leave and go home because the hardest time to have confidence is when you're not working and that is, hands down, the most important time to have confidence.

I was offered a role on a comedy pilot for Spike and at the same time I got an audition for this AMC pilot called *The Killing* and I was like, "Wow, this looks really good, I'd better go read for it."

So I went and read for it that day, and when I left the room, I said, "This is mine. I nailed this." And they called and said, "We've got interest and we definitely want to test him, but we're not going to be able to do it for two weeks."

And I had probably the biggest decision that I had up to that point in my career—take an offered job for good money, or turn down that job and take a chance and test for this show against four other actors. It was a really difficult decision. But I said, "This is mine to lose, and I'm going to get this."

So I turned down the other pilot and I tested for *The Killing*. And I am thrilled I ended up getting it.

And the other show never got picked up and never went to air.

KW: *That took a lot of courage. I don't think many actors would do that.*
EL: It's difficult, it's definitely difficult, but again that comes down to the confidence and belief.

KW: *How do you maintain confidence when you're not working?*
EL: Don't ask me. I mean you either have it or you don't.

KW: *What would you say are two or three of the smartest things that you've done for your career?*
EL: Being in an acting class and meeting people, networking, going to events and parties, really doing everything I could to become knowledgeable about this city. And learning how to not just act on a stage, but act on camera—and all that came from acting classes outside of USC.

I think that trying to rest on your laurels and your degree when you get out here is difficult because it's a whole different animal than theatre school.

But first and foremost, just by continuing acting. You know if you go talk to a lawyer and you say, "How many hours a week do you practice law?" And he says, "Well, every day from eight in the morning until eight at night."

Well, as an actor, you have to do that on your own. You know? So you need to be acting every day. And when you leave school and come out here and you're waiting tables or bartending that becomes difficult. But you've got to find time to do it. Because just like anything else, if that's what you want to do for a living, you damn well better make sure you're doing it every day, even when you're not getting paid.

KW: *If you could change one career decision, what would it be?*
EL: You know people have asked me that and to be completely honest with you…none. I just think that everything that I've done has influenced me in one way or another. And even if it's been a terrible movie or a role that I wish I hadn't done, it's taught me how to approach [things] differently.

KW: *Last question. All of the statistics tell us that acting is an incredibly difficult profession. At any given time there are far more actors out of work than are working. However, you've defied those odds, enjoying quite a bit of success in your career, and I'm sure more to come. In addition to everything else you've told me, how have you done it?*

EL: [*Sighs*] Hard work. Just hard work, you know. And luck along the way. I'm not one of those people who is going to tell you that none of it is lucky. I was extremely fortunate to find representation that believed in me and that believed in me when things were really not going well and I couldn't get a job to save my life. And they continued to send me out and continued to give me opportunity and I was incredibly, *incredibly* fortunate in that regard.

But, you know, all of that was because of hard work and they knew how hard I worked and they knew that I would be able to get past it.

And I think talent. You know, you've got to have it. You've got to have confidence, you've got to have talent, and you've got to have perseverance. Those are the three things that, if you're going to make it, you've got to have.

Eric Ladin Success Team Member

TRACY STEINSAPIR

Ken Womble: *Tracy, you're one of the owners of Main Title Entertainment, a talent management company in Los Angeles. Could you tell me what you're looking for in an actor that you want to sign?*

Tracy Steinsapir: You know, it's like a blind date. I just can see it, and if I think I can sell it, I'll sign the person. I'm definitely looking for a hard worker, that's one sign I'm looking for in a young person for sure, because it takes so much dedication to make it. Otherwise it's just a gut feeling.

KW: *When you first met Eric Ladin what was your impression of him?*
TS: Young and funny, and that was probably the main reason I signed him. I was an agent at CAA [Creative Artists Agency] and I had left and started my own company with my business partner, Stewart, and Eric's one of the first people we met.

KW: *Why did you decide to get into talent management?*
TS: I mean, basically just to own our own business; you don't have to answer to anybody.

KW: *Eric mentioned in an interview that as a young character actor he's a tougher sell than a leading man and that he really needs a manager who understands who he is and believes in him. And he credited you and your partner, Stewart Strunk, as those kinds of managers.*
How important is that type of understanding between an actor and their managers, and could you give me an example of how your belief in him plays out in everyday practice?
TS: Well, I think that if you're a good looking guy or girl someone knows how to get you in the door, it's easier. But if you're a character actor, you need to have someone represent you that knows what you can do. I know that Eric can do comedy and drama. I know that he can do period. I mean he's recurring on *Boardwalk Empire* right now.

I have another client, Meagen Fay, who's a character actor, and I always knew she could do accents. And when I first started my company, there was a part on *Malcolm in the Middle*, a recurring role for a German woman that was like ten years older than her, but I knew she could do it. The casting people didn't want to see her and I fought super-hard to get her in and she got the role and she ended up doing like fifteen episodes.

So, I think that if you're a character actor you absolutely have to have a team that knows how to sell you.

KW: *Was there anything else about Eric that kind of struck you as special?*
TS: You know, personable and he seemed like a hard worker to me. He does what it takes to get the job. I think that a lot young people who come to Hollywood are the best looking kid in their high school class or college, and they think it's going to be super easy and it's just not. You have to work really, really hard. That's the only way that you can be successful.

KW: *How long have you worked together?*
TS: He was one of our first clients. Eleven years.

KW: *And he hasn't been in the business a heck of a lot longer than that I don't think.*
TS: He actually had two other managers before me for like a year each. And I have to say as a manager I almost think it's easier to represent people who've had other management before me be-cause then they can see how good me and my business partner are—because we work really hard and get people into rooms if we believe in them.

And I feel like I have really good taste and I think that the casting directors and the producers and the executives and the show runners know it. So, if I say, "See this person," usually I can get my people in the door, because I don't sell a lot of people.

KW: *Eric talked about being proactive in looking for acting work. He said, "It's all self-discipline." Could you share an experience about how Eric is proactive in his career and in your relationship together?*
TS: I think the most important thing is that he's willing to do pretty much anything. He just doesn't say no and think he's too good for anything and he trusts Stewart and I. I think that proactive is just being available and being around. You know a lot of actors go on vacations and aren't available all the time. He's always available and he knows that's what it takes.

KW: *And I would think some actors might say, "Well, of course, I'll be available." But then when push comes to shove other things come up.*
TS: Yeah, exactly.

KW: *What would you say was Eric's first big break as an actor and what did that do for his career?*
TS: Well, his first really major break, I think, was the *Mad Men* recurring as January Jones' brother.

But the first year that we had him, he tested for a pilot called *Mullet Brothers*. It was about two brothers from the South; I think they were seventeen. And he went to a costume shop and bought a mullet wig, and that's what he wore when he tested for it. He didn't get it, but it was amazing that he went that far to try to get the job because there are a lot of actors that won't go that far. They'll think, "Oh they can just imagine me in a wig."

But if you do something like that, I think it says two things: number one, people in this business aren't as creative as you think they are, so it shows them, "I can easily be a mullet kind of guy;" and number two, I think it shows producers and directors that, "Hey, I'm going to work really hard; I'm going to take the extra step to go get a wig." And that was one of the things that impressed me the most about him in the first year that I had him.

KW: *Eric and I talked about being relatable in auditions, as he called it, "being great in the room." How important is auditioning well and being great in the room for an actor?*
TS: I think that's really, really important. That's one of the most important things.

I think that when you get a job as an actor it's for three reasons: it's because you do a good job and because you were great in the room—and when I say great in the room I mean work the room, be nice to the casting director, maybe crack a joke, be personable—and the third reason, I think, is luck. You know, there's always a little bit of luck when you are successful.

So I think that working a room is super important because a lot of those producers, creative people, whoever's in the room, it endears them to you, and they can see what you're like to work on a set, that you're really easy. And it just shows that you're honest and you're real.

A lot of the actors that I've represented, that are no longer with me, think they know better and that they don't have to go the extra mile to work a room. And they're bitchy and they're not nice and I don't think that those kinds of people succeed as much as the other kind of people. There are some people like that who succeed, but the ratio isn't as high.

KW: *Since you've been working with Eric, he's moved from occasional guest starring roles to recurring roles and just recently to series regulars. It's been quite a journey. Could you tell me about that journey and what you see for the future?*
TS: Well, he was a series regular on *Generation Kill*, even though that was a miniseries, and that was about five or six years into

our relationship. And then right after *Generation Kill* he booked a half hour pilot for CBS called *My Best Friend's Girl*. So I would say five years into it he started getting pilots.

You know, with some people it happens quicker, usually the pretty people it happens quicker.

I think that a lot of times you have to start with guest stars so people get to know you and so you get to know what it's like to be in a room, how to audition, all that stuff—and then recurring roles.

My business partner and I always shoot for high profile shows when we're talking about TV because I think that that's what gets you noticed. I have a guy who recurred last year on *American Horror Story*, he played Jessica Lange's love interest, and he got so much attention from that. And those kinds of roles are almost better than a movie a lot of times because people watch those high profile shows.

KW: *What do you mean by high profile shows?*
TS: I call them blue chip shows, you know, like *The Killing*, *True Blood*, *Dexter*, *American Horror Story*, *Boardwalk Empire*. I mean those are shows that decision-makers watch—any kind of decision-maker—casting people, producers, directors, show runners.

I have a client that recurred on *Californication*. And during pilot season, every room she walked in—*Californication* was on at the same time as pilot season—people talked to her about that role.

Casting people and creative people want to hire a known commodity. So I think that if you're recurring on a high profile show when you walk into a room the decision-makers already feel secure that you're a great actor and other people believe in you, so you're already three-quarters of the way there.

KW: *Eric and I talked about talent and he said, "Everybody might be given opportunities at the beginning of their career, but you* *have to be good to stay in the game." How important do you believe talent is for an actor to be successful? And how important has it been for Eric?*

TS: Well, first of all I think that acting can be taught but not everybody can learn it. Most people can learn acting, but believe me, I've had some beautiful, beautiful people that cannot learn it. And maybe they'll book commercials, but other than that, they're not probably working that much.

And I think what Eric means by that is when you first get to town, if you have someone good representing you, you'll get in rooms, there's no question. The casting directors, the first people that see you, the first gatekeepers, they'll see anyone if Stewart and I recommend them. But to get in the room a second time you can't fail the first time. Or maybe you will, but it'll be a year or two later.

You know, these people don't forget, so if you're bad...I think talent's really important, but I also think that there are people like Brad Pitt that probably weren't the greatest actors in the beginning but learned and got a lot better. I think that happens a lot in Hollywood. It just goes to show hard work pays off.

KW: *What kind of feedback do you get from casting directors and directors about Eric, and are there one or two things that he consistently does right?*

TS: Well, first of all, he's super funny and personable in a room and everyone loves being around him. I mean, if you just had a baby, he'll remember that. If your kid just graduated from high school, he'll remember that. He's great at just being a really nice, caring human being.

That, and also being prepared. I mean he's got the stuff memorized, he's read the script, he's prepared at least one or two different ways. If you prepared only one way and they want you to do it a different way, a lot of actors get freaked out and can't do it. If the casting or creative people like you, they're going to be giving you adjustments. But if you can't do the adjustment, then you're not going to get the job.

KW: *What are some of Eric's best qualities as a performer?*
TS: Well, he happens to be extremely innately talented. He's a hard worker, and he's very, very personable. Those are the three most important things. He's just a nice person. And when you're around nice people, you want to work harder for them because I've been around, believe me, some really bitchy people and you don't want to work that hard for them. You know, you still represent them, but you're not going to go the extra mile. With Eric you're going to go the extra mile because he appreciates it and he's worth it.

KW: *If type has been important for Eric, what part has it played and does he have a clear idea of his type?*
TS: That's the great thing about Eric, he's a true character actor. He really changes from scene to scene. For example, about four or five years ago, right after *Mad Men*, we were trying to get him in on some kind of political pilot, as a young senator or something. And we called the head of casting at CBS because he'd just booked a CBS pilot the year before, and he goes, "I don't think Eric Ladin can play that role," and I go, "He was January Jones' brother on *Mad Men*," and the head of casting at CBS says, "That's not Eric Ladin," and we're like, "Yeah, that's Eric Ladin." And we sent him the tape and obviously it was Eric Ladin.

I mean that's the sign of a great character actor—a head of casting doesn't even know that it was the same guy. Eric is different in every scene. It's unbelievable.

KW: *How important has Eric's belief in himself been, and have you had a personal experience with him that illustrates that?*

TS: Yeah. Right before he got *Generation Kill,* he didn't work for a whole year and his agents dropped him. But he believed in himself and Stewart and I believed in him and I remember we took him out to lunch and we told him, "Don't worry about it." And we represented him alone I think until he got *Generation Kill.* You know, you have to believe in yourself because you're getting so much rejection. It's the only way.

KW: *How else would you describe him as a client?*
TS: I got to tell you, the best client ever. Working with him makes it a dream. All I have to say is I'm grateful to have him as a client. I wish I had all Eric Ladins. I do have a lot of nice people.

KW: *Last question. All of the statistics tell us that acting is an incredibly difficult profession. At any given time there are far more actors out of work than are working. However, Eric has defied those odds, enjoying quite a bit of success. How has he done it?*
TS: Hard work and talent, but mostly hard work. Having a great attitude and not giving up.

Eric Ladin Success Team Member

ROSS DINERSTEIN

Ken Womble: *Ross, you are a producer and partner at Preferred Film and TV in Los Angeles. Could you tell me a bit about your company and the films you produce?*
Ross Dinerstein: We are an independent production company. We make three to four independently financed films a year, with a specialty in genre films that get theatrical releases all over the world and speak to an audience that loves sci-fi, thriller, horror and supernatural movies.

And we sell completed films that are looking for domestic distribution rights, between thirty and forty movies a year.

KW: *How long have you known Eric Ladin?*
RD: I've known him since we were born. Our grandparents were friends. Our moms were roommates in college. He's my oldest friend.

KW: *And you grew up together in Houston?*
RD: Yes, we did. And we went to school and Sunday school together. When I moved to Los Angeles in 2004, Eric was really the only person I knew.

KW: *What were some of your early impressions of him?*
RD: He's the most confident person I've ever met. He has the most amazing stage presence and ability to entertain and take over a room in any situation that he's in. And I mean that as a compliment.

KW: *What do you mean by take over a room?*
RD: When he walks in, he owns the place and he can make everyone feel like that he's their best friend, but it's very genuine. He's a very good person and has a very deep understanding of people's personalities like "That person is going to want to talk about football" or "That person's going to talk about their family" and is able to really listen.

KW: *How important is that for an actor? Because it seems to me that some actors, especially younger ones, are under the impression when they go into a room that it's all about the audition and it's not so much about the relationship. You're talking about the relationship between the actor and the people in the room?*

RD: Yes, very much so. Look, everybody out here is very talented and Eric is extremely talented. He has that in spades. But it's that extra sort of intangible element that not a lot of people have—that is what you notice. It's like a spark. People might be as talented as Eric, but they don't have that ability to connect on a personal level. He's intelligent; he's prepared. He hasn't just read the sides; he's read the script. He's done research about the producers, and he's done research about the director. He comes in prepared where most actors just come in, read their lines, and leave.

KW: *Can you give me an example of that? Has he told you about an audition or an interview that went particularly well?*
RD: We've talked about it at length because I spend a lot of time casting my movies. And I always ask him questions because I'm always surprised how unprepared some of these actors are, not even Googling the movie and stuff. The thing that I criticize actors for doing, he doesn't do. He does the exact opposite.

If Eric doesn't know about something, he calls me because typically I know more about it than he does because of my resources and what I do for a living. Eric does the due diligence because that's just his personality and, in order to be successful, you've got to work harder than everybody else because there are so many talented actors out here. What is it that you're going to have that's going to set you aside from everybody else? And Eric has that. He goes that extra step.

KW: *What would you say was Eric's first big break as an actor and what did that do for his career?*
RD: It's a good question. I remember early on he got a bunch of commercials. And the commercials were paying the bills, were getting him a lot of national exposure, but I really think his first

big break was probably getting hooked up with Tracy, his manager. Her belief in him and her guidance has been really incredible.

As far as the first big role that put him on the map where people could say, "He's the guy that played this," I think was *Mad Men*, when he was Betty Draper's brother; just the level of actors on that show and being in scenes with John Hamm and working with Matthew Weiner. I think that was the first time he really was like, "Okay, I belong here."

And I think *Generation Kill* was really a game changer for him too because he was going through a period where he was starting to question things. And that was an HBO series with the guy from *The Wire* and he was going to Africa and working with all those great actors. I'm not exactly sure which one came first.

KW: Generation Kill *came first, but I think they were both very important from what he told me. And he mentioned that when folks in the industry saw him on* Generation Kill *that helped put him on producers' lists.*
RD: It did.

KW: *What is a producer's list and how important is it for actors to get on them?*
RD: It's just kind of an industry term; it's like being on their radar. It puts him in a different stack when you have all the headshots. You know, he has a body of work that he can point to and most people know *Generation Kill*. It sets him aside from the millions of other actors out here.

KW: *Eric talked about being proactive in looking for acting work. He said that "It's all self-discipline." From your own experience, how is Eric proactive in his career?*

RD: You know, he's in it to win it. He's out here for his career. And I know way too many actors that come out here because they want to meet girls and they want to have fun and they want to go out, and it's not a job for them.

Whether Eric's working or not, he's up every day at the same time. He has this routine: he reads the trades, he reads scripts, he goes to the gym, he goes to acting class, he coaches, he does everything. It is a one hundred hour a week job for him.

Other people that I know sleep 'til noon, they go get lunch, they take a nap, they go out, they party, they drink, whatever. And Eric's never been like that. It's always been a job. I would say that Eric works as hard, if not harder, than anyone because he knows he needs that edge. And those are the actors that are successful. Not the ones that are out at the club on a Tuesday night.

KW: *And that can be sort of deceptive to young actors because in the media they see stars doing crazy things and they may get a wrong impression. They don't realize how hard it really is and what they should be doing.*
RD: Exactly. You know, as a producer, if I'm meeting with someone that is one of those kinds of Hollywood club people my concern's going to be are they going to show up on time? Are their eyes going to be bloodshot? Are they going to show up drunk? So I'd rather have someone that's not in the tabloids, that's professional, than someone that's out and about all the time.

KW: *As a producer you focus on the business end of the film and TV industry. How knowledgeable should an actor be about the business?*
RD: As much as possible. If you're not keeping up with the trends how are you going to adjust? You know, seeing what pilots are being picked up and what shows are in development and really paying attention to what Netflix is doing; all that stuff I think is

very important for actors because it affects them as much as it affects us on the business side.

KW: *Eric told me about screen testing for* The Killing, *but in order to do that he had to turn down another job offer. He took a chance and it worked out well. How important is it for an actor to be willing to take those types of career risks?*
RD: It's very important. And that, again, goes back to having really good people in your life as your representatives and other actors you trust and trusting your gut.

I was one of the people Eric talked to about that. And at the end of the day it came down to AMC has incredible programming, and he has had a good relationship with them from *Mad Men*. It was maybe not as much money as the other opportunity, but it's going to be a better show and it'll be a more memorable experience and better for his long-term career.

KW: *Eric and I also talked about talent. He said, "Everybody might be given opportunities at the beginning of their career, but you have to be good to stay in the game." However, sometimes when you turn on the TV you see an actor who you may not think is that great. So, how important is it for an actor to be talented to be successful? And how important has it been for Eric?*
RD: I think talent is the most important thing. There are always other factors that come into casting decisions—foreign value and studio decisions and political things and friends of friends. Sometimes a director will like somebody and a producer will like somebody else, and sometimes the directors win and sometimes the producers win; most of the time everyone's on the same page.

At the end of the day if the actor's not talented, they might be given one or two opportunities, but they're not going to last. And if you want to have longevity in your career as you evolve from a twenty-two year-old kid to a thirty-five year-old man, you've got to be talented.

And that is something with Eric. He's going to have a long career because of his work ethic, his perseverance and his talent.

KW: *What are one or two things that casting directors and directors say about Eric's work?*
RD: It's consistently that he's extremely talented and he's a great guy.

KW: *What are some of his other best qualities as a performer?*
RD: His ability to do comedy and drama.

KW: *And that leads me to my next question. How important a role has type played for Eric, if it has played a role? And does he have a clear idea of his type?*
RD: You know, I don't think it's played that big of a role. I think he's pretty much able to adapt. When he was younger, he was always having to play the high schooler, and I don't think that really was interesting to him. As he's become more mature, I think he's really enjoyed playing older roles.

KW: *How important has his belief in himself been for Eric?*
RD: I mean look, this is a very tough business, and his ability to not sweat the small stuff, to not let rejection affect him and just to keep at it every day is why he's been successful.

KW: *How would you describe him overall?*
RD: I mean, I'm biased, he's one of my best and oldest friends, but he's a survivor. I mean the guy came out here when he was eighteen-years-old, has worked as hard as anyone I know, he's

been very successful. He's created a life for himself out here. He's a great person, he's a great friend, and he's a great actor.

KW: *Okay, last question. All of the statistics tell us that acting, as we've talked about, is an incredibly difficult profession. At any given time there are far more actors out of work than are working. However, Eric Ladin has defied those odds, enjoying quite a bit of success. I don't know if you can think of anything else, but if you can…how else has he done it?*
RD: I think it's really what we've talked about: his work ethic, his discipline, his perseverance, and his positive attitude.

KW: *Wonderful. Anything else you'd like to add?*
RD: I think you've picked a great subject. Eric is a success story, and I think people can learn a lot from what he's done.

What are the keys that have led Eric Ladin to a successful acting career?

His business plan started in college

Eric understands that in the competitive world of acting he needs every advantage he can find. So, he chose to attend college at USC in Los Angeles, the entertainment capital of the world.

He gave himself an even bigger edge on the competition when he spent his last two years of college the way most actors spend their first two years out of college—taking professional classes, getting an agent and booking his first paid acting jobs.

He works hard and takes complete responsibility for his career

A professional actor must be resourceful, not only in creating a role but in creating a career. Without an office, a boss to answer to, or a 9-to-5 schedule Eric understands that, "It's all self-discipline," and so creates his own structure. Ross Dinerstein and Tracy Steinsapir agree his work ethic is second to none. And it is a testament to the complete responsibility Eric takes for his career.

He is an outstanding auditioner

Eric knows that auditions are the pathway to work and so prepares for them just like work. From watching "a ton of TV," to understand the variety of dramatic styles, to finding out the history of a project, Eric does everything necessary to prepare and then deliver in the audition room.

Ross and Tracy believe that Eric's confidence, strong acting choices and ability to create rapport make him unique—and irresistible to directors.

He has a great team that believes in him

When a year-long drought in acting work got Eric dropped by his agents, his managers stayed the course. Soon after, that faith paid off when Eric booked his first job as a series regular in *Generation Kill*, a turning point in his career.

His decision to do high quality shows put him on track for a high quality career

Eric focuses on, what Tracy calls, "blue chip shows, shows that decision-makers watch." They both know that these series, with superb writing and high artistic standards, position Eric as a great actor and a known commodity.

He has established himself as a character actor with a specific prototype

Eric is a character actor with a variety of roles to his credit, from a redneck Marine corporal on *Generation Kill*, to a "stuck up brat" on *Mad Men*, to a diabolical doctor on *Big Love*, to a cut-throat campaign manager on *The Killing*. Tracy points out that he "changes from scene to scene," and Eric has, indeed, displayed a tremendous range.

However, there is a common thread to these characters as well—they are all compromised in some way. Eric's ability to play a range of characters within this prototype is a defining characteristic of his career to date.

He takes risks

Sometimes, if an actor is talented and lucky, he receives competing offers—certainly a nice problem to have. Yet, it's also one that requires careful consideration because the decision he makes could have a tremendous impact on his career.

Eric faced such a choice when he had to decide between taking a good job that was offered to him or screen testing for another job. *He decided to take a risk* by turning down the offered job and auditioning for *The Killing.* That risk required faith, and Eric's faith in himself resulted in a series regular role and a big career boost.

Talent, hard work and perseverance

Eric Ladin has created a successful acting career by being conscious and specific about what he wants and then taking *action* to achieve it.

Both Tracy Steinsapir and Ross Dinerstein agree that he's done it through immense talent, hard work and a willingness to persevere no matter the circumstances.

KRYSTA RODRIGUEZ

CHAPTER 3

All Kinds of Self-Preparation, All the Time

KRYSTA RODRIGUEZ

Krysta Rodriguez was born and raised in Southern California and was most recently seen on television as Ana Vargas in the second and final season of the NBC musical drama, *Smash*. After the second season of *Smash* concluded, Krysta returned to her theater roots to star in the Broadway musical comedy *First Date*, opposite Zachary Levi.

Krysta made her Broadway debut in the musical *Good Vibrations* and continued to perform on Broadway in the original casts of *Spring Awakening* and *In the Heights*, and the revival of *A Chorus Line*. Krysta later went on to originate the role of Wednesday Addams in the Broadway production of *The Addams Family*, with Bebe Neuwirth and Nathan Lane. Other theater credits include the *Encores!* production of *Bye Bye Birdie*, the national tour of *The Boyfriend*, directed by Julie Andrews, and the title role in the musical *Gidget*, directed by Francis Ford Coppola. Krysta has also seen on television in *Gossip Girl* and on film in *The Virginity Hit*.

Ken Womble*: Krysta, where did you spend your childhood?*
Krysta Rodriguez: In Orange County, California. I was always in the choir, the one who was singing the loudest, and always doing all the choreography correctly and everything. When the other kids were kind of staring off into space, I was always very focused from a young age with performing.

KW: *Your mom once told you that you could do this as a career. What prompted her to say that and what effect did it have on you?*
KR: I was doing a dance recital and in the car I told my mom "I want this. How do I get more of this?" And she said, "Do you know you can do it as a job?" And that's when I was like, "Whoa, then why haven't I been doing that?"

KW: *How old were you?*
KR: I was thirteen. About the time I started doing children's theatre a lot of those kids were at the Orange County High School of the Arts. And I wanted to be involved in that program. So, I auditioned my freshman year, and I didn't get accepted into the musical theatre program.

KW: *Really?*
KR: Yeah. So, I decided to join the production design department, and I really enjoyed it. And then I re-auditioned and I got into the musical theatre program and spent the next three years doing that. I was in a competition team for my dance studio as well.

KW: *And you also said that everything fell into place.*
KR: Yeah.

KW: *How did it fall into place?*
KR: Well, all of a sudden I knew, I mean everything streamlined forward. There was no kind of question "I want to be a veterinarian or an astronaut." It was like "this is it."

KW: *Could you see the path, step by step by step?*
KR: Yeah. I think I could. I remember saying, "I'll go to the arts high school and then I'll go to Juilliard and then I'll be on

Broadway, and then I'll come back and perform at the performing arts center in Orange County," which I did years later.

KW: *Was that* The Boyfriend *tour?*
KR: That was *The Boyfriend* tour. Also, OCHSA had their graduation there, so I graduated high school in the theatre.

KW: *Wow.*
KR: Yeah, all very full circle moments. My life is very cyclical. [*Laughs*] I have a lot of completions of things.

KW: *That's not always true for people. You're lucky.*
KR: I know people who might say at that age, "This is what I want to do," and *not* have it click and go the way that they think it will. Of course, mine has not been, you know, anointed in the perfect way. But it's been very—great.

KW: *Also, at OCHSA you played the title role in* Gidget, The Musical. *What was that like to work with Francis Ford Coppola at fifteen?*
KR: It was awesome. I knew who he was, but I didn't know him in the context that so many people know him, *Apocalypse Now* and *The Godfather*. And here he was directing and writing *Gidget, The Musical* for his granddaughter. We would call him Uncle Francie—just a lovable, wonderful man.

KW: *You were cast in* Gidget *after being rejected from the program a year and a half earlier. What did that tell you about yourself? Was that pivotal at all?*
KR: Yeah, definitely. A lot of my story is about doors closing and finding other ways around them, or knowing a different direction was where I was supposed to go. So not getting accepted into the

musical theatre program was devastating at the time, and I'm so grateful for it now. And it definitely made the *Gidget* experience that much sweeter, of course.

KW: *So from OCHSA you moved to New York and attended NYU. Was that difficult to go from the west coast to the east coast?*
KR: I went to New York with my family when I was six, and we saw *Fiddler on the Roof*—that was my first Broadway show. And I *loved* it, and I loved the city. So from that point on it was very focused that I was going to go to New York.

And then after *Gidget* happened I got a lot of press for it. And I was approached by a lot of agents, and I started to kind of drift into that film and television world. We were driving up every day [to Los Angeles], my mother and I, changing in the car, doing my homework on the way home. And it wasn't going as well as I wanted it to and it wasn't feeling as satisfying.

So I auditioned for NYU, UCLA, Boston Conservatory and USC. I got in everywhere, but the two that I wanted to go to were NYU and UCLA. So that was the moment where it was like, "I've always thought that I was going to go to New York and now this new opportunity has presented itself. Do I stay in LA and try and do TV/film or do I make that leap?" By that point I was a little burned out on the LA scene, and I was ready to go to New York.

KW: *So you started at NYU, and were going back and forth between NYU classes and professional auditions?*
KR: Not a lot of professional auditions. They don't let you audition for school projects when you're a freshman. I did meet with the New York office [of KSR Talent], auditioned for them, and they said they would sign me on. And I auditioned for *Bye Bye Birdie* and got it—in the ensemble. It was really cool because there aren't a lot of shows with a bunch of young people in them.

KW: *But you seemed to have found all the shows that* do *have young people in them—five Broadway shows.*

KR: Well that's another timing thing, you know. I mean there are so many things that worked out well for me when I was out there, the young shows, the pop rock.

KW: *It seems that so many of the things that you're talking about have to do with timing, and some people might call it luck. Is it luck, or being in the right place at the right time, or did you sort of create that?*

KR: I wouldn't say luck as much as I would say right place at the right time. I am never sitting waiting for opportunities to arise. I am working until the opportunities make themselves available. It's me making sure that I know how to sing pop rock when all of a sudden they say it's time to sing pop rock and know that I can still work on my legit voice so that's ready when someone needs it too. You know, it's all kinds of self-preparation all the time until another force comes in and opens up an opportunity for me.

KW: *So, you left NYU and they didn't accept you back or you agreed to disagree?*

KR: No, it wasn't like a terrible parting. It was a leave of absence. I kept deferring my enrollment, and they even gave me an extra fifth semester in good faith. Then I got *Spring Awakening* and couldn't go back.

KW: *Was* Spring Awakening *a turning point, the moment that you said, "Okay, career starts here in full tilt."*

KR: I guess so. I mean I had already done *Good Vibrations*, so I had already been on Broadway at that point, which did not feel like a career arrival.

KW: *Why not?*

KR: Because it was a flop, because it closed after four months. And I was a swing so I barely got to perform on stage. So that kind of felt like the opposite of arrival, it felt like, "Is this really what I wanted to be dipping my toe in?"

So then I got the tour of *The Boyfriend*, which was really rejuvenating. I loved that experience. I met my best friends in the world. I got to travel with Julie Andrews. I got to come and perform in my hometown. It really refreshed me in a lot of ways and kind of made me feel like "Okay, this is what I get to do." We toured for nine months and did two hundred forty-two performances, and I never missed a show because I was ravenous, I was hungry for performance.

So that's when I came back to New York, I went back to school, finished the summer semester there to try and get my degree and then started my fall semester.

I saw *Spring Awakening* Off Broadway, and I called my mom and said, "I'm going to be in this show. I know it's going to Broadway, and I'm going to be in it." And she was like, "Do you want to swing again?" I was like, "I don't care. I will mop the floors if they let me in the building."

And then I got *Spring Awakening*. I think it was kind of the career igniter, but also it was an eraser. It kind of replaced, redid my Broadway debut in *Good Vibrations*.

This was the one time that I wanted something so badly, and it ended up being the thing that was supposed to happen. Because so many times the thing that you want so badly, you're just so blinded by it, that you can't realize it's not the right thing for you, that there's a better opportunity for you. And this happened to be both of those things converging and it was really magical.

KW: *Your next Broadway show was* A Chorus Line. *Tell me about your audition for that.*

KR: I auditioned for it while I was on tour with *The Boyfriend*. I was in Canada, and I flew in for the audition. And I was cut in five seconds. It was the shortest audition in my life. We did the combo across the floor and they were like "Bye!"

A year and a half later they called me to audition for the role of Bebe. And so I was like [*sighs*] "Sure." I hadn't danced in forever because I was sitting in that chair in *Spring Awakening* for nine months. And so I was like "it'll be a free dance class."

And I auditioned all day on Monday and it got pared down. All of a sudden it was the end of the day and it was me and one other girl. And I called my agent and I was like, "I might get this job and I don't even know that I want it." She was like "Just calm down, if you don't want it, don't go to the callback." And I labored about it.

But then I talked to a friend of mine who's also a Broadway performer, and I said, "But we just won all these Tonys [for *Spring Awakening*]." And she's like, "Exactly, you just won all these Tonys. You're done; you did what you can do in a new show. Now, it's just riding it out. Go play a *lead* in another show." And so I was like, "Yeah, okay."

And so I went to the callback and we had to do the audition in the theatre alone, by yourself on the stage with the creative team in the audience watching you—very much like the show. So that was scary. And I got the job that afternoon. It was quick. It was two days. And then I ended up in the hospital because I dehydrated myself.

KW: *You were not used to dancing that much.*

KR: Uh huh. I was literally negotiating my *Chorus Line* contract with IVs stuck in my arm.

KW: *You booked the lead in a pilot called* Iceland. *Could you tell me about that?*

KR: I flew out to LA to test for it in the middle of my last week of performances of *Addams Family*. It was a crazy experience. Actually, being in theatre prepared me for it in a great way because you have to go into a room of like twenty executives and do your performance.

So I got that job and then went back to New York and finished up my last four performances of *Addams Family* and then flew back to LA and shot it. It was a half-hour, single-camera comedy, very much in the vein of *The Office* or *Community*. It definitely fed my desire to do more television.

KW: *You played Ana Vargas on NBC's* Smash. *Could you tell me about the circumstances leading up to your audition?*

KR: I was living in LA for about a year and actually ended up having to move back to New York because of some personal things. I didn't have a job and didn't really know what I was going to do, but kind of threw myself back into the New York scene, which I actually missed a lot, and did a lot of concerts and benefits.

So, I got the audition for *Smash*—and I had watched the first season and enjoyed it and had a ton of friends on it—and so I was like, "Oh, this is cool." But it was a new regular character and to me it was sort of a long shot.

And I went to the audition and the executive producer, Josh Safran, was there in the room and they introduced me and he said, "I know who you are. I wrote your episode of *Gossip Girl*." I was on *Gossip Girl* back in 2008, and I was like, "Oh, my gosh!"

And then he said, "I've seen you at Joe Iconis' concerts." Joe Iconis is a very indie-focused composer in the musical theatre business, so I was surprised that this Hollywood executive knew about Joe and had seen me in the concerts. And I was just blown away because a lot of times your New York world and your television world don't really collide.

So I had a great audition and I left thinking, "You know, regardless of what happens this guy knows me and likes me."

So then I remember it was the morning of the Fourth of July, and I woke up and I had like fourteen missed calls from my agent. And so I call back and my manager says, "Well, the bad news is that they don't want to test you for *Smash*." I'm like, "Okay," and she says, "Because they're just going to give it to you."

And I was like "*What?*" I couldn't fathom that. I mean, I had been living in LA and had gone through, you know, endless rounds of auditions for things and being put on hold and not getting it and testing, and now I didn't even have to go to a callback. I literally just had one audition and about four days later had the call.

This was a Wednesday and they said, "You're starting work on Monday." It was completely a whirlwind. My life changed instantly in the way that only it can when you're in this business. I woke up that morning going, "Oh gosh, I have to pay my rent this month," and then all of a sudden I had this job.

KW: *That is a great story.*
KR: It was amazing, yeah.

KW: *So, it sounds like your callback for* Smash *was the concert that Joshua Safran saw you do.*
KR: Yeah, exactly; my audition was *Gossip Girl* and my callback was the concert and my test was my first audition.

KW: *It seems ironic that you came back to New York sort of out of necessity, yet your timing couldn't have been more perfect.*
KR: Yeah, absolutely. I like to be very prepared, to make sure everything goes right. But most of the time my career and the

way things have worked out have had nothing to do with me, just having me relax and go with the flow.

Even though I can go back in my life and career and realize how things have worked out so perfectly, I still don't allow myself to trust all the time.

KW: *You mentioned how cyclical your life has been, going from an arts high school to Broadway and then back to the Orange County Performing Arts Center. And then you returned to Broadway in a sense with* Smash, *only with the much bigger audience that television provides.*
KR: I know. I can't get away from it.

KW: *Maybe an obvious question, but was your role on* Smash *a turning point in your career?*
KR: Definitely. Now I can say I was a regular on a television show, which is really hard to do. Usually on pilots you're doing one episode and hoping it gets picked up, and then if it does maybe it only airs two or three or four times. My recognition factor has definitely gone up.

KW: *So, you've enjoyed living in New York again. Do you think you'll stay?*
KR: Yeah. I think I will stay as long as I am able to. You know, my roots are still in California. But I think I would like to be out there with a job and sort of settle.

My roots are here as an adult and I feel most comfortable. I feel most in my element to really conquer my career from this place. We'll talk again in two years, and I'll be somewhere completely unexpected.

KW: *So, do you see yourself going back to Broadway?*
KR: Yes I do, definitely. It will always be my first love, and with the right project, it's definitely something I would want to consider.

[And the right project came along just weeks after this interview when Krysta starred in the Broadway premiere of *First Date*, a romantic musical, with a book by *Gossip Girl* writer Austin Winsberg.]

KW: *Have you had a mentor along the way who's helped you, or even inspired you?*

KR: Oh, I haven't had just one. I mean there are many, many people that are really influential in my life. When I was fifteen and saw Susan Egan in *Cabaret* on Broadway that just blew my mind. She was extraordinary. And she went to OCHSA and was a famous alumnus. And now she's a friend of mine. And we've worked together and she is so giving and generous with her advice. It's mind-blowing to me still, that people that I've looked up to are so lovely and generous and just helpful to other people who are coming up in this business.

I saw Sutton Foster in *Thoroughly Modern Millie* and that was life-changing, and now she's also a friend of mine. She taught a master class at NYU and said something that sort of changed my life, "Other people's success is not necessarily your failure." And, it blew my mind because it's a hard thing to know, especially when somebody else is always getting something that you want.

You know, it's hard to remember that this business, as much as it is about talent, it's simply about math. There is one part and seven thousand people, and it's literally just a math equation that doesn't equal out. So, you have to kind of relinquish control in that area.

I auditioned for the *Hairspray* movie and got very far and didn't get it. It was one of those that just made me cry and cry and cry because I wanted it so badly. And had I been shooting that in Canada that summer, I wouldn't have been able to audition for *Spring Awakening* which started me on this path of Broadway that

I love. And I know for a fact that there are people who auditioned for *Smash* for my part who are saying now, "Thank God I didn't get that part on *Smash* because I got this other thing."

So, everybody's path is so completely different and you really don't have to compare yourself. If you look back at it, you can see how everybody is doing their own thing, and there's room for us all in our own little niche. So, I definitely believe that that piece of advice from Sutton was a mentally extraordinary thing to have in my toolbox.

Another person that I credit a lot is my friend Megan McGinnis. She's a Broadway performer and was in the workshop of *Good Vibrations*, and we lived together. She's eight years older than me and she was so, so open and generous and giving to me in that time as somebody who didn't know what they were doing. She kind of took me under her wing and we became best friends—we're still best friends. I was the maid of honor in her wedding.

KW: *What do you think really works for you at auditions?*
KR: When I started booking jobs, I realized what I did best and what I'm not so good at and was able to highlight the things that I do better. I think a lot of people will tell you once they learned who they were and felt comfortable with themselves, that's when all the pieces fall into place.

KW: *So what do you do best?*
KR: I think I have a natural quality that's becoming the fashion in musical theatre. I am also not a typical ingénue and I'm not a typical character actress, so I think making my own brand in the middle has worked well. And if there are shows that fit that, like *Addams Family*, it's a perfect fit.

If there aren't, then there's probably going to be somebody better than me. So if there's something in the middle, I don't know that anybody else can corner that market like me and a couple of other people.

KW: *You're sort of talking about type here.*
KR: Yeah, yeah.

KW: *What do you bring to an audition when you book it?*
KR: I don't know; I really don't know. You have to ask people who gave me a job. I think I use acting in everything that I do. I act when I dance, and I act when I sing, and I act when I act. In *In the Heights* the dancing is very intricate, but it's also about acting it and having an intention for every move.

I'm not going to be a Rockette dancer, somebody who is just doing pretty motions, because I don't have the technique for that. But I'm able to bring a believable acting quality to choreography that makes you want to pay attention.

KW: *How important is your belief in yourself as a performer?*
KR: You have to believe in yourself. I think my career started to solidify when I realized what I do rather than trying to do something else, trying to fit into a mold. I realized, do what you do and some of them will like it, and you'll be right for their show. And other people won't. And that's fine. I think that sort of self-awareness is very important.

Belief in yourself is hugely important because this community and this business is fickle. You know, one day you're up, next day you're down. It's very common. Your show's a hit, the next show's a flop, the phone's not ringing for some reason and then one thing will happen and then it'll ring again.

I had a voice teacher once tell me, "You could be in Carnegie Hall and have a thousand people applauding for you and one person who's booing." You can't always be listening to everybody.

If you listen to the one bad person, you're doing yourself a disservice to the nine hundred and ninety-nine other people. And if you just listen to the nine hundred and ninety-nine, you know, you're not maybe challenging yourself.

So, you have to let the influences in correctly. I don't read reviews. I don't think that they're helpful, especially in a Broadway show because they come out once the show is done. You're not going to change it. There's nothing you can do. So, I think there is something to be said for being singularly focused.

KW: *What are one or two of the smartest things you've done for your career? And if you could go back and change one career decision, what would it be?*
KR: Well, I think probably one of the smartest things I did for my career was move to New York.

I really think that coming at the age that I did and going to school here, where I felt like I was safe and I didn't need to get a survival job; I learned the ins and outs of New York while I was auditioning for things so that when I was ready, I was ready, and it happened to be before school was over.

But, you know, I never claim to have the answer or the correct way. There's no secret key that I'm holding onto that I can give to you and tell you how to get to Broadway. Everybody's path is entirely different. For me, I just felt like being in New York at that young age and getting it in my bones and learning the whole system was very important so that I was freer in my auditions and didn't feel that neediness that can happen when you're unemployed or when you're waiting tables and really hating it.

Another experience that sticks out in my mind is when I auditioned for *Addams Family* the first time, for the very first reading, and I did not get the role of Wednesday. They liked me but I was sort of an untested product in many ways. Even though I had done four Broadway shows, I had never really lead a show. So they were like, "We're going to give it to somebody that we know, that we trust, that is a tried and true product…but we'd like to offer you the ensemble."

And I was like, "Well, how am I ever going to get out of the ensemble if you're going to give me the ensemble?" You know, it's like a Catch-22. They don't trust me with their role because I've never done it, but they won't try me. So, it was definitely an ego blow.

And I kind of toyed with turning it down. I was very busy at the time and I was like, "You know, to sit in the back…I don't know that I necessarily want to do that."

And I talked to my agents about it and then I was like, "Know what? Why not? You never know what happens out of these things. I might as well." And I knew that I was right for this part and knew that they were just maybe a little scared at that point and unsure. You know, it's hard to cast someone in the first reading two-and-a-half years before it's going to be on Broadway and stick with them.

So I decided this way when it comes back around I'll know the show, I'll know the tone of it. I'll have met the people and they will have gotten to know me.

So, I did it, I did the ensemble. And I sat in the back and people came up to me regularly and said, "Did you audition for Wednesday? You should. That'd be a good part for you." And I'm going, "Yes, yes I know."

And then I auditioned again months later, when the show came around again, and got it that time.

And I remember the writer, Rick Elice, telling me much later on that one of the reasons they trusted me with the part is because they thought it was such a humble and noble act from me to take the ensemble when I didn't necessarily want to do it. And they thought, "This is a girl who's a team player. And we want her on our team."

KW: *It sounds like that was a great example of doing what you have to do, or maybe what you should do, even though it's the hard thing to do.*
KR: Right. And sometimes it's not always the right thing. Because if you really want to stop being in the ensemble, at some point you have to stop being in the ensemble.

But this one just felt a little different. Once I got past the initial ego, it was like, "No, this is a great opportunity and Nathan Lane is in this and, you know, Marshall Brickman and Rick Elice, who are titans in the literary community." I'm like, "Just get over yourself and do it."

KW: *It seems that because that took you from ensemble roles to leading roles on Broadway, it was a pretty big turning point for you.*
KR: Yeah, definitely.

KW: *All of the statistics tell us that acting is an incredibly difficult profession. At any given time there are far more actors out of work than are working. However, you have defied those odds, enjoying quite a bit of success in a relatively short time in your career. In addition to all the other things you've told me, how have you done it?*
KR: Persistence. It's number one. I mean there's just no other way. You can't let one person deter you. You can't let five people deter you. If you believe that this is what you're supposed to do, and you have some positive reinforcement that you are capable of doing it, and you are good at it, then you just have to keep going.

I think my entire career path has been a bunch of "no's" before there's a "yes." A *bunch*. I didn't make it into the musical theatre department in high school my freshman year, so I did the tech department. But then I tried out again. I wasn't Wednesday the first time, but I tried out again.

There are many things where a door closes and another one opens, but there are many things where you just don't take no for an answer. I couldn't get an audition for *Spring Awakening*, and I went to an open call. I did it myself.

If you're doing it out of your heart and you're not hurting people in the process, just keep going, just blast through it because you'll come out the other side eventually.

Krysta Rodriguez Success Team Member

MEG MORTIMER

Ken Womble: *Meg, you're a partner at Principal Entertainment, a bicoastal management company. Could you tell me a bit about your company and the mediums you work in?*

Meg Mortimer: Sure. My company represents actors, writers, directors, producers and we manage them, which means that we have a smaller amount of clients than an agency might have. Therefore, we pay more personal attention to what their particular needs or talents are at any particular time. We also produce films, normally, when one of our clients, a director or a writer, is involved.

KW: *What are you looking for in an actor you sign?*

MM: What I'm looking for in them is first of all their look. I want to know what their age range is and their marketability. But most important, I want to know can they go from zero to sixty with me? Because my role as a manager is to take actors and expose them to bigger opportunities than maybe their agent might do.

I'm not interested in somebody who's going to be slowly working their way up. I want to know when I put them in a room that they're up to the talent level and the confidence level of the people that they are competing against for a role, people with experience.

First I need to be passionate about them as a performer and have a vision for them that I share with them. It usually happens when I'm a big fan of their work.

KW: *What was your first impression of Krysta?*
MM: I first saw her in *The Addams Family* workshop. I was there because my client, Kevin Chamberlain, played Fester. Krysta comes out as Wednesday, and I am just like, "Who is this girl?" I mean immediately she grabbed my attention. And it was her poise and her confidence and then, of course, her singing and acting talent.

So I asked Kevin, "Did you enjoy working with her?" He says, "Oh yes, she's marvelous." And I said, "Well, would you mind passing along my information to her and see if she's interested in talking to me?"

We hit it off immediately. I was just bowled over by her the minute I saw her.

KW: *In performance what are some of her best qualities?*
MM: Krysta has a gorgeous voice. But she acts the song. She inhabits it. She inhabits the character.

I saw her go on in *In the Heights*—it's so funny because she's playing this Hispanic character and she really isn't Hispanic, she's got some Spanish in her, but it's not like she's Puerto Rican. But I believed her. I thought she was amazing. And she says to me, "I'm not a great dancer." She was terrific!

KW: *Krysta was in* Spring Awakening *and then* A Chorus Line *and then* In The Heights *in quick succession—and all this before*

The Addams Family. *What was she doing right that got her all this work?*

MM: I think Krysta is just special. She works really hard. She's very committed. And she stands out, you know. She has a great look and she presents herself so well.

KW: *How important a role has type played for Krysta and does she have a clear idea of her type?*

MM: Krysta and I have had conversations about that, and she's very wise about where she fits in. She makes very strong choices when she goes into an audition, understanding who she is. So she's not trying to act like something else. She's giving it her spin and if that's what they want, they're going to go with it. And if they don't want that, then they're not. But I think that's why she gets such excellent feedback all the time.

KW: *In her book,* Acting Q's, *Bonnie Gillespie said, "Working performers seem to have tapped into a sense of authenticity that most aspiring actors search for." It sounds like that's what you're saying about Krysta.*

MM: Yeah. She understands what she brings to a role and what makes it special. And Krysta knows that she's going to play the beautiful girl, but she's not going to play, you know, the bombshell necessarily. She's going to play the more interesting, fun-loving character. She knows when she fits in, and if she's not as clear, she still goes for it and gives it her own flavor.

KW: *It seems like it takes most people, and even actors, a long time to get to know who they are—*

MM: Mm-hmm.

KW: —*and Krysta talked about knowing what she does well and knowing what she doesn't do so well. It kind of takes the heat off a little bit, but it's also very instructional, it seems to me, when you go into an audition knowing what you bring to the table.*
MM: Oh, absolutely. I have never been in an audition room so I can't speak from experience, but my guess is that the minute an actor walks in the room they get a sense if they're interested in them or not. And a lot of it has to do with the confidence with which they walk in, you know, not apologizing. Everybody's nervous; I would think that every actor who goes into an audition is usually nervous. I mean I would be petrified. But it's how they channel that energy.

KW: *How important has her belief in herself been for Krysta?*
MM: Her self-confidence plays a huge part in her success. Krysta went out to LA to test for *Iceland*. A very small percentage of actors that I've worked with book a pilot the first time they've ever tested because it's very, very, very stressful, these screen tests for television pilots. There are all different kinds of players who are weighing in. They say that the executives at the studios sometimes don't give the actor a lot of feedback in their faces and their mannerisms because they probably want to see if they can withstand the pressure of having to do a show. You know, whether it's in front of an audience or in seven days. And she did it. I mean she went out and she booked the pilot. And she did an excellent job in it and made a lot of fans at the studio and at the network.

KW: *You said the feedback's terrific. What kinds of things do casting directors say about her?*
MM: I really don't go into detail with casting directors, but I can tell by their tone of voice. I mean they might say, "Oh, she was good!" Or they'll say, "I loved her, she was terrific." Now, some-

times she doesn't get the role because the director has a stronger choice for that particular role, but it's important to me that my clients continue to get excellent feedback whether they get the role or not. It's just a matter of then, what's the right role for them. You know, it's just a matter of time. Whether it's a drama or a comedy, Krysta always gets excellent feedback.

KW: *When I asked her what she does right at auditions, she said, "I really don't know. You have to ask people who gave me a job."*
MM: [*Laughs*] I know, because you see, that's it, that's the mark of a true artist. Because they just go in their zone. It's like you don't ask a painter, "Why did you make that paint stroke?" You know what I mean? It's the same thing with acting. If an actor is that measured that they're so aware of every moment, then they're probably not invested in what they're doing. They come from what their talent is. That's why they're special. They have a gift; they're an artist.

KW: *How would you describe her overall as a client?*
MM: Oh, she's a dream. I love working with Krysta. She's wonderful to talk to. She's very wise. She has a lot of insights. She's a pleasure to be around. I mean she's just got such a sparkling personality. She's prompt; she's prepared.

Actors always say, "I want an agent." But you'd be surprised, you get some clients who don't return your phone calls, who don't let you know if they're confirmed, who are always running late. Those clients tend not to be my clients for a long time because I have no patience. Because if I'm working harder than they are on their career, then I think we need to part company.

But Krysta is very invested. She's a great client to have. And also I see a future for her. I see where she could go. I don't have a crystal ball, but I know she can always rise up to the challenges that are put in front of her.

KW: *All of the statistics tell us that acting is an incredibly difficult profession. At any given time there are far more actors out of work than are working. However, Krysta has defied those odds, enjoying quite a bit of success in a short time. How has she done it?*

MM: She's talented! [*Laughs*] She's really, really talented. I don't know what else to say to that. Sometimes it's just right place, right time. You know?

But I've got to think it's bigger than that with her. She's got a really big gift. She's also got a real modern feel to her and yet she can be period. So that also has added to her success. But you can have all of that, and if you don't have the talent, it really doesn't matter at all.

Krysta Rodriguez Success Team Member

LORI SWIFT

Ken Womble: *Lori, you are the former Director of the New York Office of Kazarian, Measures & Ruskin. Could you tell me a bit about the mediums that you worked in at the agency?*

Lori Swift: Sure. KMR is a bicoastal agency, and I was the director of the New York office for twelve years. I represented actors for TV, film and theatre, including both rising and established stars on Broadway, TV and film, from newbies coming out of school to very established Tony winners.

KW: *Before you became an agent, you were both an actor and a casting director. How have those experiences been beneficial in your work with actors?*

LS: As a professionally trained actor, I have such a love and respect for actors and an understanding of what they need to have to go on an incredibly difficult journey. Actors need to not only love to audition, but also be really prepared and skilled in their craft. My experience as a casting director really helped train my eye and hone in on talent that I personally respond to.

I try to find those people who I'm not only in love with, who I think are superstars, but who have a constitution about them that makes you want to work with them and go on this journey with them. And having acted in my early years, I have such a deep respect for the process, and I'm very understanding of the emotional needs that come with the territory. I am just one hundred percent supportive of an actor's process.

KW: *When you say actors need to have the constitution, do you mean a sense of will, a sense of confidence?*
LS: Yes. I mean having the drive, the inner peace and the trust while embracing where you are at all times. Talent in someone is the initial draw for me of course. But peace, trust, drive and ambition are qualities in an actor that have determined who I have loved to work with.

KW: *Right, exactly.*
LS: There are probably many, many other things we can talk about that add to that constitution, but those four, I think, are like a diamond that illuminate you as a person and performer.

Skill and hard work, along with a constant curiosity about the world, is also a big part of your makeup. That's so important, and it contributes to you as an artist and as somebody who people want to be in the room with, and work with: traveling, reading, writing, and studying other performers and artists are all ways that are going to enrich you as a performer all the time.

If an actor is living their life to the fullest, in their person and in their craft, then they are going to be a natural magnet. I think that if you have that kind of trust and curiosity you are going to present yourself as confident and not come off as desperate to be hired for a job.

KW: *To start our conversation about Krysta, how long have you worked with her and what was your impression when you first met?*
LS: I worked with Krysta for about ten years. She came in and sang. And she was a beauty; a young, very self-composed student at the time, an NYU freshman. I was very taken with her, she had very expressive eyes, and she seemed very soulful. She said, "I want to do musical theater." Then she sang, and I thought, "Okay, this is not your typical musical theater candidate." I think that's why she excelled so much in it—because she stands out.

I was looking at her going, "She needs to be doing all mediums right away." From the get-go with Krysta, I thought she needs to be getting in rooms even if she's going to be leading with Broadway shows first. This is an area [TV and film] that she has to start getting used to because it's going to be a big part of what she does, too.

KW: *Soon after you started working together, she was cast in the* Encores! *production of* Bye Bye Birdie.
LS: Right.

KW: *How significant was that for her career wise?*
LS: Well, it was a great stepping stone. It's not like there are a lot of nineteen-year-old girls with a Broadway credit. She was one of the chosen for that big show that tons of girls tried out for. That created a real curiosity for people to say, "Oh, I want to see more. What else can she do?"

So as it turned out, she booked these back to back shows in New York while she was going to school—starting with *Good Vibrations* on Broadway, then going into *Spring Awakening*, then

In The Heights, then into *A Chorus Line*, and then *The Addams Family*.

KW: *It's unbelievable the run she's had. I think industry folks typically want actors to fill a slot in a type, so what is her type or how is she sort of in between?*

LS: I don't necessarily like to even box somebody into a type. If I do, it's because I need to start someplace with a performer, and they will grow and I cast a wide net and try to expand them. I like to see how an actor can sort of flower out into a lot of things. Krysta wasn't somebody that I had to do that with because I just had a visceral response to her charisma and her stage presence.

Like the way that happened with Donna Murphy. When Donna Murphy was young, she was sort of a young character ingénue, and then as she matured, she became like a vessel almost. She can do a lot of different things, and that's what I see for Krysta. She has this kind of ethnic feel to her, and yet she could do more mainstream roles.

For most of her teenage years and early twenties, she was in the New York scene and honing her craft at school, and she was working on these great, young ingénue and character parts. And then she booked her first TV show, *Gossip* Girl; you know a very smart, Ivy League, kind of edgy chick. And she does have that kind of persona if you want to talk about type. There's like an edge to her, there's somebody who has style.

She did that movie that Will Ferrell produced called *Virginity Hit* where she was more of a fun loving, sidekick sister type. She has a very easy and comfortable place within herself where she seems to live—you can kind of veer in so many directions. She invents the type, you know.

KW: *What kind of feedback do you get from casting directors and directors about her auditions?*

LS: She makes quite an impression in a room, and she's a serious contender for just about any role. If a role doesn't go her way, it could be a matter of her type, or she doesn't fit in with the rest of the team's idea of what they want the show to be. It's not because she didn't go in and do a great job. She makes strong choices and connects with her audience. You know, she really is magnetic in an audition room.

KW: *How much does talent play in that for Krysta?*

LS: A big, big part. There's a quality in Krysta that I would equate with talent that has to do with an awareness of herself in space, how she naturally moves, and what kind of charisma that produces. It's kind of uncanny. The way she is able to embrace her talent, channel and share it is uniquely her own.

KW: *It seems to me that she kind of does that naturally. She doesn't have to effort those things that you're talking about.*

LS: That's right, it's effortless for her. It's fluid. There are girls who are working too hard trying to do what just comes naturally for her, and I really think that's a gift that she has. And what she does with it is a big part of her talent—her natural ability to channel these qualities and just make it look effortless.

KW: *If you could cite three actions, skills or beliefs that have made Krysta successful, what would they be?*

LS: I think three big ones would be having a vision, setting goals and applying herself to meet those goals. Like "Okay, I'm going to get these credits, but I'm also going to finish school while I'm auditioning and performing. And my aim is to get a lead on Broadway." And she accomplished that.

We talked a lot about auditioning and performing and her talent and her craft, her work ethic. And all of that is great, but I think that this ability to fulfill the big picture for herself is a real skill. And it requires focus and tenacity and an ability to just get it all done, and a belief in herself to do it.

I think that she comes from a great, solid upbringing and had a lot of love in her life that helps her put things into perspective. And so long as she continues to have the drive and focus and wants to be telling stories and wants to continue to grow as an artist, I think that she's really in a great place.

What are the keys that have led Krysta Rodriguez to a successful acting career?

She made the decision to become an actor

The encouragement Krysta's mother gave her at thirteen, suggesting she could make a profession of performance, gave Krysta direction. A few years and a few strong performances later "everything streamlined forward," and Krysta eliminated the possibility of any other career. She made a clear decision to become an actor.

She has found her essential qualities and knows her type

Audiences love to watch actors who are as real and complex as humanity itself; actors like Krysta who know and play their essential qualities. As to type, Krysta's natural quality brings to mind neither a traditional ingénue nor a character actress. She has created her "own brand in the middle."

She is a great auditioner

Meg Mortimer and Lori Swift raved about the responses Krysta gets at auditions. Why are her auditions so well received?

When she walks into a room she knows who she is and radiates relaxed confidence. And when the audition starts Krysta's laudable acting and singing skills are abundantly clear. Krysta knows how to put together all the elements of a winning audition package.

She is talented

Krysta is a skilled actor who has honed her craft through thousands of stage performances and multiple TV appearances. Her management team highlighted her innate qualities as well—natural charisma and self-awareness—qualities that make her immensely attractive to audiences. Meg summed it up best: "I think Krysta just is special...she stands out."

She has confidence

Lori believes the confidence Krysta developed in her happy childhood, and uses as a performer today, has kept her steady on her show business journey.

She has good timing

Good timing often leads to good luck, and Krysta has had both. Arriving in New York just as pop rock musicals like *Spring Awakening* and *In the Heights*, with roles perfect for her voice and brand were taking off, got Krysta her start on Broadway. Performing in a string of concerts with a prominent television producer in attendance got her a leading role on NBC's *Smash*.

Krysta's good luck and timing have led to interesting roles in great shows—and to significant advances in her career.

She is a pleasure to work with

Entertainment industry professionals tell me repeatedly how they like to work with actors who are responsible, friendly and cooperative. When I asked Meg to describe Krysta as a client, she called her "a dream." Lori expressed similar sentiments.

She's perseveres, no matter what

Krysta's decisions are proof of her determination to get what she wants, no matter the circumstances. Although she had already performed on Broadway, she made the decision to audition at an open call, with unknown and untried actors, for *Spring Awakening*. Although she had already played leading roles, she made the decision to take an ensemble role in *The Addams Family*. Both these decisions were difficult to make; perhaps because they felt like steps backward, yet led Krysta to giant steps forward.

She has a clear vision for her career and puts it into action

About her life and career Krysta said, "…things have worked out so perfectly." Lori talked about Krysta's vision for the future and how she backs up that vision with action. She began planning—and fulfilling—that future in high school when she decided to be an actor and her decisions have been strong and clear.

In just a few years she has accomplished more than many seasoned performers, and because she is working both hard and smart, I believe that for Krysta Rodriguez, the sky's the limit.

TONY YAZBECK

CHAPTER 4

There's a Higher Power Involved

TONY YAZBECK

Tony was born in Riverside, California. Upon moving to Pennsylvania at age four, he started taking dance classes after watching Fred Astaire on television. He is now Broadway's foremost song and dance man.

Tony's Broadway credits include *Chicago* (Billy Flynn), *Gypsy* with Patti LuPone (Tulsa, Outer Critics Circle Nomination), Irving Berlin's *White Christmas* (Phil Davis), *A Chorus Line* (Al), *Oklahoma!*, *Never Gonna Dance*, and *Gypsy* with Tyne Daly at age eleven. Off Broadway credits include the *Encores!* productions of *Little Me* (George Musgrove), *On The Town* (Gabey), *Gypsy* (Tulsa), *The Apple Tree*, *A Tree Grows in Brooklyn*, *Pardon My English*, and *Fanny Hill* (York Theatre). Regional credits include *On The Town* (Barrington Stage), *Far From Heaven* (Williamstown Theatre Festival), *Animal Crackers* (Goodman), *Irving Berlin's White Christmas* (Paper Mill Playhouse), *Sycamore Trees* (Signature), *Antony and Cleopatra* (Hartford Stage), *My One and Only* (Goodspeed), *Singin' in the Rain* (MUNY), and *Harmony* (Alliance). TV and Film credits include: *As The World Turns*, *All My Children*, *Smash*, and *Every Little Step*. Tony serves on the panel and as a master teacher for The National Young Arts Foundation.

....

Ken Womble: *Tony, how did you get your start in show business?*

Tony Yazbeck: I started actually as a tap dancer when I was four-years-old. I was put into dance class and I knew that's where my heart was. And the voice really didn't come until I got to college.

I didn't really focus on it. I just thought I was a dancer who performed well and wanted to be in shows.

And so finding that out in college and realizing, "Oh, I can sing classically if I want. I can sing all different styles," that was a big surprise to me.

KW: *It sounds like you were intent on this from the beginning. Your first Broadway show was playing a newsboy in* Gypsy *starring Tyne Daly. What was the audition and the experience of doing the show like?*

TY: Well, I was eleven-years-old and I was dancing nonstop in Pennsylvania. I was involved with a dance studio there, and I was competing and performing a lot. And my mom made it a rule to really practice, practice, practice. I mean my work ethic started real young. I knew all the old movie musicals. That's sort of how I got started. I watched the old movie musicals on TV; Fred Astaire and Gene Kelly were everything to me.

And so my mother gets a call that somebody knows of an audition in New York. This was the first audition I had gone on, and there were over one hundred boys there. The audition was actually at the St. James Theatre on the stage, which doesn't happen much anymore—it's usually in a studio—but it was kind of thrilling just to be there. And they needed a kid who played the clarinet, tap-danced and sang. And lucky enough I had done all these things. I was playing clarinet in the marching band.

And moments later when I was downstairs in the basement of the St. James in sort of the green room, the casting director comes down, and my mother and my father were there, which was a thrill because they were divorced then, and he says, "You're starting in three days, get ready. You got it." I remember jumping up and down and just yelling, I was so excited.

And I got my Equity card and the bug started. And for me that whole experience was about the community—the theatre—the community of people around you and how much love there is in a cast. And watching Tyne Daly from the wings sing "Some People" every night was just thrilling, you know? Watching Bob Lambert play Tulsa instilled in me later on how I wanted to start looking at this number and finally put it on stage myself.

So, it was neat. As a child you take everything in, children are like sponges. And it stays with you.

KW: *In the more recent version of* Gypsy *you were cast as Tulsa. How much influence did that experience, as an eleven-year-old watching from the wings, have on you?*

TY: It had a lot of influence, honestly. And I think the reason is because you bring who you are to every role. Tulsa has sort of a dark side. He's very passionate, he's a romantic kind of guy and he's a dreamer. And he just wants out. He wants to make it out there. And he doesn't even know if he has a say because he's been put down his whole life. I related so much to that. So I was able to just bring who I was to this part.

Going through my family drama as a kid and, you know, back and forth, my mom and my dad and then watching this guy sing "All I Need Is The Girl," this amazing scene, song and dance, I think what I understood most was the underlying dark magic of that song. I just got it. I understood that it was all in the heart.

And it was Arthur Laurents who directed me in this one. So going in to audition for him, I knew exactly what he wanted without even him saying anything. And it sort of worked. And it's always nice when you walk in the room and you do your number and the director's crying and it's for the right reasons.

That was a great moment for me because I really felt like what I took as a child was the right thing.

KW: *And after college, around 2000, you moved to New York and started working right away.*
TY: Yeah.

KW: *Was there momentum going on there?*
TY: You know it's interesting. Everything happens for a reason. I feel like God sort of blessed me right away. I went on a leap of faith. I left school after my third year. I was broke and I couldn't pay for school and I was sort of miserable with where I was in my life. I just lost some confidence.

And I left school and I had a hundred bucks on me and I called my drama teacher from high school and I said, "Is there anywhere I can stay?" because I didn't know anybody in New York at the time. She said, "I know this woman who went to the same high school as me and she lives in Queens and you can stay on her couch." So I go out there, I have my two bags and I walk in and she immediately said to me...it's just weird, she says, "Have you been seen or submitted for *Annie Get Your Gun*? there's a national tour going on of the Broadway show." And I said no. She said, "Well, I'm an agent. I'd love to submit you."

And I thought, "Wow!" I really had no idea. And I said, "Of course you could. That would be amazing." But I don't even think she knew what I did, or I just told her what I did and she saw that I had a good look for the stage. And I also had callbacks for two other shows that week, for *Chicago* and a callback to play opposite Angela Lansbury in *The Visit*. And within the next month I booked the national tour of *Annie Get Your Gun* with a full production contract, which I stayed with for eleven months.

That was the biggest, best thing that could have happened to me because I was fresh out of school. I was able to have an amazing experience on the road with all these great people, pay off my debt from college and then come to New York with enough money to get my own place. So that forwarded my career to where I was a little more confident, and I could really audition in New York and go for it.

KW: *That's an amazing story. Who was the agent?*
TY: Her name's Diane Riley over at Harden-Curtis. I left them years ago, but she was a sweetheart for doing that for me.

KW: *So, within a month you had booked* Annie Get Your Gun?
TY: Yeah. I actually booked it within a couple weeks.

KW: *That's incredible timing and luck. How do you think that happened?*
TY: It's just kind of crazy. I just have faith in what I do. I haven't had an actual everyday American job in New York.

And it's kind of interesting to me. You work and work and work forever. And when you start playing leads in productions you wait for those right roles to come along. You don't even take the things that are offered to you sometimes because you feel like it's not the right direction for your career. But I've been lucky enough to be able to find those roles in the last six years or so since I've really started to say no to playing in the ensemble and yes to playing roles and getting my career going more as an actor.

KW: *Was that a conscious decision not to have an outside job, or is that the way it's fallen?*
TY: It just sort of the way it's fallen. I mean I've been on unemployment a couple of times and that's something I think every actor has done because our line of work is so in and out. You can be working for a year, all of a sudden you have two or three months where you're not working. And then you get a job. So, there are always these breaks.

The thing is to start realizing what else you can do to fill that time. I love to teach different techniques in musical theatre like Viewpoints that help with performance. I just love the fact that I can constantly work in my career in one way or another in creating.

KW: *How do you prepare for auditions?*
TY: I work my butt off. I don't even feel comfortable going in for auditions anymore unless I'm so prepared because I won't do my best work, and if I don't do my best work, I feel like I cheated myself. I try to make it so that there's no excuse I didn't get it, other than the fact that it's out of my hands. Other than it's my look or my type or it's just not right, you know, that kind of thing.

A lot of times now you're given the material for the show. You don't even sing your own thing anymore. So you're printing off maybe ten pages of sides and two songs. And I call a coach and pay somebody to help me through this music or I already know it. Or I work on it with a friend. I try to memorize as much as possible.

But at the end of the day, what I try to do is instill myself into the character as much as possible. Because they know after the first bar of music you can sing. They don't need to keep hearing that you can sing well. They need to know that there's somebody there. They want to know the truth. They want to see somebody who is going to move an audience. That's what's most important, you know. It doesn't matter that I kicked a leg as high as everyone else, it doesn't matter that I'm singing the best notes, it doesn't.

And I really believe that life experience has a lot to do with it. You're basically telling an audience that they're not alone and that this is real. And if you can do that, then I think you have a pretty good chance of getting a job.

KW: *I hear that over and over, that sense of self. Was there a moment, or an experience, that made you realize how important that was?*

TY: I guess I've had a lot of different moments like that. And they usually happen when you go into a room and you don't expect anything. You don't put any pressure on yourself. Sometimes the best auditions are when you don't think you could ever get this job, and then you have absolutely no nerves, no pressure. You don't want it. You should never want the job. You should just do your best in a room because the jobs sort of pick you.

KW: *Can you give me an example of that?*
TY: At Trinity Repertory Theatre they saw me as Bernardo in *West Side Story*. I did my thing and they loved me and wanted to call me back. And before I left I said, "Listen, I don't know if it's okay to ask, but who I am is Tony. And I would love to show you these scenes and songs. It's in my heart. It's what I am." And she was open. I did my thing, she was moved, and she said, "You were right. This is who you are." I ended up getting that part, and it really was a dream job for me because I always wanted to play it.

Another instance: I got to meet Tina Landau, an amazing director. She was directing a new musical [*Sycamore Trees*] at the Signature Theatre in D.C., written by Ricky Ian Gordon, which was awesome. And I walk in there for this smaller part, and she looks at me and goes, "Will you come back tomorrow and read for the lead? Here are the sides." And there's like this three page monologue. She wanted me to look at in a day, and I just thought, "Oh my gosh. Okay. I'll give it a whirl."

And this was a part that I would never think that I was right for. He was shorter, skinnier, kind of nerdier, you know, but he had a heart. He had a major heart. And I just thought, "Wow. This director saw the essence of who I am, and she wants me to play this part." Normally you walk into a room and most people have a blind eye and they just are not open.

And I came back in. I wasn't necessarily memorized, but I said the lines truthfully, and I emotionally went to where I went to, and she gave me the job. Those are the times where you feel like true theatre happens, you know.

Or you meet somebody that is going to influence your life like Tina did. When you walk into auditions open, usually things happen. As much as you want to make clear choices, you still have to be open to anything that can happen in that room because that's true theatre for me, the spontaneity of the moment.

I started to really get what makes a good audition and why people get roles. I think it's because you don't care in the best way. You walk in there with a completely open heart, ready to do whatever is required in that moment. And it's helped me understand that it's really not about talent as much as it's about opening yourself up.

KW: *That's wonderful. You just gave me about four quotes that I'll probably put on my wall!* [Laughs]
TY: Oh good. Yay!

KW: *When you book a role what kind of feedback do you usually get from your agent or director?*
TY: You know, they don't really do that much any more.

KW: *No?*
TY: I'm pretty bold in rehearsals. So I go right to the director, and the director tells me exactly what's going on most of the time. I want the truth. I want to know if I'm doing something right or wrong so that I can keep working on it.

Jay Binder is one of the casting directors that I've loved over the years. He's such a supporter of mine. When *On the Town* was happening at City Center *Encores!* he said, "This is your role, this is who you are." And I got that job and it was one of the most amazing experiences. So these people forward your career and support you in doing it.

If you can find directors and choreographers that collaborate with the actors, it's really the best experience. I love it in the rehearsal room when I feel like you have your role as the director, you have your role as a choreographer, I have my role as an actor and we all respect each other's roles. If we can all just put our heads together and find the best product, it's going to be a better theatrical experience and an open forum to just create.

KW: *Do you feel free to have that dialogue, let's say, at a callback for a show? Do you have that sort of interaction with the director?*
TY: At a callback you're trying to just explore different choices and let this director know that you are not one-dimensional. He wants to know that in an instant this person can change their viewpoint on how they're doing something and feel like they've created it for themselves and not just been told to. And if they find an actor that can do that, isn't set in their ways, they're so happy.

I guess the best thing that I've learned in this business is knowing how to talk to people and how to get what you want in the most politically correct way. Being able to be bold and yet gracious and kind at the same time. That's an art form, you know?

KW: *Sure.*
TY: Networking and creating with these people and understanding how to really play the game.

KW: *Right. How do you network yourself?*
TY: I just keep trying to keep lines open with people all the time. If I find out there's something going on that maybe my agent hasn't told me about, I tell him right away, and I always find out if I know

somebody who's connected to that project. I'm very comfortable writing an e-mail myself. And a lot of times when an actor is bold enough to just say, "Hey, what about me for something?" you become an agent for yourself, you know? And you have to. You cannot let your agents help you get jobs the rest of your life. Your career will never happen for you.

KW: *When you find out about a project do you let your agents know about it and work in coordination with them?*
TY: Yeah. I would let them know first thing. And then they would work on it, and I would work on it at the same time.

And now I have a manager as well, so I have three sources. We all work on different angles to get the same thing going. Sometimes this person might know somebody and this other person might know somebody else.

KW: *Was there a moment when you decided not to fall back, to be an actor and nothing else? And if so, what motivated that?*
TY: I'll be honest, I might as well have been four-years-old when I knew this was all I wanted to do. You know, there's a girl in *Every Little Step* [a documentary film Tony appeared in] who says, "If you know you're going to fall back, you'll probably fall back."

KW: *Right.*
TY: And she's kind of right, you know? The truth is you've got to be so set and so confident in knowing that—and I tell this to students all the time—"If you love what you do so much and you feel compelled to do it and there's a passion and there's a fire burning in your heart to do it, you're probably meant to do it." There's some kind of force that says *you* have a mission to do this; which means you're probably going to succeed, as long as you are focused and going in the right direction to do it.

And that's kind of a faith way of looking at it, sure. But for me to have a four-year-old mentality of, "I want to dance, I want to dance, I want to dance," it's just mysterious to me. And there wasn't really another thing in my head of what would I do.

There are people in this business, and I know some of them, that do it for the fame and do it for the money, and they're trying to get ahead, and they don't even know why the heck they're doing it. And it's sad because they're not open in an audition room. They're not out there to change somebody's life and make some art happen on the stage. And that's just the wrong reason to be in this business. I think the more you just focus on work and you focus on art and you focus on creating, the money will just come.

And I know that's easy for me to say because I've been sort of blessed, but I really think that you have to have a sense of faith in this business because it's art, you know? Not like a daily job. You're not going to know that you have a salary coming in every week and that's just how it is. You've got to have a belief that this is going to happen. Or else, gosh, you're just going to worry yourself to death. You know what I mean?

KW: *What would you say is your best quality as an actor?*
TY: I'm open hearted. I was trying to say that a better way. I'm not afraid to tell the truth with my heart. It's like with *Gypsy*—underneath there's a dark current of joy. It's like a dark light always happening within me from everything I've gone through, all the shit that has happened to me in my life. But then it's knowing that there's hope at the end of the tunnel and joy there. There's so much joy in what I do and how I want to live my life, and I think people see it. And that's something they don't see all the time.

KW: *It sounds like you're very congruent, what you want is very aligned with what you're doing and what you're getting.*

TY: Yeah, I think so. I mean, a lot of people say, "Oh, you're the song and dance man; nobody sings and dances and acts like you, you're the triple threat." I've heard from some people it's like there is a truth, an openness. And that's something that really doesn't have much to do with talent, you know?

That's the thing that actually speaks to somebody. You know, the talent is just the stuff that helps get that to them.

KW: *What part would you say that momentum and timing have played in your career?*
TY: Sometimes a show comes up that you've been wanting to do forever and you're like, "Wow! I'm the exact age for this show, and I'm perfect for this." Timing is a lot in this business.

KW: *Can you give me an example?*
TY: *A Chorus Line* was a big one because I knew about the show back in the day, but now I was close to this character's age. I wasn't even going in for this part [Al]; I was going in for Mike. And then they saw me in the room; they just went, "You're Al," and I thought, "Great! Whatever! He's a role in the show, right?" And I thought, "I think everybody in that room thinks I'm the one for this part. That must mean something." You know, I was here for a reason.

Getting the job as Tulsa [in *Gypsy*] was a different story because I basically fought my way into the room for that job, and I wasn't stereotypically what they were looking for, and all the odds were against me because of the way I came across. They thought I was a little too old, and all I knew was I knew how to communicate it. And I called the choreographer of the show, and she helped me get into the audition because I couldn't before.

And there were six of us, and I was the only one that looked like me. You know, there's five other shorter, skinnier, blonde guys and me. What the heck am I doing here? But you know what? I knew what I was doing there. I was there because I was supposed to be there. I just felt like this is the time. I had been waiting to play this role my whole life.

And we went to City Center, not thinking it was going to Broadway. And then four months later you get a call, "You're going to Broadway, they want you as Tulsa." And you're thinking, "What? Wow! What is happening?" And it's being directed by the same director, going back to the same exact theatre you did it in as a kid, and you're playing the role you always wanted to play. It's just like, "Okay, there's something divine here going on."

That was kind of perfect timing. Something felt very meant to be.

KW: *What would you say are maybe one or two of the smartest things you've done for your career? And if you could go back and change one or two things, what would they be?*

TY: Well, one of the smartest things is about a year before *Chorus Line* I decided, along with Jay Binder, I wasn't going to take an ensemble job ever again because he believed that this was the time I needed to start playing roles—do principal work.

And it was hard for me. I was really in debt at the time, and I just felt like, "How am I going to do this?" And a couple weeks later I got a couple of offers for ensemble work—they were good money jobs—and I had to say no. That was one of the best things I've ever done. And it was scary, you know? But knowing that there's a big power in "no," in turning something down and saying, "I feel like something is coming."

And within the next couple of months, I got to play Tony in *West Side Story,* and I played this character Matthew Mugg in the national tour of *Dr. Dolittle*, and I just thought to myself, "Wow! I'm starting to do it now."

And then I did an Off Broadway show called *Fanny Hill*, and then right in the middle of that run, I got the call that I was offered Al in the Broadway revival of A *Chorus Line* and it just sort of blew up from there. And I haven't taken an ensemble job since.

KW: *Was Al in* A Chorus Line *a breakthrough role for you?*
TY: It was a breakthrough because I knew that it was going to get coverage, people in New York were going to see this production. And to be able to have a character on the line and have my face front and center was a huge deal because now I was able to go, "Hello, New York, this is what I do; I'm a principal performer."

KW: *You were a replacement for the role of Billy Flynn in the Broadway production of* Chicago. *You must've done a hell of an audition because you seem a little young for the role.*
TY: Well, that's what I thought. It was my manager's idea for me to go in for it. And I told him, "Really? I think I'm too young." And he's like, "Yeah, but they're looking younger right now and they want some fresh blood. And Tony, you're the type, you're thirty-two years old, you're not a kid anymore, you're a man. These are the types of roles you should be going in for."

So I went in, absolutely no expectation at all thinking, "I'm not going to get this." And I'm looking at the guys around and they're all at least ten years older. I've seen them in Broadway shows and it was great because I didn't care. I didn't put any pressure on myself, no nerves.

And it was a director that I'd worked for before—in *White Christmas* on Broadway—Walter Bobbie. And he was laughing and happy and he was like, "That was a great audition." I walk out and two days later I get a call that I was approved for the job and I'm just like, "What?" completely surprised.

KW: *Okay. Last question. All the statistics tell us that acting is an incredibly difficult profession. At any given time there are far more actors out of work than are working. However, you've defied these odds, and you've had quite a bit of success in your career. How have you done it?*

TY: I'm going to be honest with you, I believe there's a higher power involved. It's the only way I can say it. And I'm not trying to be humble, I just feel like there's something else up there looking after me. I've believed it my whole life. My parents always supported me, and I worked my butt off in dance class, and I worked to improve my voice, and I really tried to be bold in this business, like a lot of people do. Why is it that I think that I got there specifically? I don't know. But there's something out there that said to me, "You're supposed to do it this way. This is your path."

And, you know, we all have the decision to say yes or no. And I think my own decision to just accept this challenge proved okay for me. It's kind of a mystery because I know a lot of actors who are amazing performers, who still have not been able to get their break.

I don't really credit myself that much. I just credit my creator and go, "Thank you for giving me the strength to get through this." Because it's too hard of a business to simply say that I did it all by myself.

Tony Yazbeck Success Team Member

JAY BINDER

Ken Womble: *Jay, you're the owner of Binder Casting in New York. Could you tell me how you got started in show business and what led you into casting?*

Jay Binder: It was a fluke. I had a friend that was general managing a production of Edward Albee's adaptation of the Nabokov novel *Lolita*. And Frank Dunlop, who was at the time an incredibly famous English director, and Edward Albee were having trouble casting it.

And Leonard Soloway, who was the general manager, called me and said, "You know a lot about casting. Would you go down and meet Edward Albee and Frank Dunlop?" And I said I would be happy to go down and meet them. And of course, I thought the first thing they were going to say to me was, "Could you find us a thirteen-year-old girl to play Lolita." And I was petrified, of course. And Edward turned to me and said, "You know, there's a part of a one-armed actor in my play. Can you find me a one-armed actor?" I said, "Left-armed or right-armed?" And I got the job.

KW: [Laughing] *That's a great story.*
JB: It's true.

KW: *Did you say left-armed or right-armed seriously or…*
JB: No, I said it with a twinkle in my eye. I looked at Edward squarely in the face and thought to myself, "Yes, he's serious, but also this is a test." Not could I really find one, but am I a person with any irony? Because certainly one needs irony to cast an Edward Albee play.

KW: *You've cast over fifty Broadway shows, both musicals and straight plays. What are some of the challenges unique to each?*

JB: Well, since I started doing this, it is almost impossible to produce a play on Broadway without a major star. If a play originates at Manhattan Theatre Club or the Roundabout or the Public or Playwrights Horizons that fortunately gets remarkable reviews and moves without a star, well that's a different case. But, without a star, it is almost impossible to produce a play commercially on Broadway.

Musicals are different stories. I mean, there are very few star-driven musicals. We could've never done *Nice Work If You Can Get It* until a star was attached because, while it's not a revival, it's the kind of show that needed a name, a reason to see it other than Gershwin music.

KW: *When you bring in an actor for an audition, what are you looking for and what are some of the things that you expect of them as professional actors?*

JB: Well, the main thing you look for is an actor who has an innate understanding of what the character is and the style of the play. You need to walk in and, without being told anything by a director, you need to understand the play and the part and give a performance.

Some directors don't give any adjustments, but there are some directors that if they see a spark of what they're looking for they will get up and work with you. But that doesn't happen a lot. I always say that in America "audition" is a noun and in England "audition" is a verb.

KW: *Oh, interesting.*

JB: So, what I expect of a professional actor is for them to have done their homework, to come in and have a point of view about the material, to have read the entire play, to be on time and to have followed the instructions that we give the agent to give to the actor, like what kind of song we're looking for. I expect that someone comes in prepared to do what they need to do to the best of their ability, whether they get the job or not.

KW: *Right, because if they don't get that role they want to come back and see you again.*
JB: Well, of course. I mean, if there's somebody that I think is talented and I bring them in several times and they don't get a job I don't give up on them.

I met Christian Borle many, many years ago when all he had been doing was a non-Equity tour of *West Side Story,* and I would bring Christian in for a lot of things and couldn't get him arrested. Christian was not nearly as formed then as he is now, but people grow. People that you have faith in, you have to have faith in—like I do with Tony.

KW: *That's a great segue. So, when you first met Tony, what was your impression of him?*
JB: I can't remember exactly when we met. You know, Tony defined the role of Al in *A Chorus Line* in a way that it had never been defined because in the original company Michael Bennett was thinking of cutting that number. And his masculinity paired with very good casting of Kristine [Chryssie Whitehead] made that number show-stopping.

And also, to have a real masculine Tulsa in *Gypsy* was what Arthur Laurents was looking for. Tony is incredibly smart about what he thinks is best for him, and if he respects you as a director, he's completely collaborative and really listens.

In *Gypsy* the *"All I Need is the Girl"* dance is designed for a very specific body type. So, what was wonderful was that Arthur

Laurents, the director, realized how special Tony was and allowed him to make the minor adjustments that made it *his*.

He's a genuine actor and a leading man. He's no longer a juvenile. What becomes very difficult is for someone to redefine themselves—which his management team is working to do—into things other than musical theatre, because he certainly could have a TV series in a heartbeat.

And fortunately, because of the relationship, when I cast Tony in *White Christmas* the director, Walter Bobby, saw Tony for who he was and cast him in *Chicago*.

KW: *That was his first lead in a major musical on Broadway.*
JB: Right, although Tulsa being a supporting role and *A Chorus Line*—that's when he began to get noticed. He is a very serious young man who wants to do nothing but his very best, and I have such respect for that because he's a perfectionist. And I think that's incredibly important.

KW: *Before* Chorus Line *Tony had done a lot of ensemble work on Broadway.*
JB: Oh I know, and I had him in the chorus of a couple of musicals at *Encores!*: *A Tree Grows in Brooklyn* and he was in an old Gershwin musical called *Pardon My Irish* just as a chorus dancer—which must've, you know, frustrated the hell out of him.

KW: *He made the decision around the time of* Chorus Line *to only play principals, which he's done since. In the Broadway musical world, how difficult is it to move from ensemble to featured roles?*
JB: Well, you know, you have to make the decision and then you begin to earn it. There are people that are capable, and there are people that are not. He's somebody that's capable. And if you're talented enough, you made the right decision.

KW: *It seems like that would be a pretty big risk, especially for somebody like Tony who works mainly in the theatre because you have to turn down other jobs.*

JB: Yes, you have to be willing to not give in, and you have to be willing to deal with yourself financially. But Tony's a very strong man. Tony is a very focused and dedicated person. You have to have a certain type of personality to do that.

KW: *Tony told me the same thing you did about his audition for* A Chorus Line—*that he felt he was perfect for it and that you guys, on the other side of the table, felt that he was perfect for it too.*

JB: And Tony getting *Gypsy* was very tricky for me because he was in *A Chorus Line*, which was my show. But he was determined and when he got that part he deserved it.

KW: *He told me that he "…wasn't stereotypically what they were looking for," in the role of Tulsa, that he looked really different from some of the other guys who were called back. So what did he do that won him the role?*

JB: Well, he can act. And he was so credible as a young boy, but he projects such a strong masculinity. The story being told between Louise and Tulsa is done in very few words, and she has an immense crush on him, is in complete awe of him.

When we started this production of *Gypsy,* it was Arthur Laurents' intention to explore this play in a way it had never been explored before. And indeed, he succeeded in that because it was an experience that went beyond theatre, it had such a sense of reality. And that was the whole company, Patti [LuPone] and Laura Benanti and Boyd [Gaines] and even down to the character men who had small parts. And I think that Tony was a wake-up call to everybody about how to envision that role for this production.

KW: *Tony talked about how important it is to have passion in pursuing an acting career. Have you had an experience with him where you felt that? And how important do you believe passion is for an actor?*

JB: I think it's deeply important. And some people may misinterpret that passion because so few people are as passionate as he is, in the way he is. And so, if Tony doesn't get a job, it's very possible he shouldn't.

KW: *Because?*

JB: It may be the wrong team for him. I've never known him to come into the room and not do what I said and be utterly and completely prepared to do what he needs to do. And I have tremendous respect for that.

KW: *From your experience, are there one or two things that Tony consistently does right at auditions?*

JB: Yes, he consistently comes in and makes you notice the fact that he has a point of view about each role that he's auditioning for. I mean he's not somebody that's ever ignored. He comes in and he's discussed because he has that strong a personality. He's not, you know, "Next," and not talked about.

KW: *What would you say are two or three of his best qualities as a performer?*

JB: Oh, I think his best qualities as a performer are the fact that he has a deep soul and that he has a beautiful voice and that he can dance. He's a genuine triple threat. And I also think that, in the right piece, clearly he doesn't have to sing or dance.

KW: *How important a role has type played for Tony, if it has played a role?*

JB: Well, you know, it does play a role. I mean, he's not all-American because he's dark and he's swarthy. And so there are certain times when that's not what the director's looking for, and no matter what you do, you can't change the director's mind because he has a very certain vision. I long to see Tony play a villain that ultimately ends up with a heart of gold. I mean, he may be a little past it, although with the right Vera, who would be better than Tony Yazbeck in *Pal Joey*? Nobody, you know?

KW: *How important a role has talent played for him, and how important role has belief in himself been for Tony?*
JB: Equal, because he has talent and he has gigantic belief in himself. But also don't forget no matter how confident somebody is on the outside there's insecurity, and I think that you can't be gifted without ignoring your insecurities. And as he's maturing he's not allowing that part of him to show. He uses that part of him to his advantage.

KW: *Last question. All of the statistics tell us that acting is an incredibly difficult profession. At any given time there are far more actors out of work than are working. However, Tony has defied those odds, enjoying quite a bit of success. In addition to all the things you've told me, how has he done it?*
JB: He's done it by being damn good. You know, he walks in and he's got tremendous conviction and inner strength. He could easily have been in a featured chorus role in *Kinky Boots*, but he would rather go off to do the right play for not a lot of money if he feels that's the right thing for him to do. He has passion and he also is an incredibly decent human being.

Tony Yazbeck Success Team Member

RICHARD SCHMENNER

Ken Womble: *Richard, you're a talent agent at Paradigm in New York. Could you tell me a bit about how you got started in the entertainment industry?*

Richard Schmenner: Like many people in the agency business, you always start out wanting to be up front, you know, living your childhood dreams. I had studied acting and theatre; I'd gotten an MFA. I came to New York and realized that being an actor was something I wasn't really cut out for. But I did want to be part of the business.

So a friend suggested that I take a look at the agency business and, like most people, I started out being the receptionist and I moved into being an assistant and then I was a commercial agent and then I moved into what I really wanted to do which was represent actors for theatre.

KW: *Do you do mainly theatre?*
RS: Our agency does everything. I do a little bit of everything. I mostly do theatre, some film and a little television.

KW: *Paradigm is a major bicoastal talent agency.*
RS: Correct.

KW: *And it seems to me from looking at your client list that you represent both stars and working actors.*
RS: Yeah.

KW: *So, what are you looking for in an actor that you want to sign? For example, do you want accomplished actors with strong* *credits, or are you looking to develop talented actors who may not have worked as much?*

RS: It's always more fun to work with actors that you can develop, that you believe in to help them get launched. I was, once upon a time, Felicity Huffman's first agent and Allison Janney's and we sort of got them rolling in the world of television.

We're pretty selective and like to keep our client list to a manageable number of people. And there are just so many people that you can start each year. There are no overnight successes. Everyone pays their dues—other than Julia Roberts.

KW: *Why do you think everybody pays?*

RS: I think the casting community and the directors here want to know that you can deliver the goods basically. And it takes some time.

We tell people when we take them on, we're not expecting you to get the job of a lifetime in the first year with the agency. Actually, we're happy when you get callbacks. And if you're not the part, the casting director still thinks of bringing you in continually. So, it's about lining up those relationships. Casting directors love to help launch a talented actor's career.

It's a matter of going in and being consistent so that everybody knows this is a person who has the talent, can deliver, is not a flash in the pan. It's somebody who is grounded and can go the distance with their career.

KW: *How did you start working with Tony?*

RS: He had come to us from another agency. He has a manager, James Suskind; we're fairly new to the management team. But the whole idea of getting a manager and changing his agency—we like to think that we're one of the premier agencies here in New York—is to really up his profile as far as the business is concerned, to get him into those leading roles in Broadway shows and expose him to some film and television opportunities, which he hasn't had a chance to go up for before.

KW: *What was your first impression of him?*
RS: I was always taken by Tony because he has great stage command. He's somebody your eye's going to follow. You know, he engages with the audience.

I remember really registering with him when he did *A Chorus Line* on Broadway, and I thought, "Oh, this is a guy who's really passionate about what he does." And he's a great song and dance man, of which there are very few. So it is a marketable talent that he has.

KW: *By that do you mean there are great singers and great dancers, but it's hard to get them both in the same person?*
RS: Yeah, and somebody that has a lot of sex appeal. His idol was Gene Kelly as a kid growing up, and he filled in doing *Singin' in the Rain* this winter out in Chicago playing the Gene Kelly part. He was fantastic!

KW: *When I asked Tony how he networks himself, he told me that if he hears about a potential acting job he finds out if he knows someone connected with it. How do you work together with him on projects?*
RS: Well, because he is well established in the community and he has a great fan base, people call on him to come in to do the workshop or do the reading or actually do the part if it's coming about.

So it's a matter of just connecting with the producers and the director and saying, "I know you've been talking to Tony," and finding out the details about the project and what we can do to further it along.

KW: *Tony told me that one of the smartest things he's done is to decide not to take any more ensemble roles in musicals. Were you working with him then?*

RS: Yes. We sat down with him and discussed that. It was like, "We want to get you out of the ensemble and into the principal player, leading role." And sometimes you have to be brave enough just to say no. We want people who have goals and obviously that's what Tony has in mind too. He wants to move beyond where he started.

KW: *On Broadway, Tony played Al in the 2006 revival of* A Chorus Line, *and then Tulsa in the 2008 revival of* Gypsy. *Both are featured roles. In the Broadway musical world how difficult is it to move from ensemble to featured and leading roles?*

RS: It's not easy. I think it takes a certain charisma, a certain drive. You know, I see a lot of shows, I look at a lot of people in a lot of choruses and you can spot the people who are just popping. I can usually tell if somebody can act if they just say one line because it's got to have a ring of believability to it. When somebody who has little stage time kind of captivates your eye and your ear, you know there's something beyond what they're doing now.

I mean there are so many chorus people. There are so many musicals. There are so few jobs beyond that. And so it's a very competitive world, and Tony has proven that he can move beyond that. He still has several mountains to climb, but he certainly climbed out of the ensemble.

KW: *But did he do it by saying no, or just having faith, or the agency being aggressive in his career?*

RS: I think it comes down to the person. You know, he just is a unique talent. I think we're aggressive in trying to get him in doors, but we can't get you the job.

KW: *About the time you started working with Tony, he was cast as Billy Flynn, one of the replacement Billy Flynns in* Chicago *on Broadway.*
RS: Indeed.

KW: *How important was that for Tony's career? And was it a turning point?*
RS: I think it is a turning point because it's definitely the leading man in a Broadway show, and it just proves to everybody that this is something that he can do.

And the show has been running for what, almost fifteen years? And they've had a variety of stars, non-stars in that part. They always need somebody who can sing and can dance, but they need somebody who can be kind of devilish and charming and wily, and he was able to bring all of that to it.

And they also need somebody who's the captain of the team. I mean if you look at a Broadway show as if it's a football team, you need a leader. You need somebody who the chorus and everybody else is going to look up to. And he has those capabilities. You know, he is not only a leading man, but he is a leading person. He's very smart; he's very savvy; he's got real good people skills.

You're working in a community. You know, an artist can go to his attic and paint, a musician can go and just record by himself, but an actor needs a community to realize their art. And it's great to have somebody who can be the leader in their community.

I think if you're going to be a leading player you need to be a leading person because sometimes you have to stand up for yourself or you have to stand up for the persons that you're working for. All of these are million dollar productions, there are a lot of investments riding on it, and you need somebody who can stand up to that pressure and has the integrity of their beliefs.

KW: *Tony told me about his audition for* Chicago, *and I was kind of struck because he's in his early to mid-thirties and in my mind Billy Flynn is in his mid-forties.*
RS: He was a young choice for them.

KW: *And it just seems to me that he somehow convinced them that he was the right person for the role—or were they just going younger anyway?*
RS: No, I think he convinced them that he was the right person. They have been through a lot of Billy Flynns, and they're always looking to add something new, but I do think he was a young choice for them. But, you know, he's got a maturity about him.

KW: *For a production of* West Side Story *at Trinity Rep, he was brought in to audition for Bernardo but convinced the casting people to let him audition for Tony and then he was cast as Tony. I thought that took a lot of courage to walk in and say that.*
RS: You know, it does.

KW: *What does this say about him as a person and as a performer?*
RS: I think he has great belief in his abilities. I don't think you hold yourself out to do something that you don't think you can do. I mean he really believes that he could play Tony.

KW: *What kind of feedback do you get from casting directors and directors about Tony's auditions, and are there one or two things that he does consistently right?*
RS: He is always prepared, which is very key. I mean there are some people that wing it, that really don't study the lines. They'll either go in and they're glued to the sides or they're paraphrasing, which most people just loathe—because they want you to say the

words as the author has written them. And he goes in with the right attitude; whether it's his part, he always is a choice for the part.

KW: *By always a choice do you mean he's always sort of a possibility?*
RS: He's one of the top three or four choices for the role.

KW: *What would you say are some of Tony's best qualities as a performer?*
RS: He has a great smile. If you could've seen him doing *Singin' in the Rain,* they had to hand out tarps to the first three rows because he was getting everybody wet. He was having so much fun and the audience was with him. You know, just kicking that water up and letting it fly, and there was just such a great camaraderie between the actor and the audience which is what you want anytime you go to the theatre. He is charming and he has appeal and that's not easy, not every player comes with that. And he has abandon, which I like in an actor.

KW: *Could you expand on that just a bit?*
RS: I like somebody who's free in who they are as a person, and they're able to get out there and just fly. They don't stick to the page, per se. They are able to take something and bend it to themselves and get out there and hit a home run each time. They don't always take the safe choice, which can be boring.

KW: *They go beyond what's written sometimes.*
RS: Exactly, exactly.

KW: *In her book called* Acting Q's, *Bonnie Gillespie says that, "Working performers seem to have tapped into a sense of authenticity that most aspiring actors search for." Do you feel that's been true for Tony?*

RS: Oh sure. In the world and in the roles that he's done so far, yeah.

KW: *How important a role has type played for Tony? And does he have a clear idea of his type?*
RS: Oh yeah, he knows exactly what he can do and why he's unique.

KW: *How important a role has talent played for him?*
RS: Oh, 100%.

KW: *How important has his belief in himself been for Tony, and have you had a personal experience with him that illustrates that belief?*
RS: I think it's very important and he's got a lot of confidence and he's got dreams and ambitions. And we share those. We wouldn't have made a team unless we didn't think we could succeed.

KW: *How would you describe him overall as a client?*
RS: He's kind of the ideal client. You know, he's not shy about calling. He's not shy about saying, "This is something that I want to go up with." He's good about sharing feedback so that we know what's working, what's not working. He shares his ideas. He listens to yours.

KW: *He struck me as somebody who seems so congruent, very single minded about his career.*
RS: Oh yes, definitely.

KW: *Okay, last question. All of the statistics tell us that acting is an incredibly difficult profession. At any given time there are far more actors out of work than are working. However, Tony has defied those odds, enjoying quite a bit of success. In addition to all the other things you've told me, how has he done it?*

RS: Absolute determination—absolute belief in his abilities. You know, he has a great deal of confidence and it shows. He's not shy. He's out there to be the performer. He's out there to deliver the goods every time.

What are the keys that have led Tony Yazbeck to a successful acting career?

He works from faith and "luck" follows

Faith is a powerful force for Tony. Starting with the "leap of faith" that took him to New York, to his first agent being his first room-mate from whom he booked his first national tour, Tony thinks his "luck" has been a result of the faith he has in himself. He believes "this is going to happen."

He prepares thoroughly for auditions

Tony leaves no stone unturned when preparing for auditions. From the technical to the emotional he takes complete responsibility for the quality of his auditions.

He's on a mission from the heart

Tony knows audiences come to the theatre to be moved, so he reaches deeply into his soul to tell the truth, *his* truth in every performance, whether for an audience of 1,600 on a Broadway stage or an audience of one in an audition room.

Tony's willingness to trust his heart has won him respect from his success team and roles from such innovative directors as Tina Landau.

He networks assertively. Tony doesn't just sit back and wait for the phone to ring. In concert with his agent and manager, he researches upcoming projects and does everything he can to get into auditions.

He has a great team

An actor's fans are not only found among audiences, but among the agents, managers, directors and casting directors with whom he or she works. And these fans enthusiastically promote their actor's career. Richard Schmenner revels in the collaborative relationship he and Tony share, calling him, "kind of the ideal client," and Jay Binder has not only pushed for Tony to get roles, but offered meaningful career advice.

He has never had a fallback plan

At the age of four Tony decided he wanted to dance; he wanted to be an actor. And he's never even considered another career.

He is talented

Jay and Richard clearly believe that Tony's talent has been huge to his success. How? Tony brings his own unique vision to every role. An impressive example is his portrayal of his dream role, Tulsa, in the 2008 Broadway revival of *Gypsy*, in which Tony shone—just like the show's stars, all Tony Award winners. Because he pops on stage, Tony commands attention from audiences and also sings and dances extraordinarily well, making him that rare commodity in the theatre, a true "triple threat." There is not a weak link in Tony's musical theatre performance package.

He takes risks

Tony's reps told me his decision to move out of the ensemble and into principal roles required courage and confidence, the courage to pass up offered work and a steady paycheck (which Tony did more than once), and the confidence to trust that the work he wanted was on the way. When Tony started booking role after role, his willingness to take this risk—and succeed—put him into a small and elite group of principal performers working on Broadway.

He is a leading person

Broadway musicals have a lot riding on them, both artistically and financially. So, a cast needs not only a talented leading actor, but as Richard said, "a leading person," a strong presence for the rest of the company. His intelligence and people skills enable Tony to play this role perfectly. Tony's leadership is also evident in audition and rehearsal rooms where he has learned to get results by being "bold and yet gracious and kind at the same time."

He believes divine intervention has been central

Ever since, as an eleven-year-old newsboy in *Gypsy*, Tony stood in the wings of the St. James Theatre watching Bob Lambert play Tulsa, he knew he was destined to play the role. Yet when his time came with the 2008 revival of the show, Tony had to fight to get into the audition room and fight again to change minds about the role being played by someone younger and lighter. Finally, against all odds, he was cast as Tulsa.

Tony believes that divine intervention was clearly at work and has been at work for him his entire career, his entire life, guiding him from one success to another.

JAMES EARL

CHAPTER 5

One Hundred Percent Comfortable in Your Skin

JAMES EARL

James Earl was born and raised in Los Angeles. His first television appearance was on the Nickelodeon show *Drake & Josh*. Shortly after, Earl filmed his first guest-starring role on the hit television show *ER*. Following that role, he landed his first feature film, *Gridiron Gang*, starring The Rock. He scored a recurring role on NBC's *Las Vegas* and Fox's *Glee*. Earl has also guest-starred on shows such as *CSI: Las Vegas*, *Crossing Jordan*, *Community*, *Cold Case*, *Bones*, *Weeds* and *No Ordinary Family*. In between shooting, he spends time recording music with his group The Future III. He also mentors at-risk youth from his childhood neighborhood.

....

Ken Womble: *James, you were born and raised in Los Angeles. How did you become interested in acting?*

James Earl: The middle school I went to had an after school program called Inside Out where at-risk kids that didn't do well at school would go to get extra credits. And it was an improv program where actors and artists came and volunteered their time. And at the end of the program, we showed it in front of the school and then we went to USC, it was sponsored by USC, and we did a showcase there.

KW: *Were you interested in acting before that? Did you think it would be something that you'd like?*

JE: Kind of. You know, growing up your first thing is, "I want to be a doctor, I want to be lawyer." Me, I wanted to be a police officer because I thought that would be a way to keep out of jail. I used to always watch TV—I love movies. So I liked the arts, but I never understood it until I started doing it.

KW: *You said to keep you out of jail you wanted to become a police officer. I take it you're from a rough neighborhood?*

JE: Yeah, I grew up in South Central Los Angeles. I'm literally from where the LA riots started. Growing up I didn't even realize that because my mom made sure that we all were in the house safe. And I used to always ask, "What happened to these buildings? What happened to this place?" And she used to just say a fire happened or stuff like that. But when I grew up and I actually started hearing about the LA riots, I realized I grew up two blocks down the street where it all started.

And to know that's a part of my history has inspired everything that I do now because a lot of people don't really do good coming out of there. A lot of people either end up dead or in jail or on drugs, or in situations they don't want to be in. And a lot of people don't understand how important it is just to believe in yourself and figure out what's good in your life that you *can* do. And programs like Inside Out helped me to see other outlets, you know, acting programs.

KW: *It sounds like you were determined to get out, even if it hadn't been acting.*

JE: Yeah. I was determined to just do something good with my life. My sister was the only person in my family to ever graduate from college and get a master's degree, and she actually became a psychologist. And so I felt obligated to kind of do something good as well.

Growing up I wasn't a good kid. My mom, she's a private duty nurse, so she had to get jobs close to my school because I would get suspended, you know. I was the class clown, fall out, used to do all types of stuff at school. I used to make stuff up like, "Yeah, I'm like doing a movie with Denzel soon," you know, "I just did a song with Dr. Dre," just stuff that I used to imagine growing up.

KW: *And now it's really happening.*
JE: Yeah. And now stuff is actually coming to life.

I ended up moving out to the Silver Lake area, and I got a different aspect of life. I wasn't just in an environment of all black and Latino kids. I'm in a mixture of blacks, whites, Armenians, all different types of people. And I got into doing theatre there, too.

In eighth grade they invited a group of the kids from the theatre program to this thing Nickelodeon was doing up in this house in the Hollywood Hills, and Nick Cannon was there, Amanda Bynes. It was like a house party every day, and they would play music videos, and they always had kids come. So I got to go there like three times and kind of experience what's it's like to be on set. And, you know, Nickelodeon, they keep it fun, snacks everywhere, it was crazy. So I was like, "I want to do that again."

KW: *And your first TV appearance was on Nickelodeon on* Drake and Josh.
JE: Yeah, exactly.

KW: *So did that come from that connection you made in eighth grade?*
JE: No, that was totally separate because in eighth grade what happened was my mom was making a phone call, and she called a wrong number and the number that she ended up calling was an agent and he was like, "I have a buddy who has this management

company," and she was like, "Yeah, my son wants to be an actor." And she ended up calling the management company.

We come in, and he's like, "No, maybe when you get a little older," da, da, da. But this one lady there really liked me. She was like, "I'll take him. Let's see what we can do." They had acting classes, so I did a few acting classes and a showcase where I met with some agents.

I'm probably like in the eleventh grade at the time. I went to Hollywood High. And they have an acting program, but they didn't let me in their acting program because of my record. You know, I was a troubled student coming up, so they didn't really think I was appropriate for the acting program. They didn't know that I was already an actor and they really didn't care.

So the first job I ever got was a Toyota commercial. And it goes well; it runs for a while so people see it. And I get another audition for Nickelodeon for *Drake and Josh*—the lady loved me. The next day I was working on the show but only had two lines. But those two lines got me a recurring role on the show. And that kind of started the career.

ER was my first time auditioning for big, prime time TV. There was a full room of producers and this is a recurring role, you know, four episodes, so it was a big deal. And I did it and I was nervous as hell, but it kind of worked for me.

And then everybody at Hollywood High was like, "James we didn't know you were an actor," da, da, da. "You want to join?"

KW: *Then they wanted you.*
JE: Yeah. And I was like, "No, I'm good. I'm happy where I am. I'm about to graduate anyway, so it doesn't matter." So I kind of just left that alone and continued to act and go forward. You can't get mad at that because, you know, if people don't know who you are, people don't understand. Some people, it just takes them a longer time to notice your skills.

After I did *ER* there was a little break. It was like a year or so and I was working at Coco's. I was washing dishes and cleaning, you know, just to keep some money and gas in my car. And during that time I'm kind of like, "What am I doing?"

But that's when I started to understand about the whole patience aspect of the industry, how you have to be patient and how a lot of people can't go through those drops because they just don't know how. They never had to go through anything like that in life. It's very important to understand patience and how you might be working today and you might not be working tomorrow. And it might be a couple months that go by where you're not doing anything.

So I graduated from high school, high school's done, I'm kind of just floating around a little bit and the opportunity for this movie [*Gridiron Gang*] came up. And it was the first time I ever auditioned for a movie. The casting director, Sarah Finn, was really awesome, and she gave me the opportunity. She saw something in me because I came in and read for one role and then she was like, "Oh, I have this other role that I think you should read for," the role of Matlock. And I ended up getting that.

And it was my first time ever doing a screen test. A film screen test is different from a TV screen test because you're on the soundstage and there's like fifty people in the dark that you can't see. And the TV screen test is just you and the producers in a room. So it was a big deal. The Rock was in there, I didn't even know it; I was a big Rock fan, I was into wrestling, so I was like, "Whoa, I'm about to work with the Rock."

The physical and emotional requirements of it were somewhere I've never been because for three weeks we had to do football every day pretty much, and on top of that we were filming in a prison with real criminals in there. It was crazy, you know.

I really got to understand how, when you're on set you've got to make sure you're there, you're on time and you do your job. This one scene I did I wasn't really feeling it—I was nervous. And when we were done I was like, "Damn, I messed that scene up. I was horrible." And something happened where we had to reshoot it. And I got it down, I got it perfect.

And when I got done, I was walking with the director and I told him, "You know, dude, the first time I did it I felt horrible about it and thank you, I'm glad we got to do it again." And he was like, "Well, it doesn't always happen like that. So, make sure you're on your A game; make sure you got it together."

That was one of the most fun times though. I will never forget that.

KW: *You booked a pilot called* Awesometown *for ABC. Do you think that attitude of, "Now I know what I'm doing and feel comfortable" affected that audition and helped you book it?*
JE: Well, that situation was crazy because I did this show called *Glory Daze* and the producer was friends with the producer from *Awesometown,* and he was trying to figure out roles and he was like, "Hey, maybe you should bring James Earl in."

So they called me in and when I read the role I got it. The description was for a white guy, like it was totally opposite of who I am. But I learned to make stuff me, just be myself but kind of switch it. And when I went in, I didn't even know all the dialogue, but I knew the mentality and I knew the presence.

You know, if I was producing the movie, I have to be confident in the person that I'm going to hire. I have to make sure that I'm mentally confident and I'm mentally prepared.

Like sometimes before an audition I'll stretch, I'll breathe, you know, I make sure I get my breathing right. Sometimes people go to auditions and they're out of breath because they're nervous and their blood pressure's going up, heartbeat's racing. You got to get all your levels to zero and then go in.

KW: *I've never heard that, "Get your levels to zero."*
JE: Yeah, you got to be able to bring it down, so when you go in there, you can control what you're doing.

KW: *Do you think that's affected your work and your booking?*
JE: Yeah. Mainly the confidence though. Anytime anybody asks me for advice I'd give them on acting I tell them confidence. That's it. That's the main secret to acting.

I feel like the producers are our audience. They have the same mentality. So I need to make sure that they believe in what I'm doing even if I don't get it. That's my whole thing. Even if I don't get the job, as long as I go in there and I know I was confident, I gave my all and I was happy about it. You can't really get mad if you don't book a job. I mean, it probably wasn't for you, you know. Next job.

KW: *That's great you've developed that attitude. I think a lot of people say that, but there's a big difference between saying it and actually doing it. It sounds like you're doing it.*
JE: Yeah. I was on avail [being available for a commercial shoot] for a Boost Mobile campaign, and when I went in to audition, I went in as the character. At the end of the day I want them to understand that this is what I'm presenting to you, this is the character, this is my vision for it and if you like it, great! Let's do this! And if you don't it's all right. You have plenty of options out here.

KW: *So, did you come in costume?*
JE: Yeah, they wanted a genie, not your typical genie though. But what you think a genie would be nowadays. So I was like, "Well, let me be a hip hop genie." And so I put on a jacket with some

shine on it and a chain and I made a kind of scarf little genie thing. And I went in and I had this calm attitude about it. I wasn't like, "Hey I'm the genie." I was like, "Hey, what's up?" you know? I just made it my own. A lot of times actors are scared to do that, but I feel like that's very important.

KW: *How did you develop that attitude? How did you learn that?*
JE: Trial and error. And I learned a lot from other people's mistakes. I'll go to an audition and I'll see somebody doing something and I'll be like, "Okay, I'm going to make sure I do *not* do that."

KW: *You mentioned* Glory Daze *earlier. You were cast in your first role as a series regular on that show in 2010. Was that a turning point for you?*
JE: Yeah. That was a major turning point. When I first went in for *Glory Daze*, the role was a big fraternity guy, a big buff guy, like the discipline guy at a fraternity, you know. And so I went in with the same mentality, and the director loved what I did. But they didn't know if the network would want me to play that role. So he was like, "I want you in this regardless. [So] I'm going to give you this role," which was like a two-liner role, just to put me in it. So I was like, "All right, cool."

And so I go to the table read and one of the producers came up and he's like, "We want you to read the Turbo role and the other role." And this is with the network, like a hundred people in the room. So when it was time I just gave it my all—boom! You know, I just took off and I was real energetic with it and I kind of used that nervousness and excitement as energy to help me get through it and they loved it.

So after I left the table read, they were like, "Okay, you're not going to do that role, you're going to do the series regular role."

KW: *Wow. That's a great story. So, was that role also written for an African-American guy or for a white guy?*
JE: No, it was written for a white guy.

KW: *And you said he's like a big buff guy. You're a big guy, but you're husky.*
JE: Yeah, I'm husky. I'm not buff.

KW: *So, what you did changed their minds?*
JE: I was still Turbo, but I was more of like a football linebacker, team coach, like, "Come on guys!" [*claps his hands*] I was still that big guy, but I added some comedy that made it a little funny. So, the network liked it, and they were like, "It's a go."

KW: *The improv class you had taken earlier probably paid off at that moment, huh?*
JE: Yeah, learning improv was the best thing that could happen to me because I learned how to use my imagination first rather than learn how to read dialogue.

KW: *It seems like you know how to book, from what you're telling me. So what do you think they're looking for?*
JE: I mean they're looking for what the character description is. We actors feel like we could do every role. We feel like we could be Superman, we could be Batman, everything. But you have to really be realistic with yourself and be like, "Okay, what is my range? What am I good at? What can I bring to this?"

KW: *So, that kind of dirty word some actors call "type."*
JE: Yeah, when somebody's sending you out for something, they're sending you out according to what the character description is, a type of person. So it's like either you have the

physical attributes that it says in here or you're able to bring that to life.

KW: *What would you say is your type?*
JE: For a while my type was like high school football jock. Now, what is my range? I can do comedy, I can do drama, I can do some action stuff. I think the reason I'm doing more comedy is because I like to have fun.

When I get a character description, I break it down. A lot of people say the back story, but sometimes you just got to work on who that person is: like the description says, "Eighteen, overweight, shy, high school dropout." I'll break that down. You know, "Why am I that? What's the reason for that?"

I'm going to tell you this though. A lot of times in auditions I don't even do that. I literally read the lines and go in and just say them. And put a little twist on it. I haven't even had to act really. Ninety percent of the work I've been doing is literally me being myself, or a personality of somebody I know, or some personality that I actually have.

KW: *Interesting.*
JE: Yeah.

KW: *So you did* Glory Daze *for just one season.*
JE: One season and then we got cancelled.

KW: *That must've been rough.*
JE: Yeah it was rough. But I think I got over it well. Because now my thing is, "What's next?" I'm not going to get stuck on anything anymore. I'm not going to get like, "This is it, this is going to change my life." Because if that doesn't happen, then what am I going to do? You know?

KW: *And around the same time you were cast in* Glee.
JE: Oh, yeah.

KW: *And that's probably what you're best known for.*
JE: I know, that's crazy.

KW: *What was your audition like?*
JE: I only had to audition one time, and when I went in, I think I had to say two lines. That's it. Real easy. And the casting director, I remember him telling me, "I loved you in *Gridiron Gang*." And I was like, "Hey, thank you, man!" Nobody ever noticed me for that movie.

KW: *You got cast for just one episode of* Glee *and then you ended up doing many more episodes.*
JE: Yeah.

KW: *So how did that happen?*
JE: I did one episode, they liked it, and they just kept calling me back.

KW: *Did they tell you why? I mean, was it to do with your relationship with the other character, Dave Karofsky, your buddy on the show?*
JE: I think they liked the Karofsky and Azimio thing. They liked that a lot, so I think that's what kept it going.

KW: *What was it like to be on one of the hottest shows on TV?*
JE: Umm, I don't know. It was cool. But I didn't feel the fame aspect of it. When they called me back for the second season, it was bigger and everybody knew it worldwide, da, da, da. And I'm hanging out with them and it was cool. But I didn't feel like I made it; I didn't feel like I was a part of the phenomenon.

It's awesome to be driving and you see a billboard and you're like, "Oh, snap, I'm on that show. That's tight." And I get these letters from these kids, and they're always like, "Hey, we love your work" and they're real supportive. And they come from all around the world, too, like Australia, Brazil, places I want to go. And that's inspiring, you know. So I'm grateful for *Glee* because it has got me some recognition.

KW: *Was it a turning point for you?*
JE: Yeah, definitely. I think I've got a few opportunities because of *Glee*.

Where I feel I am now is I just want to find a home. I'm tired of the constant back and forth, auditioning, trying to get on a show. And somewhere that's solid and this is my job and this is what I'm doing.

KW: *And make a nice living at the same time.*
JE: Yeah, making a nice living. Because one of my main reasons for doing it is, one, because I like to do it, and two, because I like to pay my bills. [Soon after our interview James found a home when he was cast as Derrick, a series regular, on the new TBS sitcom *Ground Floor.*]

This is a business for me. This is not just a hobby. And a lot of people let that pressure of being in business kind of break them because when you're not making any money then you're not paying any bills and they feel like their life is falling apart.

KW: *Could you describe an audition where you felt like you just absolutely nailed it?*
JE: Well, the *Glory Daze* audition when I did the table read; that was my callback. I did it exactly how I thought about doing it. I felt like it was no holds barred and hearing the laughs fed me to do it even more, like, "They're laughing—good, good, good."

KW: *So the producers were laughing?*

JE: Yeah, the network, everybody was laughing. It was the first time anybody had heard me do it. And Tim Meadows came up to me and was like, "You're funny as hell." And I was like, "Whoa, you're Tim Meadows, dude."

KW: *You said you had "no holds barred." What do you mean by that?*

JE: Like I had nothing holding me back. I had no nervousness; I had no anxiety. I was just one hundred percent comfortable in doing what I was doing. And that's what it comes down to. You have to be one hundred percent comfortable in your skin.

KW: *Not trying to please them.*

JE: Yeah, yeah, because if you're trying to impress the producers… I mean, if they're looking to see what I'm going to present, then I need to be in my best mind state so I can present it in my best way possible.

KW: *Would you say that training has played a significant role for you? Or has it mainly been on the job training?*

JE: I feel like the acting training when I was kid helped. As an adult I learned more from doing and experiencing rather than going to a class and having somebody tell me. You know, I was more of a hands-on kind of learner. I literally learned from being on set and working with directors. That's my acting class. You know, rehearsing.

KW: *That's the best acting class.*

JE: Yeah. The best acting class is rehearsing with the director. The director I just worked with, Jessie Perez, was awesome. He is one of the best directors I ever worked with because he was hands-on.

He wasn't trying to overdo it. He was like, "Let's make it good. Let's make it real. Let's make it funny."

KW: *Have you been typecast? And if so, has that been to your advantage or your disadvantage?*
JE: Well, it comes to a point where whatever opportunities you have, you have to take those opportunities. I mean people feel like they're getting typecast, but at the end of the day an opportunity's an opportunity and you're doing it to get to the next opportunity.

You know, for a while I was tired of doing football roles. I don't want to wear another football suit. I don't ever want to put on another football helmet, you know? But then I started realizing that as I go along and people start to see my abilities, more opportunities will open up for me. And that's exactly what's been happening. As I got older I wasn't just this big guy. I could do comedy; I could do drama; I could do all this stuff.

But I don't really put too much energy in the whole typecasting thing. That's not my concern. My concern is booking jobs and paying bills. But at the same time, I want to make sure I'm doing something that I like to do and that's good. And so far, a lot of stuff that I have been doing has been that.

KW: *And it seems like you have an attitude about the profession of doing it your own way. And you've learned the ropes by doing it rather than having other people tell you how to do it.*
JE: Right, because that's how they did it. The way they made it isn't going to be how you make it. I'm not going to be on the same road that Will Smith was on because that was Will Smith's road. That was how he made it.

And a lot of people don't understand that. They watch *E True Hollywood Stories* and feel like this is how you make it—this is what you got to do. And everybody's path is different. And until people understand that, they're going to be in the same place. Everybody in your acting class isn't going to make it.

KW: *Most won't.*
JE: Yeah, so that's just how it goes. You know. And you have to figure out how you're going to do that. And for me it's just straight determination, being determined to do whatever, by any means necessary, to make sure I give my all and do a great job.

KW: *That's a great quote. I've heard it said about the acting profession if you have a fallback plan you'll fall back.*
JE: Yeah.

KW: *Do you believe that?*
JE: That's one thing I learned from Will Smith. Don't have a Plan B because it takes away from Plan A. You know what I'm saying? It's only Plan A. If you have Plan B and you have Plan C, then you're going to automatically go to those because you know you have them.

That's something he said on the *Inside the Actor's Studio*. I watch that a lot. I like to hear other actors' stories. You can take things from different stories, but you kind of have to put it into your own perspective.

KW: *Put it into your own story?*
JE: Yeah, put it into your own story, your own situation. That was one of the biggest things he could ever say to me because that's how we were taught to live—have a backup plan. And realistically some people *do* need a backup plan. Everybody can't just have a Plan A.

KW: *Have you made that decision not to fall back?*
JE: My backup plan is entertainment. If I don't act, I'm going to produce some music, and if I don't do that, then I'm going to write

something, and if I don't do that, then I'm going to be a PA, and if I don't do that, I'm going to be a grip and if I don't do that, I'm going to do something in the union. I'm going to figure it out because there are so many opportunities available in this industry—it's endless.

KW: *What would you say, James, is your best quality as an actor?*
JE: My best quality is I keep it real. That's the one thing I hear a lot—it's real.

KW: *And you're drawing from your own experience, your own life.*
JE: Yeah, all from stuff that I've actually been through or somebody I know. It's all roots from somewhere within me, you know, it's not just made up.

KW: *Have you had any mentors or people who inspired you along the way?*
JE: Yeah, my whole career I've had mentors and people who've inspired me, people who just helped me guide myself into the right direction, people who I still am in contact with to this day.

KW: *You talked about going in with confidence. Where does that confidence come from?*
JE: One day I was nervous at an audition and I just got mad at myself. I was like, "You don't have time for this; you don't have time to get nervous. Either you're going to do this or you're not going to do this. You need to believe in yourself, you need to get rid of all this nervousness because that's not why you're here."

KW: *It sounds like you made the decision at that moment that you were going to be a successful actor.*
JE: Yeah, I was going to do it and give my all and not let the nervousness win the battle. You can't.

KW: *What are one or two of the smartest things you've done for your career?*
JE: Fired my old manager.

KW: *What was happening there?*
JE: Well, I had a manager who reached the end of his career, and he was just literally living off his clients. But I didn't know that because he didn't live in LA. I didn't see him for some months, and then I got a job and we got to meet up because we had to sign some paperwork. And when we met up, it was like, "Who is this guy?" And literally the next day I called him and told him. Split.

You want a manager who's bringing stuff to the table and not just collecting. You want a manager who's actually working for you every day to make sure that your career's being managed properly and that the right opportunities are being sought out. You know, just being on top of stuff.

And I learned that I have to manage my own career. I can't depend on my managers. And if I'm not working on a set, then I need to be working on why I'm not working on a set.

KW: *What part, if any, has timing played? Has there been a sense of timing for you?*
JE: Yeah, because a lot of people when they come to Hollywood feel like they're going to hit it off immediately. And I'd rather climb up than just be at the top. I'd rather grow with my career rather than my career outgrow me.

KW: *That's smart.*
JE: Yeah. And I mean a lot of times people don't want that; they want the big success first. And then they want to relax and come back to reality but that's really impossible to do.

KW: *How important is your belief in yourself as a performer?*
JE: It's super important. It's one of the key factors. You don't believe in yourself then who else is going to believe in you? Nobody's going to believe in you.

KW: *If you could change one thing in your career what would it be?*
JE: I don't know. I literally feel like everything that happens is meant to happen. I feel like every mistake that I've made has changed me for the better and I've learned from it. It's made me who I am today. I don't feel like there's any way to filter that. Things happen for a reason. It's life. You can't manipulate life, you know. If I didn't get a job, it wasn't meant for me. If I made a mistake, I was meant to make that mistake to learn a lesson.

KW: *Are you sure you're just twenty-five?*
JE: Yeah.

KW: *I think you're about forty! You don't look it, but your maturity kind of defies your years in some ways.*
JE: I grew up around older people. I'm young but I've been through a lot of stuff.

KW: *All right. Last question. All of the statistics tell us that acting is an incredibly difficult profession. At any given time there are far more actors out of work than are working. However, you have defied these odds, enjoying quite a bit of success in a relatively short time. How have you done it?*
JE: I just stay out of the negative bubble. And I have that whole mentality of, "This is my plan, Plan A, this is what I'm going for."

KW: *So you're just staying focused on your dream.*
JE: Yeah, just staying focused on the dream and letting opportunities come in. I feel like when you put too much pressure on the career then it feels that pressure and you're going to stop yourself. You're going to stop that wind, that wheel from spinning because you're putting too much negative energy in there. You just got to let it go.

James Earl Success Team Member

PATRICK WELBORN

Ken Womble: *Patrick, your bio is pretty eclectic. You were a producer and designer and for two years taught drama.*
Patrick Welborn: I did teach drama for two years, a fun two years. I was a lighting designer at the time and the headmaster of the school was a friend of mine and agreed to let me go away if I had a lighting gig, you know, install a design and then go through tech week and get a show open.

KW: *Did you teach acting as well as lighting design?*
PW: It was just a general theatre course where you teach what a proscenium is, what a designer is and roles in theatre, you know, the principles of our art.

KW: *Have those experiences affected the way you work with young actors?*
PW: I would hope so. Hopefully I get to hold a little bit of all of my life experience and it makes me a little bit wiser. If not, I'm in trouble, huh? Most of us get our introduction to entertainment through storytelling or the art of suspending disbelief.

KW: *What are you looking for in an actor you want to sign? [Patrick is a talent agent and partner at Allegory Creative Management in Los Angeles.]*

PW: I think a lot of agents look for marketability and look; none of us escape aesthetic. But to me the older I get the more it goes back to the storytelling issue. You find people who have an ability to not necessarily always play themselves but to bring some element of themselves into a character that is different from them and tell a story.

I'm looking for people who have that ability to understand that what we do is a collaborative art, so it's not all about them. You're not a kid jumping on the diving board yelling for everybody to look at you; you're actually bringing a service to an audience. And story is the one place we get closure; it's the one place that we get to suspend our disbelief and kind of step away. It's kind of a carnal hunger.

KW: *That's a great quote. You represent James Earl. How long have you worked together?*

PW: Seven years.

KW: *What was your first impression of him when you met?*

PW: James is a really unique individual. He's come from a harder world than most of us are used to or aware of, and I think that allows him to bring something to our world that we want to understand. I think that kind of feeds into his ability to tell stories. He brings emotions that are a little more weighted than the average twenty-five year old Caucasian kid who grew up in the suburbs.

He grew up in South Central Los Angeles and in a room testing with forty execs in suits, whatever drama most of us would bring into the stress of that situation, he's seen a harder life. So I don't think he cares. He doesn't get stressed about the small stuff.

But he's also remarkably talented. He's extremely intelligent, and being a kid in South Central, he doesn't shy away from, you know, playing a gay role or playing the boy that beats up the gay kid. He's done both. He brings some real essence of him into both roles. And it's believable.

KW: *Yeah, I was really impressed talking with him, and after a while I said, "Are you sure you're just twenty-five?"* [Laughs]
PW: [*Laughs*]

KW: *"You seem like you're forty as far as what you know about life."*
PW: Well, he was that way at seventeen. You know, he lived with a single mother; she was a nurse down at USC hospital which is in the worst possible neighborhood. And his drama in his life was, were family members going to live? Was he going to live?

The first big feature we put him on was *Gridiron Gang* and it shot out in Castaic, at one of the correction camps. And they had to go through security, and there were a bunch of kids in the yard and two or three kids ran over to the fence and yelled his name.

And I come from a fairly privileged background. You know, it's one of those moments where you understand, you're watching these two kids talk through a fence.

KW: *You mean he knew these guys who were incarcerated?*
PW: Yeah, he even convinced the director to let them play in some of the scenes. But you sit and look at it and you realize, two different paths, same spot.

And, you know, it's a testament to his mother who is a really strong, brilliant woman, but also to James. He made smart choices. And acting from his world was not necessarily the most masculine thing to do, but he didn't care and he pursued something he was good at and in the long run it paid off.

KW: *James told me that his first TV role was on Nickelodeon's* Josh and Drake *at seventeen and that kind of started his career. His two-line role became a short, recurring role. He got upgraded his first time on TV. It seems like they really liked him.*

PW: I don't know that he's ever been on a set where he hasn't been really liked and adored and part of it is also he's the fish out of water, and comfortable being the fish out of water.

On the set of *Glee* he was standing next to this blonde chick and everybody was kissing up to her. And they were sitting there talking and she really liked rap, and James likes rap, so they went into this conversation. And finally he had to look up who it was because he didn't know. He'd spent all day with Gwyneth Paltrow; he had no clue. And now he and Gwyneth are hip hop buddies.

KW: *Soon after* Josh and Drake *he got an even larger recurring role on* ER.

PW: Yeah, on *ER* he did a four or five episode arc, which was brilliant because it was the season cliffhanger and then opened the following season. And it was art imitating life. It was a kid who grew up in the projects who was taking care of his brothers and sisters because his single mother was working.

KW: *And in* Gridiron Gang *about two years later he portrayed a high school football player. That it was his first audition for a movie and he booked it. What does that say about him?*

PW: It says his agent is a *genius*.

KW: *Of course!*

PW: No, I'm just kidding. It does say that he's one of a kind. I mean he's a rare, rare find. It's the combination of being a tough inner city kid, yet being emotionally available and with sense enough to act. And I don't think you find those traits come together often. I think that he goes in and he does it better than anybody else.

KW: *How much of a break for him was* Gridiron Gang?
PW: I think it was a big deal. I think anytime you get a major, high-budget motion picture it's a big deal. I mean, it would've been bigger if he was not so specific an archetype. I'm purposely steering away from the word "stereotype."

The thing about any performer is you play a range of roles that you're right for that an audience will go along with. So he's kind of stuck in...he's not going to [be] Brad Pitt but neither am I.

KW: *Not many of us will be.*
PW: You know, it's one of those roles that if he was a twenty-one year-old Caucasian kid with blonde hair and blue eyes that looked remarkably hot, he'd be a billionaire by now.

KW: *Because...*
PW: Well, just because there's more material written for those archetypes than there is for James. I think especially early in his career he was cast as a gangbanger with a heart or, you know, the inner city kid with trouble...it was a recurring theme.

One of the fascinating things about a pilot he was in [*Awesometown*] was that the breakdown came out for a twenty-four year-old Caucasian aspiring sex addict. So that was a conversation that he and his manager and I had with the writer, "Hey, think about James." And he talked to the casting director; she called me one Friday night and said, "Patrick, that was absolutely not at all what we were looking for, but it was the funniest thing we've seen all week."

So they spent the weekend rewriting all of *Awesometown* to try to fit him in and, to be honest, I think it made the script far more interesting. Because early on it was four twenty-five year-old white guys of similar kind of type, so sometimes it was hard to decipher whose dialogue was whose. And all of a sudden you read the script where they'd rewritten for James and it was more interesting.

KW: *You sometimes hear feedback that James is funny and authentic. Anything else to add to that?*
PW: I think there's always an "aw" moment with James where people don't know how to identify with him yet. A couple of times he's had feedback where it was really funny, but it was not all right or appropriate, but more often he sinks into what we send him into.

I think I habitually forget anything that's not…I have a paternal aspect to my agenting job and it's sort of like if somebody knocks my kid it's their loss. I hear the good things.

KW: *And it sounds like he hears the good things, too. That's something we talked about, how he tries to avoid the "negative bubble."*
PW: I have never seen him with a negative attitude, ever. He's always positive, even when he's not working. I mean God bless him, it's rare, but there are moments where he'll go a month or two and he doesn't have a job and instead of getting nervous or uncomfortable he goes and sets up a music studio and flies around. He went to New York and to Holland last year. He figures when the time comes, it'll come. That's the fantastic thing about working with James—he just trusts.

KW: *He trusts that he's going to get more work?*
PW: He trusts we're doing our jobs, he trusts that he'll work and it makes it easier. There is no tension between actor and agent. Not to say an actor shouldn't know when their agent isn't working because there are plenty of agents that don't. But when you've got

a good thing, know it. And I think that's James. He knows he's built a solid team. That's the great thing about working for him is we appreciate each other.

KW: *He told me you take him out to dinner at Lawry's?*
PW: Lawry's, that's always our celebration place. We'll eat prime rib, (a) because I like to eat, and (b) because he likes to eat.

KW: *That's nice of you.*
PW: It's fun.

KW: *In 2010 James was cast on a series called* Glory Daze. *Would you say that was a turning point for him?*
PW: No, I think that year *Glee* was probably more of the turning point, as odd as it was. The first few seasons of *Glee* it was such a runaway hit. You know, it's a weird business that we're in. In television and film audience makes power. I don't know that anybody saw *Glory Daze* where, you know, everybody saw *Glee*.

KW: *In what ways has* Glee *enhanced his career?*
PW: It just made him more visible. You know, the larger your audience the more viable you are. The more people that recognize your name or recognize your face, the easier my job becomes.

KW: *Meaning you can get him in for things easier?*
PW: Oh yeah. There are a lot of casting directors who don't remember *Glory Daze*. You know, it shot nine episodes on TBS and went away. And if the casting director doesn't recognize the name of the show it goes in one ear and out the other. If you say, "Oh, he's Azimio in *Glee*," even if they don't watch the show they at least recognize the character. So it gives us that ability to force him into rooms.

KW: *He told me that this is a business for him, not just a hobby. Could you give me a couple of examples in your work together of how James treats acting like a business?*

PW: I don't work with an actor who doesn't treat this business like a business. I mean that's the quickest way that will get you dropped off my list is if you start to treat it like a hobby. If you don't find a way to put forty hours into your career every week you're not a professional in it.

I think part of that with James is a survival tactic. He's always had to keep himself busy to stay out of trouble.

KW: *James told me something interesting: he said that "your path is different from the person next to you." It seems that he really understands his own uniqueness. How has that helped him?*

PW: I think it's helped James because he allowed himself to be different than some of the role models around him growing up. I forget the independent film that he shot that he did a gay role in. I thought that was really fantastic and brave of him. That's not something that you would allow yourself to understand normally, growing up in the neighborhoods he grew up in. It's well outside of acceptable for that area.

KW: *What would you say are some of his best qualities as a performer?*

PW: Intelligence. He's extremely self-aware. He knows who he is, he knows what he can do, he knows his boundaries. And I think there are a lot of people out here who aren't self-aware. So you get ego instead of reality and I think he has no ego; there's no unearned ego.

KW: *How important a role has type played for James and does he have a clear idea of his type?*

PW: Certainly. After the first four or five years of his career, we all had a clear idea of his type and where it was a huge asset because he had the ability to be emotionally honest and play that type which is not emotionally honest. It built his résumé early on because he was the guy who could do it.

Now he's into a transitional period in his life. It's been hard because we have to fight against some of that and change perception to expand that type.

KW: *Are you able to expand his type because he has more exposure now?*
PW: Yes. If his résumé wasn't what it was, casting directors would hang up on us.

KW: *That's no fun.*
PW: Well, I'm used to it. [*Laughs*] I'm certainly used to it.

KW: *How important a role has talent played for him?*
PW: I think that talent is ultimately important, certainly the biggest thing. Success in our industry is talent meeting action. There are plenty of people who are talented who don't do enough with it. He's talented and he takes action. He doesn't ever let his mind get to a stasis point; he doesn't stop. All of my successful actors are the same way.

I think there are kids who may not be as talented as some of their competitors, but the fact is they work harder, they work more often, they're persistent and action makes up for the deficit.

KW: *Does that action include networking?*
PW: He makes friends very easily, he does musical shows, he does improv shows, he's always sending me a clip of something he did for free or he and his friends got up on stage at the Viper Room and just started to play.

He never gets to that point where he's sitting on the couch waiting for something to happen. He's not waiting for somebody else to bring his career to him.

KW: *How important has his belief in himself been for James, and have you had a personal experience that illustrates his willpower or his belief in himself?*
PW: I don't think any of this would have happened if he didn't believe in himself. The amount of strength it takes to believe in yourself and go against the world you know and go into a world you don't. I mean it was sort of like stepping on an alien planet for him. And I think that takes a lot of inner strength and not caring what other people say, because I'm sure there were people in his high school and friends that looked at him like, "You're crazy."

KW: *He actually mentioned when he started at Hollywood High they didn't let him into the drama program. And then he booked the* ER *episodes and they asked him into the program and he politely declined.*
PW: [*Laughs*] He's a nicer man than me because I wouldn't have been polite about it.

KW: *How would you describe him overall as a client?*
PW: Loyal, full of honor, respectful, respectable and a very decent person. He's a good, honest man.

KW: *That's really saying something.*
PW: Yeah, I mean it's easier for clients like that because you fall in love with them a bit, and if you love somebody, there's a passion to be involved and to take action for them.

KW: *I don't think some actors understand that aspect, that it's a two-way street between agent and actor.*
PW: I think that's probably a universal truism, lately, of not understanding that in any business relationship. We lose value if we lose familiarity, and we lose respect for each other. I think at the end of the day all of this is human relationships, and you're not going to work for somebody if you don't care about them as a person.

KW: *All of the statistics tell us that acting is an incredibly difficult profession. At any given time there are far more actors out of work than are working. However, James has defied these odds, enjoying quite a bit of success in a short time. In addition to all the other things you've told me, how has he done it?*
PW: Well, if I could ultimately answer that I would be a billionaire.

KW: *I hear you.* [Laughs]
PW: As an agent who cares about his clients deeply, I wish I knew what made any of them successful because I would do that.

James is not passive. He's talented and he's self-aware and he doesn't let ego get in the way of his progress. He doesn't have expectations that are unreal. He understands where he is in his career and what he can play at this time and where he can stretch and do something new. He brings something that's honest about his life to the character and does that in an active fashion.

I think that's what makes him successful.

James Earl Success Team Members

MATT FLOYD AND NAISHA ARNOLD

Ken Womble: *Could you tell me a bit about your backgrounds and how you got into talent management?*
Matt Floyd: Well, I've been all across the board. I started out at a small agency called Diverse Talent Group. I wanted to try out casting and simultaneously worked in post production and it was not what I wanted to do. So I got into management and went over to Luber Roklin, fell in love with that side of it, was there for a little over a year and a half and then came over here [to Untitled Entertainment].

KW: *Naisha?*
Naisha Arnold: I actually went straight from college to an agency called Coast to Coast. Untitled offered me a job and I've been there ever since, about seven years. I've always known that I like to work with clients in some capacity and management seems to fit the bill.

KW: *What are you looking for in an actor that you want to sign?*
MF: I think the most important thing is just the dedication to it, someone in whom you can truly see the passion and the drive and the determination to pursue it.

NA: What I look for is similar to what Matt said. It's really about someone that I'm passionate about because it's such a tough, tough industry.

It's hard to tell sometimes. Initially I think someone has the drive, and then after working with them, I realize they really don't have it. I love someone who has an athletic background because I think they understand you need to have that drive.

MF: I mean, whether you get referred clients or you just see some-one at a showcase, the first thing that catches your eye is their talent, obviously, and then you go from there. And if they do have the drive and the determination, it's just the complete package.

KW: *You represent James Earl. How long have you worked together and when you first met, what was your impression of him?*
MF: He was a client at Luber Roklin when I was a manager there, and when I first met him, he was just the nicest, most down to earth and talented guy.

He approaches every situation with the same calm. It doesn't matter if he's reading for a casting associate or if he's in a network test, he approaches it the exact same way. And I think that's a large part of the success that he's had. He's calculating, but he's still very laid back with it and he's always prepared.

NA: Right. I think it's also the confidence he has. And that's sort of what I noticed when Matt brought him to my attention. You have to have confidence without the ego.

KW: *It seems like there is a lot of pressure in being an actor. So, could you give me a couple of specific examples of when he was calm and it paid off?*
MF: We've sent him out on a ton of auditions. During pilot season he tested on a half-hour pilot and he was going to network and before he went in I was like, "Don't psych yourself out, you know how to do this, you've done this before and you've succeeded in this before. You've just got to go in there and do your thing."

And he told me, "It's just another audition, man. That's all it is."

KW: *James told me that his first TV role was on Nickelodeon's* Josh and Drake *at age seventeen, and he was cast in a two line role that became recurring. He got upgraded on his first TV role.*

NA: We weren't with him at that time. But we did hear about it, and it's so phenomenal because these things don't happen often. Which I think shows how talented James is.

MF: When we worked with him at Luber Roklin, he never ever had bad feedback and he was booking a ton then. It's just his world; I mean he just gets it.

KW: *It seems auditioning is a tremendous skill; it could be the most important skill you have as an actor.*

NA: It definitely is, first and foremost. We tell all of our actors that you can have all the theory and the background down, but if you don't know how to show it when you're starting off auditioning, nothing can come of it.

MF: They always look at if you're off book, if you get the character, if you understand the material and convey it in the way that they're looking for.

But the most important thing, I've always thought—and casting directors are kind of the gatekeepers on this one—is can you take direction in the casting room; because if you can't take direction in the casting room, you're not going to take it from a director on a set.

KW: *In 2010 James auditioned for a new series called* Glory Daze. *He was cast in a small role, but at the table read was asked to read for a bigger one and then was cast in that role. It was written for a buff white guy, and of course James is a husky black guy. He seems to have done this a few times. He goes in and changes people's minds.*

MF: I'll send James in to play a white nun. They'll re-write it.

NA: Yeah. [*Laughing*]

KW: *Really? A white nun?*
MF: Yeah, 100%. The writers are there at the table read and they're like, "Wow, he is perfect. This is a completely new scene," because it's always a blueprint. When they get to the table read, they have a great idea of where it's going, but sometimes these actors just blow them away and they're like, "All right, so we're going to have to rewrite this for him."

KW: *James played a recurring role on* Glee *for three seasons. Was that a turning point for him?*
NA: Yes, of course. For where he was at that time to be on a show like that which was so popular and to play such a controversial, interesting character is always a turning point for anybody.

MF: Not to mention the fact that Gwyneth Paltrow was in there at the time.

NA: Sure, that was great too.

KW: *Yes, I heard that story. And he didn't know who she was at first.*
MF: No, he had no idea.

NA: You know, he's just like, "Hey, what's up?" What's so great about James is he's a cool guy, you know, somebody you want to hang with.

KW: *How important is that, if you're a director or a writer on a show, to cast somebody you want to hang with?*
NA: I mean, incredibly. I always tell clients it's about the relationship, everything's relationship. Who do you want to hang with for

fifteen hours a day, and if it's a TV show for potentially the next six years. You know there are a lot of talented people out there, but not a lot of people you want to be with all day long.

MF: Completely agree.

KW: *What is James' overall approach to the business and what does he do that works?*
MF: He's always prepared. He's always, always, always prepared. When I send him sides he writes me back, or if we send him an appointment he always writes or texts me back. He reads the script.

We give him advice on what he should go up for and what he shouldn't go up for, but more often than not he just wants to go in for it. He doesn't care. He's always dedicated because it's a new opportunity either way. He does his research.

That's the most important thing, is to go in there and know exactly what you're dealing with, because if you go in there blind, unprepared you're not getting the role.

KW: *Is there anything about his performance that sticks out. I mean his honesty, his strong choices...*
NA: I think he always does all of those things. We never get bad feedback about James; he is always spectacular.

I think that if James is not getting something, it's because they do need to actually cast the white nun, you know? He knows what he's doing as far as his artistry in acting; he has great comedic timing. That's one thing we hear all the time.

KW: *James was recently cast as a series regular in a new comedy called* Ground Floor. *Congratulations.*
MF: Thank you.

KW: *Anything you can tell me about his audition or the whole process of getting the show?*

NA: At the time there were actually three different shows that were very interested and wanted to test him, things that were conflicting. It was a big process, but not as far as James getting it. They always wanted him; it was just trying to navigate through what made sense for him.

It's a great problem to have for an actor, not many have this problem. But it was definitely a little bit trying in that two week time where it was like, "What are we doing? Which show is right for him to test on?" Because we knew, as his reps, that whatever he wanted to test on he was going to get.

KW: *James told me that you've got to understand that your path is different from the person next to you. It seems that he really understands his own uniqueness. How has that helped him, or made him different?*

NA: I think having that mindset just puts him ahead of the pack. You know, not going in with this jealousy. He's just going in focused on what James sees and what James wants.

KW: *You said James never gets any bad feedback. So it sounds like sometimes no news is good news. If they don't say anything is that good?*

MF: We always want to get feedback, so we can know the conversations that we're going to have with the client. Because if you hear that it's down to him and one other person, you've got to get strategic, "What relationships do we have that can drive this in his direction," you know? If you don't ever call, then you're never going to get that role because I promise you the other client's agents are doing that.

NA: It takes more than just going in and giving a good audition. Maybe they say, "Oh, we were going for this look," and we show them pictures of James that shows he can be this look.

KW: *What would you say are James' best qualities as a performer?*
MF: I went to the taping of the [*Ground Floor*] pilot at Warner Brothers. When you film a sitcom, it's in front of a live audience, and he thinks on his feet and works off of other people. He knows how to get a big laugh. It catches you off guard because we all were reading the scripts, and they go through rewrite after rewrite, and seeing a guy like him bring it to life and come up with stuff you never thought would have been in the script is hilarious.

KW: *How important a role has type played for James? And does he have a clear idea of his type?*
MF: He knows his type and when they're looking for the African-American guy in his mid-late twenties, bigger guy, we can get him in.

The initial type is always important; that's what casting's focused on. But when you get to a creative point with the producers and the writers some of that changes. Not always, but it can.

NA: I think it was Al Pacino [who said], I might be misquoting it but, "You're wrong all the time until you're right all the time." And you can see James is already doing that. He's basically right for everything because that's how good he is.

KW: *So the talent sort of trumps type at that point?*
MF: Yep, that's it.

KW: *Which leads to my next question; how important a role has talent played for him?*

MF: Everything. I mean if he wasn't talented, he wouldn't have gotten where he is. Type is one thing. You know, if you fit the bill for a role that was written a certain way and you have the talent to back it up, it's pretty hard not to book that person.

And if you're a likable person too; he can go into a room and make friends with everyone. That's the gift, he can go in there and blow them away with his performance and then they'll want to take him out for a beer after.

KW: *How important has his belief in himself been for James, his confidence? And have you had a personal experience with him that illustrates that belief?*
MF: I think he's just self-aware. That's the confidence that he has. He's told me, "I'll go into a room for a half-hour comedy, and I know how to do that, and then later in the afternoon I go into a drama. I know where I am and I can dial it down." I think it's just because he doesn't care. He's always in that competent mindset. It's kind of who he is.

NA: I think that in this business you have to have that self-awareness and that self-confidence because it's just such a hard thing to do.

This pilot season he was a newer client of ours and it was amazing to see the way he handled each audition, the way he handled going in somewhere people are thinking that you're not right and you're proving them wrong.

KW: *How would you describe him overall as a client?*
NA: Amazing. You know, funny, likable, energetic, responsible…

MF: Very responsible, hilarious…

NA: Reliability is huge for us. I mean, you'd be surprised at how much we don't have of that. That's half the job.

KW: *It seems that James' career has pretty much gone straight up. I mean, maybe a few little dips here and there early on, but he seems to keep building on each new achievement. In your experience is that typical of actors who are successful?*

MF: No, no, no. It's not typical. With him I think it's because everyone loves working on a team. He's an easy client. He never complains, he doesn't ask for much. But when he does ask, I'll bend over backwards to try to get it done. He's someone you want to work for. Every single person on our team cares for him, knows his talent and the potential that he has and we have an open forum.

His career has gone upward because he's built off the right roles, but also because of having a team that made the right moves.

KW: *Okay, final question. All of the statistics tell us that acting is an incredibly difficult profession. At any given time there are far more actors out of work than are working. However, James has de-fied these odds, enjoying quite a bit of success in a relatively short time. How has he done it?*

MF: Dedication and talent.

NA: Yeah; having a good team, consistency and dedication. I always tell people if you work at this and you stay at it and you're consistent, things will happen and it will work out for you.

You know, people aren't consistent, they're not reliable, they're not hard workers—and James is all of those things.

What are the keys that have led James Earl to a successful acting career?

He's determined to make it "by any means necessary"

James keeps it real, both in the acting craft and in the acting business. He knows how tough the industry is, so he has made a series of conscious decisions that support his laser beam focus on making it.

He was frustrated with nervousness preventing him from auditioning well, so he willed his way into getting rid of it. He learned from Will Smith that the only way to have a career—Plan A—was not to have a Plan B. And he knew he had to figure out how he was going to make it, so he became "determined to do whatever necessary by any means necessary."

He trusts his instincts then acts on them

Ever since his earliest work as an unproven seventeen-year-old in *Drake and Josh*, James has relied on his own instincts. He knew he needed training, so he took improv classes that taught him to value imagination over dialogue. He trusted his own life experiences to inform his acting, and he learned to get his "levels to zero" so he could walk into auditions relaxed.

Patrick Welborn believes James' ability to make "smart choices" stems from his tough upbringing in LA's South Central and notes how James embraces his individuality—he's "comfortable being the fish out of water."

In one situation after another James sits back and sizes things up, then makes a choice and puts that choice into *action*.

He makes every character his own

Like most actors James was type cast early in his career, mostly as jocks and tough, inner city kids.

However, his ability to bring his own unique qualities to every character have helped James *transcend* type, so much that when the producers of *Glory Daze* and *Awesometown* saw him audition, they threw out the old characters and rewrote new ones expressly for him. Not a small feat, especially since both roles were leads on television series.

This ability to make others see him in a broader way has created new acting opportunities, as Patrick Welborn, Matt Floyd and Naisha Arnold all stress.

He focuses on the positive

By centering his attention on his dream, James stays "out of the negative bubble." And even when he isn't working, he keeps a positive attitude. As Patrick noted, he "trusts that he'll work."

He has confidence

When James stepped onto an "alien planet," as Patrick called it, from the tough world of his youth to the world of show business, he actually took a giant leap that required courage. In audition rooms and on TV and movie sets—his team agrees—confidence has played a huge role in his career. And his successful track record confirms that James is correct when he calls confidence "the main secret to acting."

He is a great team player, with a great team

The relationship between actor and agent, and actor and manager is based on trust; each side agrees to work hard for the other to create mutually successful careers.

James' reps get him into great auditions, develop business relationships, strategize about job choices and negotiate contracts. James fulfills his end of this agreement by a positive attitude, reliability, thorough preparation for auditions and, most importantly, by booking job after job.

It's easy to see why his team feels passionate about working with James.

He is talented

Every member of James' team agrees that he is very talented. That talent has been proven over and over in a range of roles, from dramas like *ER* and *Glee*, to comedies like *Glory Daze* and *Ground Floor*.

Patrick summed up best why James has been so successful: "He's talented and he takes action."

GARY BEACH

CHAPTER 6

I Just Love It

GARY BEACH

Gary Beach has had a long and varied career on the Broadway stage, as well as film and television.

He was nominated for the 2005 Tony Award for Best Actor in a Musical for his performance as Albin in the revival of *La Cage aux Folles*. Mr. Beach received the 2001 Tony Award as well as the Drama Desk and Outer Critics Circle awards for his performance as Roger De Bris in Mel Brooks' *The Producers*. He created the role of Lumiere on Broadway in Disney's *Beauty and the Beast* (Tony nomination). Other Broadway credits include *Annie, Doonesbury, The Moony Shapiro Songbook, Sweet Adeline* (Encores!), *Something's Afoot* and *1776*. National tours: *Legends!* starring Mary Martin and Carol Channing. Regional: *Closer Than Ever* (LA premiere) *Lend Me a Tenor, She Loves Me* (Comet Award), *Of Thee I Sing* (Helen Hayes nomination). Television includes: *Kennedy Center Honors honoring Carol Burnett and Mel Brooks, Recording The Producers, Queer as Folk, Murder She Wrote* and *Cheers*.

A native of Alexandria, Virginia and a graduate of the North Carolina School of the Arts, Mr. Beach was most recently in the Broadway revival of *Les Misérables* and the national tour of Monty Python's *Spamalot* as King Arthur.

....

Ken Womble: *Gary, how important has training been to you in your professional career?*

Gary Beach: I think early on it was hugely important and not just the training. I grew up in the '50s and '60s in Alexandria, Virginia, which is now quite a nice town. But back then it was just a quiet little southern town. The first Broadway show my parents ever saw I was in. So what it served for me was to be around multitudes of like-thinking people, whether they were actors or musicians or dancers. I'd never been around that before. It gave me a new perspective that I wasn't that different. There were a lot of people that had the same interests that I had. And luckily for me, my parents did not fight it. They loved the fact that I was interested in it and supported me one hundred percent all the way.

KW: *I think so many of us had that feeling that we found home in a way when we got in a group of people like us.*
GB: I remember that feeling very well. I can feel it right now. I remember going to the auditorium one night, my first year there, to hear a concert and practically the whole school was there. And I was thinking, "I've never been in a room like this in my life with so many people who loved what they were doing."

KW: *You auditioned for the national tour of* 1776 *right after, I believe, you graduated from the North Carolina School of the Arts, and you drove yourself back and forth from North Carolina to New York. Wasn't that quite a long shot?*
GB: Well, you know what? It's even a longer shot because I *hadn't* graduated yet. I was in my junior year, and I went to see the original Broadway production of *1776* which opened around spring break. I went to New York, I saw it, and I fell head over heels in love with that show. I just thought it was brilliant. And I was in the school library one day and I saw in *Backstage* that they were casting the national tour. So I was talking to my speech teacher, who had had a career on Broadway as an actress, and she said, "Well, who's the casting director?" I had no idea what she was talking about. And so I went back and looked and I came back to her and I said it's a fellow named Michael Shurtleff.

KW: *Oh my goodness!*

GB: Yeah, exactly, *that* Michael Shurtleff [author of the classic *Audition*]. She said, "Oh I know Michael." And lo and behold she just picked up the phone…this is what I mean about luck and timing, right? And she said, "Michael I have a boy here who's just head over heels in love with your show, he would love to audition for it, he doesn't have an agent." I had joined Equity the summer before that doing summer stock in Atlanta, Georgia and so I had my union card. So he said, "Oh great, when can he come up?"

So I drove the ten hours, went up and I auditioned, I drove the ten hours back. I got a callback the next week. I drove the ten hours, ten hours back. I got the final callback, so ten hours up and ten hours back. And finally, on my last audition the director from the audience says, "Gary, I understand you're driving back and forth…so where are you going?" And I said, "Winston-Salem, North Carolina." He said, "Oh my God; how many hours?" I said "Ten hours." He said, "Well, that's okay, this is your last trip. Thank you for coming." And it was like, "Really?" I had no idea what he was saying. So I get back to school and a day or so later I got the call offering me the job.

So I actually went to the dean of drama and I said, "You know, I have more than enough academic credits. This is the opportunity of a lifetime to get my foot in the door." And I talked to different instructors and they agreed, and so they graduated me a year early. And the main thing for me was to get the degree because no one in my family had ever been to college. And it was such a big deal for them, you know? Stayed in, got the degree and left.

KW: *That's wonderful, because some actors don't finish up. And for me it was always a source of pride to have a college degree.*

GB: Me too! It meant everything to my family and it meant a lot to me too. And whenever I talk to students or groups one of the things I always say is stay in school. There's nothing worse than a dumb actor. I've been stuck on stage with a few of them! [*Laughs*]

KW: *Was* 1776 *your first break?*
GB: Yeah. Totally. That's why I was all over it like a bad suit. It wasn't to play the role I wanted, it was to understudy it and play a smaller role. And so two and a half months into the run we were playing Miami Beach and the fellow playing it got ill on stage and left and never came back. And I was his understudy. So, the next afternoon, Saturday, I was on. And I was on for the rest of the weekend and the rest of the week. And somebody was on my side because I started getting all the reviews. And I think it also had to do with playing the South because we were in the South at the time and that song "Molasses to Rum," it packed a wallop. And I think that people in the South heard it even more loudly than people in the North. It's the slave trade. And so the song became a highlight. And one night at the end of the song I was supposed to stand there center stage, my arms outstretched, and then storm over to stage left, grab my coat, storm off stage right followed by the whole southern delegation. And as I'm standing there center stage I see a man running down the aisle, his hands above his head and he's just whistling like a crazy [man] and cheering and he gets to the side of the stage, and I recognized him. It was Sherman Edwards, the writer of *1776*. And so I, quickly of course, ran over, got the coat and left. [*Laughs*] And as I got off stage, a friend of mine is standing there and just hugs me and says, "If you never do this again, you did it tonight," meaning that I had, I guess, knocked it out of the park. And afterwards they offered it to me. He had been sent there to see what this guy was like. So it was the ultimate audition!

KW: *So even though the other actor didn't return, it wasn't automatic that you would get the role, I take it?*

GB: No, not at all, especially on the road, well anywhere really these days, it's not automatic. In fact, I think they shy away from it because it's much easier to cast someone in a large, juicy role than someone to understudy the large, juicy role.

1776 was a very important part of my training. There I was at twenty-two, the youngest person in the cast, and around young and middle-aged character men, because that show was filled with twenty-six men or something. And all of these guys had a good deal of experience, certainly more than I had. And being around them for that year really set me up for the rest of my life, and how this thing is supposed to be done, and what to expect of it—of your life and of your career. It was such a formative time for me that I'll never forget them. You know, just being backstage with people that had done a lot of Broadway. One of the actors was a big deal up at Stratford, Connecticut, the Shakespeare Festival and Ashland—Patrick Hines—and he was a major American Shakespearean actor. And to be around someone with that experience, and we shared a dressing room quite often, and to just sit there and talk. It taught me so much.

KW: *Would you say getting that large role gave you a sense of destiny about your career?*

GB: No, that's a little strong. I didn't have a sense of destiny. I've always felt this…it's the journey. There is no destination, you know. And I have so many friends who always thought there was a destination: that role that sent them over the top on Broadway, or the Tony Award, or the Oscar or whatever. And that really is a great stop on the way to somewhere. You know? It's not the destination.

I'll never forget the first time I was nominated for a Tony. It was for Lumiere in *Beauty and the Beast* and a friend of mine called and said, "Gary, you've been nominated for a Tony Award." And I hung up the phone and I shook a bit. I felt a sense of arrival that I didn't think I'd ever get here. And I must be honest, when I didn't get it there was a little disappointment, I guess, but I never felt like, "Oh, I lost!" I've been nominated three times and every time it's great, every time it's special, and winning is terrific. There's a sense that you are now a member of a club.

KW: *And you were chosen by some of your peers.*
GB: That's right. And that's exciting, too, isn't it?

KW: *It sounds very exciting. Did you then do* 1776 *for a long run on Broadway?*
GB: They took a lot of the original Broadway cast to Hollywood to make the film and so they recast. And when that happened I went into the Broadway company. And I think I ended up playing about eight months. And I've done it on and off over the years.

KW: *And then you went on to do a number of other Broadway shows, and tours as well including* Something's Afoot *and* Annie *as Rooster Hannigan.*
GB: Loved *Annie*. I did that a long time.

KW: *How do you deal with long runs? Eight shows a week.*
GB: I love long runs. I may be one of the few actors you talk to who really likes long runs.

KW: *Why?*
GB: I like the stability it gives to your life, and I'm not just talking monetarily. I get up, I do this, I do that, I go to the theatre, I do the show. I'm coming off almost ten years of eight a week, when I first moved down here [south Florida]. I've done even longer than

that if you go back to *Beauty and the Beast,* and I seem to have a cutoff number which is huge, about 1,700 performances.

KW: *That's over four years!*
GB: That's right! And *Beauty and the Beast* I did it over a period of maybe six years, but I'd come and I'd go and I'd go to the Los Angeles company and go back to the New York company. I went up to Toronto for a few weeks.

KW: *At some point you decided to move from New York to LA. What caused that?*
GB: I had done a play called *Legends* with Mary Martin and Carol Channing, written by James Kirkwood, the guy that had done *Chorus Line,* and we were going to open at the Ahmanson Theatre in Los Angeles. And a friend of mine had moved out years before and was having success in television. He had plenty of room and said, "Hey, you can stay here while you're at the Ahmanson." Well I did. And I got into a lifestyle there. We were there for months and nightly there would be a knock at my dressing room door after the show and there would be yet more friends that had moved to LA. And I'm thinking, "If they've done this, maybe I could give it a try." I went out with the idea that I'll try this for a while and I loved living in LA.

I hated the work I got. It was pretty bad television. And you know if you don't get a series, if you're just doing guest shots, it's a pretty terrible existence. Luckily, upon moving out there, they were putting up the Los Angeles company of *Les Misérables,* the first company there. It had been running on Broadway for a month or so, so it was still a relatively new show. And so they asked me if I would do Thénardier, the master of the house. I said, "Oh this'll be nice, I know it'll run," which it did for like a year and a half, and it kept me in Los Angeles and paid the bills and it gave me a chance to get to know people. And it was, once again, luck and timing.

KW: *So you didn't find living in LA hurt your musical career? It sounds like you were doing very well.*
GB: Okay, don't quote me on this but a friend of mine said, "You're the only actor I know that moved to Hollywood and became a Broadway star." [*Laughs*] It's sort of true in a funny way. I consider Lumiere to be the first of some wonderful work that I got.

KW: *Tell me how you got offered the role of Roger De Bris, the flamboyant director in* The Producers.
GB: Well, this is how it happened. I was living in LA and it was early in 2000 and my agent got a call and Vinny Liff [*The Producers'* casting director], who had kept me working for years basically, wanted to know if I would come to New York. They were doing a reading, Nathan [Lane] was going to be doing it, he's the only name I knew really, and would I like come and do Roger De Bris? And I had, as a young man, been a big fan of the movie. And I knew exactly who Roger De Bris was and I thought, "You know, in a musical that could be really fun." And I asked my agent, "Does he still make his first entrance in an evening gown?" And my agent said, "Yes he does—but get this—he ends up playing Adolf Hitler in *Springtime for Hitler*." And I thought, "Oh my God, an evening gown in the first act and Adolf Hitler in the second. It's never going to get any better than this." [*Laughs*]

KW: [Laughs] *How many actors have had that opportunity?*
GB: I know, and so I said, "Oh I'd love to. Just tell them to call me and we'll arrange the flight." And my agent said, "Well that's just it. They want you to fly yourself in and can you stay with a friend?"

KW: *Oh my goodness.*

GB: That's exactly what I thought. Maybe a little harsher. [*Laughs*] And I said, "I can't talk right now. I'll have to call you back." I hung up the phone and I was literally sitting on the couch shaking and then, out of nowhere, came this epiphany: "Why the hell else did you play a candlestick for 1,700 performances so you could afford to do this?" So I called my agent back and I said, "Sure, I'll do it." And they sent me the script. And I loved it. We could've gone into rehearsal that day, that's how ready the script was.

And so I went to New York. And Glen Kelly [the show's musical supervisor] and I are at the piano and he's teaching me this piece of music that happens in the middle of *Springtime for Hitler*. It's called "Heil Myself" and it's sung by Hitler. And Mel Brooks is standing there, you know, just listening, and I start singing it and Mel says to me, "Are you doing Judy?"

KW: *Judy Garland?*

GB: Yeah. I said, "Yeah," because I hadn't planned on it.

KW: *It just came up?*

GB: Yeah! It was the mannerisms and stuff like that, you know. It's not like I sing like Judy Garland, and so he said, "I love it!" And I said, "Oh God, I do too!" And Glen, who is a genius, said, "Oh my God! Go get Stroman," [Susan Stroman, the show's director]. And the four of us just start talking. And then I finally came up with the thing, I could sit on the edge of the stage. Well, the four of us start giggling like children. There was this guy, [*laughs*] the worst director in Broadway history, who was going to be sitting on the edge of the stage living his dream in front of the audience.

Well, we did it at the reading. Of course there was no stage and we were all in folding chairs with music stands and everybody on Broadway wanted to be there that day. And one of the people there was Robin Wagner, who they had asked to design the set. And he told me when it came time for me to do "Heil Myself" I just stood up from my folding chair and walked to the center of the room and just looked at the audience. And they screamed with laughter because they knew exactly what I was doing. And Robin said to me a couple years later, "I knew you won the Tony that day when you just stood up and walked to the center of the room and stared at us!"

So I get back to where I'm staying, at a friend's house that night, and the phone rings. It's for me. It's a girl who was stage managing the reading, and she said, "Mel wants to know how much your ticket was."

[Later] Vinny Liff called me and he says, "Roger De Bris please." I said, "Who is this?" He said, "Vinny Liff. You're it."

KW: *How did you feel?*
GB: Oh, I felt the earth shift.

KW: *That's a wonderful story. And then, of course, you went on and won the Tony Award for Best Featured Actor in a musical for* The Producers. *Was there a sense of validation for your Tony win?*
GB: I can't say yes. I mean I had a feeling I was going to win. Because by the time you get to the Tony Awards you've gone through two other awards; they call it the Triple Crown. The Outer Critics Circle Award, the Drama Desk Award, the Tony Award, and I had won everything up to then. So it wasn't a sense of validation. There is a sense of *arrival* in that I do belong here in this group. But for me, don't forget, I wasn't twenty-eight. You know, I was fifty-something. And I think it made a huge difference. But that show—if you want to talk about magic—hardly a day passed by in that first year that wasn't just like, "Oh my God!" It was incredible.

Experiencing 9/11 through doing that show was an incredible thing, too. Tuesday night was cancelled, Wednesday night we went back to work. According to the story, [Mayor Rudolph] Giuliani actually called Rocco Landesman, who was main line producer of our show at the time, and said, "Can you get the show back up for tomorrow night?" And Rocco said, "Sure, absolutely." Giuliani knew that one thing he had to do was try to look like we're going back to normalcy. And so Broadway was open. I took the subway to work that night and I came out on Duffy Square, which is right there at the Palace Theatre, and there was no one in line. There was no one walking around. I got to 45th Street, which is a busy theatre street, looked down. There was no one in front of any theatre. I walked through Shubert Alley, turned the corner to 44th Street, looked down at the St. James and the streets were filled with people.

KW: *For your show.*
GB: Absolutely filled with people, and the street, not the sidewalk. And it became obvious that there were going to be a lot of cancelled seats because tourists couldn't fly into the city. So you had a lot of people that went there to buy these cancelled seats.

And the audience that night was the most ferocious I think we had ever faced. They laughed like their lives depended on it. Rocco actually caught me coming into the stage door and said, "You have the hardest job of all tonight." I said, "I happen to think I have the easiest job." And I was right. When I rose up out of that floor as Adolf Hitler, it wasn't lost on anybody.

KW: *It must have taken some courage for all of you to go and do that because at that time you didn't know what else was going to happen.*

GB: I don't know if it was courage, but there was that sense. And, of course, as it went on it became stranger and stranger because theatre did not do well for the first month after that. And we had some friends and cast mates that were buying tickets to their shows and giving them to firemen just to keep the show open. And you couldn't get close to the theatre it was so sold out. And once again luck and timing.

KW: *After* The Producers, *in 2004, you played Albin in the revival of* La Cage aux Folles *on Broadway.*
GB: Right.

KW: *Was coming back to a lead role on Broadway different after* The Producers?
GB: Well, yes and no. It was a huge role and this is what I thought— talk about ego—I actually thought, "Who else is going to play this?" You know, a middle-aged, sort of leading man-ish guy in drag. I mean, you know, "Hello! I guess it's what I do now." But I absolutely loved it. The best part about that was the last few months of the run Robert Goulet came in and played the other guy, George. And that was a total thrill. He was a great guy. And luckily I got to visit him just prior to his dying. At the close of our *Le Cage* we actually kissed on stage. I mean it wasn't a huge wet, sloppy thing, we just kissed. And so at the final performance we kissed, the curtain came in, and we pulled back and he looked me and said, "Well, I'll never have to do that again—maybe."

KW: *That's funny. Gary, before you were receiving offers and you still had to audition for shows, do you remember an audition when you absolutely nailed it. If so, what were you doing right?*
GB: That's a great question. I hope I have a great answer! I actually do remember a particular audition. There was a political review in

New York City at a place called Upstairs at Jimmy's on West 52nd Street. And the review was called, *What's a Nice Country Like You Doing in a State Like This*? And one of the guys was leaving, so I got a call about auditioning. They had walked me in to see the show the night before the audition, and it looked to me like the kind of thing I just love doing. It looked like they were winging it. And so I went in the next day and just started singing a song from *The Rothschilds*—"I'm in Love, I'm in Love." I had just finished doing a tour of the show and had found a hook for the song that made it seem very off the cuff. And they responded like gangbusters. It was exactly what they wanted to see. I looked like I was making it up as I went along. And so at that moment I thought, "Oh, I've got this." And I did.

KW: *Well it sounds like you understood the material and what was required of it. I don't know if it was a risk for you, but going out there and being spontaneous may have been a risk for some actors.*
GB: Possibly, right. But for me, I knew. When I saw the show the night before I thought to myself, "Oh, this is what I do. If they could all go like this it would be wonderful."

KW: *I've heard it said about the acting profession that if you have a fallback plan, you will fall back. Do you believe that?*
GB: Not necessarily, but I think if you're that uncommitted then you'll probably fall back. When you decide to go into the theatre, it's not a "decide" sort of thing. It's something you just grow up knowing. And as a young man, like I said to you, it wasn't as if I was being nurtured to do this. I had never seen a show, but I knew I wanted to be in one! And so I think that maybe for a while I had what you would call a "fallback plan." I went to a liberal arts college in Virginia for a year thinking that I would study political science and then in the middle of that year I realized that this isn't what

I want at all. I really want to be an actor. And that's when I went down and auditioned at the School of the Arts and never looked back. It wasn't like I went to New York and gave myself two years or whatever. I just went there and started working.

KW: *That was my next question. Was there a moment when you decided not to fall back? Was that during school?*
GB: Actually, yes. And honestly, I really think that that whole fall back thing was something I said to make my family feel better. [*Laughs*]. You know? "Oh, he does have a plan!" [*Laughs*]. But I don't think I ever really considered that, "Oh well, if this doesn't work out..." I just had to make it work out.

KW: *Did you just assume it was going to work out?*
GB: Well, I definitely hoped it would work out, and it was working out. You have to realize this. I was working in the professional theatre starting in college. And then upon graduating I had the tour of *1776* which was about a year. And then when that was over I went into the Broadway company. I got an agent fairly easily. It's timing and luck and being prepared. So when the timing happens and something lucky happens you're ready for it, you're prepared to show the goods and deliver.

KW: *What is your best quality as an actor and why?*
GB: I love to work. I just love it. And I'm sure you ran into this. Isn't it strange when you meet people in this business, as hard as it is, who really don't want to be there?

KW: *Yes, it is.*
GB: It's like, what are you doing here? This is hard. This is exciting and interesting and hard. And so that is probably a quality that I've enjoyed and perhaps even worked because of.

KW: *As far as what you do on stage, what would you say is your best quality? What you bring to an audience?*
GB: Hmmm.

KW: *From the feedback you've received.*
GB: Well, you know, I feel like a one-note Johnny, but people have said to me for my whole career, "You look like you're having the time of your life." And I think that especially with the roles I get to play that it's really helped. "Oh, he's playing a candlestick, but look he's having the time of his life!" [*Laughs*] You know, "He's playing Adolf Hitler, but look he's having the time of his life!"

KW: *And that's what audiences come for as well. They spend a lot of money and they want to have fun.*
GB: Yes, exactly. And those are the kind of shows and roles that I'm most often cast in. I'm hardly ever cast as a person who is into themselves, you know. It's usually a gregarious, out there, person. I think that that probably is the thing that I've heard most often in my career. Or that, you know, "You're funny." And let's face it, if you're doing musical comedy that helps. [*Laughs*]

KW: *How important to your success is your belief in yourself as a performer?*
GB: Well, of course you have to believe in yourself. I mean that's obvious. But I also think that there's nothing wrong with a certain amount of self-questioning. I think that leads you in a direction you may not have gone. You need that as a performer because how else are you going to grow?

KW: *What would you say is the best piece of advice that you've ever been given about acting?*
GB: Wow.

KW: *As a career, or a craft or both.*

GB: Oddly enough, given that question we were just talking about? It probably is believe in yourself. It all comes back to that, doesn't it? I mean, if you don't believe in yourself, how can you stand up in front of a thousand people and say, "Watch me! I'm going to be interesting enough for you to take two hours of your life and watch me."

KW: *What are the smartest things you've done for your career? And if you could go back and change one career decision, what would it be?*

GB: Probably the smartest thing was to go to New York. There were four of us in my graduating class. One guy went to Los Angeles, one guy went home and started a company and the other guy just fell off the face of the earth. And I went to New York. And we've all had nice careers, especially the guy that moved to Los Angeles...he became a lawyer! [*Laughs*] If I had been lead to go to California, I think I would've just died on the vine there. I actually did go to California and spent about twelve years, but I was more of a mature performer and I had a little bit of a reputation, which helps you there. But for me to go to New York was a great decision on my part because that's where my career was going to be.

And as far as anything I'd change? I can't think of anything. Even the bad stuff I learned from. I mean, I've worked with a couple of rotten apples over the years, but I even learned from them. So I wouldn't change a thing.

And I'm enjoying my life. I just got off the phone with a friend, a director; we're going to be doing *Hello, Dolly!* together. And we're thinking about casting the role of Dolly and, "We can do this, we can do that." It's all ongoing.

KW: *Okay, last question. All of the statistics tell us that acting is an incredibly difficult profession and at any given time there are far more actors out of work than are working. However, you have defied these odds, enjoying quite a bit of success in your career. How have you done it?*

GB: For many, many years I just went where the work was. And I think that was important for me, for the kind of career I had. You know, "Oh I don't tour, oh I don't do this, I don't do that." That's ridiculous. I did a whole year of industrial shows back in the '70s because that's where I should be going at the time. And I took great trips and they treated you beautifully, and at the time the pay was pretty good. And so it kept me going for a year until I got *Annie*. That more or less established me as working on Broadway. And I never looked back.

Gary Beach Success Team Member

MARCIA MILGROM DODGE

Ken Womble: *Marcia, you are a noted director, choreographer and teacher based in New York. Could you tell me a bit about the kinds of plays and musicals that you work on?*

Marcia Milgrom Dodge: I do a lot of revivals and I work primarily in the regional theatre. I did a revival of *Merrily We Roll Along* in Washington, D.C. with Stephen Sondheim and I've worked a lot at the Bay Street Theatre where I got to do *Tommy* and *Hair*. My husband Tony is a playwright, so I've directed some plays that we cowrote and that he's also written. I've done mysteries and comedies and musicals from coast to coast and as far as Denmark and South Korea.

I like to call myself kind of a working dog, you know? I just go where the work is and try to find new insights into material that's lived longer than me, and then I'm lucky to get to work on new material too; most recently *Sense and Sensibility*, which I'm very proud of, that played at the Denver Center.

KW: *Wow, what a résumé.*
MMD: Yeah, it's a little exhausting! [*Laughs*]

KW: *In 2009 you directed the Broadway revival of* Ragtime. *It was critically hailed and nominated for seven Tony Awards. It was your Broadway debut as a director. Could you tell me about that experience?*
MMD: I went to Washington, D.C. [the Kennedy Center] and worked on the show as if it was my Broadway show. I was working with the writers, I met E.L. Doctorow; it was a very big deal. So I approached it as if my life depended on it.

And the show was so beautifully received in Washington that the pilgrimages started, and I would hear, "So-and-so's in the house tonight," and "So-and-so's coming down," and I tried to stay very calm. I've had my heart broken many times before where we thought we had something that was going to move to New York and then it didn't.

And I was very proud of what we were able to accomplish in New York [on Broadway]. Not just because I was so proud of the production, but because of what the story of the show is and what it has to say about who we are as a culture and as Americans.

KW: *You mentioned it taking so long to finally get a show to Broadway. I think Gary's career parallels yours in that he had been working for over twenty years before he got his first Tony nomination.*
MMD: You know, that's what Gary and I probably have in common. We felt that we were doing really good work and then to

be acknowledged in New York City is just affirmation. There's a community here that is so remarkably inviting, and people like Denzel Washington and Hugh Jackman and Tom Hanks and all the other stars that come to perform on Broadway feel it.

And when you've done it and you're an adult, there's a certain maturity about you and a certain calm and confidence. I felt very confident when I came to New York; I was more than ready.

Gary had worked twenty years, I had worked thirty years before I made my Broadway debut, and Gary and I had worked in regional theatre together. The first thing we did together was *Of Thee I Sing* which was done at Arena Stage in Clinton's first term. He played Wintergreen, looking a lot like Ronald Reagan. We gave him orange makeup and coiffed his hair and it was really funny.

And then a couple years later we did a revival of *Closer Than Ever* and then he got *Beauty and the Beast.* When Gary got that, he was like a kid in a candy store.

KW: *And he told me that with his Tony nomination for* Beauty and the Beast *he felt a sense of arrival, and the role was the first of some wonderful work he got. Was his nomination for Best Supporting Actor in a Musical a turning point for him?*
MMD: Absolutely. I mean, getting a Tony nomination, particularly for an actor, is a really cachet-raising event. And the ones that win the award tend to reap a few more benefits.

So, I think that it was just a great big, door-opening welcome from the Broadway community to say, "This is where you belong. So let's spend the next twenty years doing shows here."

KW: *When you first met Gary on* Of Thee I Sing, *what were some of your first impressions of him?*

MMD: He made me laugh so hard I almost wet myself in rehearsal; and truthful and honest and musical and silly and friendly, with no ego. It's all about the work.

You know, I've been sort of lamenting the loss of those kinds of comics that really understand the Vaudeville style. It's an art form that has to be passed on and you can't really teach it. You've got to have sort of the gene for it. And Gary has that gene, you know? Everything he did was so full-bodied, full-out, ferocious and funny; the four F's. [*Laughs*] Gary Beach, the four F's. And every time I work with Gary I learn something, I am moved deeply, and I'm laughing really hard.

I just did *Hello, Dolly!* with Gary and Vicki Lewis and when we got to the Harmonia Gardens scene I just got out of their way. I was like, "I'm in the room with the Sonny Liston and Muhammad Ali of comedy. I'm just going to stand over here and if I think of something to throw in, I'll throw it in."

KW: *How much of a higher level did* The Producers *take Gary in his career?*
MMD: Well, then they offered him *La Cage*, right?

KW: *Yes.*
MMD: I don't think he had to audition…

KW: *I believe that's right.*
MMD: And I don't think he really auditions anymore. So, I think after doing *Beauty and the Beast* he was auditioning for better shows and after *The Producers* he won the position of not having to audition. And he knows everybody. I mean, he's a Broadway treasure.

KW: *And people like him. How much of a difference has that made in his career?*

MMD: Oh, I think if he was a snob or a diva he wouldn't have been as successful. I don't think people like to work with people that are not nice and lovely and generous.

I will only work with somebody once if they behave badly, unless they're stars and you're sort of stuck with them. But, honestly, the bigger they are the nicer they've been. I just directed Jonathan Pryce in *My Fair Lady*, the concert version. And I'm about to do it again. And he's willing to come to Santa Barbara to do it again just because he had such a good time.

Someone that feels they've been passed over for something carries around a lot of grudge behavior. But Gary doesn't carry around that kind of baggage. He's just so grateful when the job comes he's like, "I got a job! I'm so happy!" He has that generosity of spirit and humility which is essential for longevity.

KW: *When I asked Gary what his best quality as an actor is he said, "I love to work, I just love it." Has that love of work been important to him, do you believe? And if so, how?*

MMD: Oh, absolutely. It's like an IV; I mean, hook him up to a text and a rehearsal room and let him go. I think he really loves to work! "Let's dig in and find out. Let's make this choice, let's sleep on it, come back the next day and say, 'You know what? Two o'clock in the morning I had an idea,'" so we try it.

We did *Guys and Dolls* together—that was another really great treat to work on that classic musical with Gary—and he just came in prepared. I mean, we did these shows at Music Circus with six days of rehearsal. It's like crazy boot camp, you know? And Gary comes in off book and ready to go and he's studied it and he's made choices. He doesn't wait for the director to tell him what to do; which is the worst thing that I face every now and then.

I have a lot to deal with so I want actors to come in with big choices and then I edit and shape and throw a suggestion in here or there. And Gary and I have really found that way of working.

KW: *Do you find that most actors in auditions make big choices?*
MMD: In auditions I look for the choices. I am only interested in the ones that have given a thought about who I am, what's my relationship to the other characters, to the environment; sort of Uta Hagen's six steps. You're just going to get smarter people if they invested some time in it. And I understand the process of auditioning is exhausting and heartbreaking at times, but you've got to go out there and do the work.

And that's what Gary doesn't shy away from. He'll do a line reading that you read sixteen times and you'll go, "Holy shit, that was hilarious," or "I didn't even understand the meaning of the line until he said it." He's invested, always invested.

You know, any opportunity to work with Gary I just grab it.

KW: *What are some of Gary's best qualities as a performer?*
MMD: He's having so much fun that you can't help but have fun when you watch Gary. And he's always connected deeply emotionally to whatever he's saying or singing. He finds the meaning behind everything that comes out of his mouth. And then he has this wonderful physical elegance to his body language that is at times funny and sexy and playful.

KW: *I saw a photograph of Gary in the* Sacramento Bee; *he was reprising his role in* The Producers *at Sacramento Music Circus. And he's leaning into the other character, dressed in female garb, totally intruding this guy's space. He's like the Tower of Pisa leaning toward him. And it's just hilarious.*

MMD: He is fearless and he's always in action, he's always in pursuit of something. He's never a victim or feeling sorry for himself. Even as Nathan Detroit, who is sort of put upon, you know, "What am I going to do? What am I going to do?" He'll do anything to get what he needs. And that means sticking his tits in somebody's face if he's wearing a bra.

When we did *Forum* there's this wonderful sequence where Marcus Lycus's soldiers are following him and I think the line is something like, "Watch his every move."

And so Gary starts by just walking. And then he turns it into like a mincing, very female walk and the three boys are following him, and then he starts doing a silly dance step and they follow him, and then he finally gallops off and they gallop off. I let him loose, it was just so right; whatever he decided to do was right.

And he was consistent, you know, he didn't change it night to night. Some actors will get bored and say, "Oh, I don't want to do that tonight, I'm just going to keep them on their toes." But Gary will find the comedy and then work to keep perfecting it. That's what I love about him. Sometimes making everybody laugh in rehearsal could be the kiss of death. But with Gary, if you're laughing in rehearsal you're laughing even harder in performance.

That's what he means when he says, "I love to work!" It's like, "Okay, I found the laugh, and now I'm going to keep working on it making it better." And he doesn't get bored.

KW: *He said his cutoff point for long runs is about 1,700 performances.*
MMD: [*Laughs*]. Well, he and Marian Seldes probably have that in common. I don't think she missed a performance of *Deathtrap*.

KW: *Bonnie Gillespie wrote a book called* Acting Q's, *in which she says, "Working performers seem to have tapped into a sense of* *authenticity that most aspiring actors search for." Do you feel that's been true for Gary?*

MMD: Yes, it applies to Gary in the sense that he does it and by doing it you are true to your authenticity. You're able to be authentic because it's part of your daily life. It's like breathing. You know, you get up and you act!

I have subscribed to the Meisner approach, which is to live truthfully under imaginary circumstances, and I think Gary lives truthfully. So, whether he's doing a broad comedy or a poignant, dramatic moment he's truthful. And he's in his own skin. So, he's as authentic as he can be.

KW: *How important a role has type played for Gary, if it's played a role? And does he have a clear idea of his type?*

MMD: That's a good question because when you think about it he's done Wintergreen in *Of Thee I Sing*, Pseudolus in *Forum*, the baritone in *Closer than Ever*, Horace Vandergelder [in *Hello, Dolly!*], you know what I mean? It's like, what type is he? I don't know what type?

KW: *He's a character actor.*

MMD: He's a character actor, and I didn't get to see his *La Cage*, but I've seen clips of it and, again, living authentically in the skin of a drag queen, he's not a drag queen…you know what I mean? And then *The Producers*. He takes big bites out of everything.

KW: *How important a role has talent played for Gary in his career?*

MMD: Oh gosh, it's everything. I mean he's so talented. He is a great actor and he sings great. I think you can cultivate your craft and you can get better. But I think you've got to be born with that. He's succeeded because of it and he's envied because of it.

KW: *How important has his belief in himself been for Gary? And have you had a personal experience with him that illustrates that belief?*
MMD: When I met Gary, he was confident. So, I've never, ever felt that there was any self-doubt or self-loathing or self-pity. I'm sure he's wrestled with it as we all do, but on the surface it's never been there. I think he's always made me feel confident because he's been confident.

KW: *How would you describe him overall as an actor?*
MMD: You know, he's raised the bar for me for other actors coming to audition for me. I don't want to work with any people who are less talented, less gracious, less willing, less real than Gary Beach. I just want that to be my status quo.

KW: *What a wonderful testament to him.*
MMD: Yeah, when he asked me if I'd do this I said, "Oh, I don't know if I have anything nice to say about you, but I'll try. [*Laughs*]

He's a love and I'm so glad he's in my life professionally and personally. I mean, he's just a sweet, sweet, wonderful man.

KW: *Wow. Last question. All of the statistics tell us that acting is an incredibly difficult profession. At any given time there are far more actors out of work than are working. However, Gary has defied those odds, enjoying quite a bit of success. In addition to everything you've told me, how has he done it?*
MMD: He doesn't say no. I'm not saying he doesn't turn things down, but I think he's always up for a new challenge and a new opportunity and I'm so thrilled that he gets to field the offers now. And he pounded the pavement and he auditioned and he got cast because he was great. So, he's an example of hard work and commitment and having those blinders on. Not being distracted.

To say he's a theatre animal is key to his success.

Gary Beach Success Team Member

STEVEN UNGER

Ken Womble: *Steven, when you first met Gary Beach what was your impression of him?*

Steven Unger: Well, I'd known of Gary and I had seen his work before we started to represent him. My impression was a really funny kind of character guy, a very talented song and dance man that can do it all. And I saw him do Rooster in *Annie* with our client Marcia Lewis, but we didn't start working together until he did *Beauty and the Beast*.

KW: *So this is 1994 and he had been in the business for over two decades, and he received his first Tony nomination for that show, and then later for* The Producers—

SU: Which he won—

KW: *Which he won—and then another for* La Cage aux Folles. *So, three Tony nominations in a row, but over about a ten year span, I believe.*

SU: Yeah.

KW: *Why didn't that come sooner for him? Was it because he hadn't had the break? What's your take on that?*

SU: I think sometimes an actor grows into who they're going to be and a role like Lumiere [in *Beauty and the Beast*] was just so splashy and flashy and Gary just took it to the hilt. I think that's when people truly noticed. In *Annie* and *1776* he had replaced someone, so there's less notice there. But nobody knew what *Beauty and the Beast* was going to be on stage, if it was going to be a cartoon, or how it was going to look. And then when people realized it was a Broadway musical with great Broadway performers in it like Gary Beach and Beth Fowler, they paid more attention and I think what he did was quite special and that was a show-stopping number, "Be Our Guest." So I think people went, "Oh my God, it's Gary Beach—of course!"

KW: *He said in that show he felt a sense of arrival, and the role was the first of some wonderful work he got. Was that nomination a turning point for him?*
SU: Oh yes. I think it is for most actors when they're nominated for a Tony Award. It's sort of like you become part of another family. You're a family when you're on Broadway, but now you're part of being nominated for a Tony or winning a Tony. So it ups the ante a little bit and then people are always like, "Oooh, can we get that guy who was nominated for a Tony, or the guy who won the Tony?" It definitely puts you more out front: you're going to these press events, you're doing interviews. So it's not just about you performing in the show anymore; it's now about you being part of that other community. And because Gary is so personable, he was a hit, and he's great on the red carpet, and he's great in an interview. So I think people were like, "Oh my God, Gary Beach, he was nominated for a Tony Award. We'd love to sit and talk with him." And perhaps some other people in the casting world and TV and film were like, "Oh, we want to know Gary Beach." So it absolutely helped.

KW: *It sounds like you're saying because he was such a great guy and so personable and such a pro, people were happy he had gotten to this level in his career.*
SU: Oh, absolutely! So many people said it couldn't have happened to a nicer guy. People were just rooting for him. I think there would've been a lot of very upset people if he hadn't won for *The Producers*.

KW: *When you first interview an actor, can you tell what they're going to be like to work with?*

SU: Absolutely. We have met over the years some very, very talented and respected actors. But sometimes you say to yourself, "I don't know if I want to be in the room with this person for another hour." In my thirty years here among the people that I represent, there's nobody that I wouldn't want to take a phone call from. When you meet certain people, you just go, "Okay, this is a match made in heaven. I want to work with this person. This person is about doing the work." And that's kind of number one with me. If somebody's going to come in and say, "If you represent me, I'll always need to have the star dressing room and I'll always need to have this color carpeting in my dressing room," I'm like, "Wait a minute, you don't even have a job yet!"

I had an interview recently with this woman, very talented. I saw her in something and asked her to come in. And basically, for an hour, she told me how amazing she was. And I ended the conversation with, "I don't know why you're leaving your current agent because you're doing great." And she's like, "Well I want more, I want more. I mean, I've done twelve Broadway shows and I want more." And it was just like, "Whoa, whoa, whoa, whoa, whoa—this is somebody who will be calling a hundred times a day and nothing is going to be good enough."

KW: *Do you think in another scenario someone could've come in and given you essentially the same information, like "I want more," but put it in a different way?*

SU: Oh absolutely. A common thread here in New York is most actors want more TV and film work because it's such a theatre town. And that's going to happen for some and it's not going to happen for some. It's just the way the ball falls. But people put it, most of the time, in a very professional and comprehensive way.

I can get it right from the beginning. I don't need somebody to say, "I've starred in this and my name was above the title on this."

I think in the life of an actor, you're always looking for what's next as opposed to some of us who have stayed in the same position in an agent's shop or a professor, or a doctor or a lawyer. For an actor it's always temporary until the next job. And you can be in the biggest hit show, and you can stay with it for a year or three years, but you're going to have to start another one at some point, whether it's in film or theatre or television. And that's the life of an actor. You never know. You do a reading, which is what Gary did of *The Producers*, and then two weeks later you're going to Chicago and then coming to Broadway.

KW: *That was a perfect segue to my next question. In 2000 Gary was up for the role of Roger De Bris in* The Producers *and he told me the story of singing the song "Heil Myself" for Mel Brooks and then Brooks asking him if he was "doing Judy," meaning Judy Garland. And he said he was. And to me this seems like an extremely creative moment in an audition. What kind of feedback did you get from* The Producers *creative team?*

SU: The feedback was, "He was amazing and we're going to Broadway." I mean it was one of those showbiz stories. It was very quick. It wasn't like, "We'll know something in a couple of weeks." Sometimes you do a reading and you wait three years for it to happen. I think everybody who was lucky enough to be in that room sensed that this was so special we've got to do this now.

I mean sometimes it's that magic that happens and it's a role and an actor and they just mesh and you just go, "Wow! Who else could play this part?" So many times people do readings and then they go, "Okay, we really love you, but we have to look for a star, or we have to look for a TV person, blah, blah, blah." And you go, "Wait a minute. You've got the person who is making this work for you." And it's frustrating. But they were like, "We're going and we want Gary." And those are the nicest words anybody can hear.

KW: *That's a real vote of confidence.*
SU: Absolutely!

KW: *We talked about* Beauty and the Beast *bringing him to a higher level as a Tony nominee. Did* The Producers *take him to another level?*
SU: Oh yes. I mean, first of all, Broadway hadn't seen anything like *The Producers* in I don't know how long, a show that won twelve Tony Awards. You couldn't get a ticket for a year. And also it was happening at a time where shows weren't selling out, so all of a sudden we had this phenomenon, and he was right in the middle of it. And so that was pretty amazing, and I think it showed him in a very different way than Lumiere or anything else. So here he is in a dress and sitting at the end of the stage singing a tribute to Hitler. And it was a love fest with the show and with the role.

KW: *What would you say are some of his best qualities as a performer?*
SU: Everybody just loves Gary Beach. He's got a great, great attitude. He's a trooper. He's sort of from the old school. He's like "We're puttin' on a show, I show up, I do my job." He's just one of those guys that's like a ray of sunshine and he's really funny. If somebody asked me to describe him, I'd say he's just a joy to know.

KW: *He was a joy to talk with. He was so personable and, as you say, funny and I thought, "Well if this is his demeanor in the business, I'm sure he's very popular."*
SU: Oh yeah. Very much so. There are no airs.

KW: *In her book,* Acting Q's, *Bonnie Gillespie says, "Working performers seem to have tapped into a sense of authenticity that most aspiring actors search for." Do you feel that sense of authenticity has been true for Gary?*

SU: Oh, absolutely! Gary Beach is a Broadway star because he knows how to do it. You don't have to teach him how to dance, you don't have to teach him how to get a laugh from a line, you don't have to teach him how to sing the song. He's that authentic Broadway actor who just goes and runs with it. We've all been in shows where it may not be the best material in the world, but you figure it out to make it work. You hire Gary Beach, he's going to make it work.

Going back to *Beauty and the Beast,* I mean Jerry Orbach had done the film and it was animated, but everybody had an idea of what it was. And then here's Gary who came out there and just sparkled and flashed that smile and won them over, and the same thing in *The Producers.* It was Gary Beach's Zaza in *La Cage.* It wasn't a carbon copy of George Hearn or Nathan Lane from the film. With Gary Beach you get an original. He *is* an original. And I think that's the charm and the excitement about watching Gary Beach.

He also works really well and closely with directors. I mean, he's not somebody who you can't say, "Hey, try this," and they'll go, "Mmm, no." He'll try it. And he's had some great marriages with directors where it's just been a love fest.

KW: *How important a role has type and talent played for Gary?*
SU: Oh, he's quite versatile. I think that talent is a big part of it because I'm not sure that there are a lot of people around who could be Thénardier and Zaza and Roger De Bris. I think those are three very, very different roles.

He can stretch himself quite far. I think people were shocked when he came back and did the *Les Mis* revival. It was like, "Wait a minute, that was Gary Beach, that gorgeous guy in the fabulous dresses from *La Cage* and here he is coming out of a sewer in *Les Mis*."

KW: *How important has his belief in himself been for Gary?*
SU: You have to believe in yourself. You have to believe in your talent. But more than believing, I think you have to have a knowledge of what you're capable of. You can't bite off more than you can really chew. If someone said, "Hey Gary, we're doing a heavy duty rock-n-roll musical," he might have to think twice about it.

KW: *All the statistics tell us that acting is an incredibly difficult profession. At any given time there are far more actors out of work than working. However, Gary has defied these odds enjoying quite a bit of success over about a forty year span. How has he done it?*
SU: I think he's very particular with choosing material. And Gary's also one of the rare breeds who doesn't leave a show in six months. If he's having fun, he's going to stay. He has been chosen for some very, very special projects. *The Producers* is Broadway history. And he'll always be part of Broadway history as well. He will always be Tony Award winner Gary Beach.

What are the keys that have led Gary Beach to a successful acting career?

He seizes opportunities—at all costs

Some actors refuse to work on certain jobs or in certain locations, and their choosiness costs them. Gary's willingness to go "where the work was" created opportunities. By 2000, after almost three decades in show business, he had half a dozen Broadway shows and a Tony nomination to his credit.

When *The Producers* came along the same year, Gary was prepared, yet when he discovered he would have to pay his own airfare to perform just a reading of the musical, he was reluctant to go. As he had done throughout his career, Gary decided to make what he wanted more important than the cost of getting it by *viewing this also as an opportunity.* He took the trip and won a career-defining role that created many more wonderful opportunities.

He has good luck and timing

Over and over Gary has been at the right place at the right time dating back to one of his first professional jobs (with perhaps the longest commute by car for an audition on record) when his college professor just happened to know renowned casting director Michael Shurtleff, who just happened to be casting *1776*, a musical Gary was perfect for.

On tour with the show, Gary's luck multiplied when he was promoted to a leading role, made his Broadway debut in the show, and then signed with his first agent.

And Gary's hilarious turn as flamboyant director Roger De Bris in *The Producers* not only won him a richly deserved Tony Award, but the show's outrageous humor brought audiences some welcomed comfort after the heartbreak of 9/11.

He is inventive, funny and having the time of his life

Marcia Milgrom Dodge, a very talented theatre director, loves Gary's inventiveness in the rehearsal room, deep emotional connection and "wonderful physical elegance"—qualities that make her and other directors delight in working with him.

Also, Gary's ability to take larger than life characters and make them *real* is unique, so unique that Marcia believes he is one of the last links to the great comics of Vaudeville.

A profound love for acting is evident in Gary's engagement with audiences and has kept him going and going and going.

He is a joy to work with

Directors want to work with talented actors who offer their creative ideas and are open and friendly.

Gary scores high marks in each of these areas, with Marcia's comments serving as a primer on how actors should work with directors: "I don't want to work with any people who are less talented, less gracious, less willing, less real than Gary Beach."

He found his place in the business

Although Gary lived in Los Angeles for over a decade and worked in film and television, his first love has always been the theatre. He told me probably the smartest thing he ever did for his career was to move to New York, "because that's where my career was going to be," and his greatest successes and sweetest memories are from the theatre. As Marcia said, "To say he's a theatre animal is key to his success."

He is talented

Both Marcia and Steven agree that Gary is very talented, and this talent is validated by a long list of awards and nominations for Gary's work, voted on by his peers in the theatre.

It's about the journey, not the destination

When I asked Gary if he felt a sense of destiny from his early success in *1776*, he replied, "It's the journey. There is no destination."

He shared fond memories of discovery—when, at his first concert in college, he found himself among a creative community of people like him, and of inspired moments—when he did "Judy" for Mel Brooks.

Gary Beach appreciates the winding road his career has taken, and he has savored that journey, enjoying all the stops along the way.

JOHN TARTAGLIA

CHAPTER 7

Never Fall for "You Have To"

JOHN TARTAGLIA

John Tartaglia created and starred in Disney's *Johnny and the Sprites*, (Daytime Emmy nomination) and made his Tony award nominated Broadway debut in *Avenue Q* (Princeton and Rod). Other Broadway credits: Lumiere–*Beauty and the Beast* and Pinocchio–*Shrek the Musical*. Over ten seasons and multiple guest appearances on *Sesame Street*. Other television: *Ugly Betty*, *The Today Show*, and several other children's series. Upcoming film: *Silent But Deadly*. John is a recipient of the Theatre World Award, Backstage Award, a Broadway.com Award and more. He is a frequent guest of the New York Pops. In one of the highlights with the Pops, he conceived, hosted and directed *Jim Henson's Musical World at Carnegie Hall*. Resident director of *Avenue Q* Off Broadway. Some directing credits include *Shrek* at MUNY, and the World Premiere of the musical *Because of Winn Dixie*, written by Nell Benjamin with music by Duncan Sheik.

Other current projects include: theatrical show *ImaginOcean*—played Off Broadway and an international tour under option for TV with The Jim Henson Company; shows with both Royal Caribbean Cruise Lines and Carnival Cruise lines, Walt Disney Imagineering, Walt Disney Creative Entertainment, Dramatic Forces and more.

....

Ken Womble: *What was your musical theatre background?*
John Tartaglia: I grew up doing it—literally from birth I think I was performing. My parents are both in the business, and I've always been around theatre and stagecraft. In high school I did all

the musicals, and I used to direct some of the shows. But I moved here [New York] after high school, and I didn't have the college experience. I was doing lots of little Off Off Broadway shows, and I did a children's theatre tour.

KW: *At a young age you were part of the puppetry team on* Sesame Street. *How did that come about?*
JT: When I was twelve, I wrote a letter to Jim Henson and almost met him twice. And then when I was fourteen, I wrote to Kevin Clash who performs Elmo on *Sesame Street,* and he called me one night and invited me down to the workshop to see the show. While we were hanging out I said, "Out of all the thousands of letters you get why did you call me?" And he said because Jim had once mentioned me.

So, in a very kind of ethereal, backwards way that's how I got Kevin's attention. I ended up doing these workshops that are basically three day auditions and by sixteen I was working with them. So it was really kind of an amazing the way everything came together like that.

KW: *How long did you work on* Sesame Street?
JT: About twelve years.

KW: Avenue Q *was your first Broadway show. At the time were you in the mindset of "I'm going to continue with puppetry and go that way" or "I'm going be a Broadway musical performer?" How did those two worlds meet?*
JT: I'd always wanted to do both. One of the composers of *Avenue Q* and Rick Lyon, who was my co-star in the show, knew that I had a musical theatre background as well as puppetry so that's why they thought of me. It was kind of kismet. I mean it was definitely

a once-in-a-lifetime thing, a show that lined up so perfectly with the two things I love to do.

KW: *You were asked to be in* Avenue Q *long before it actually made it to Broadway. Was there a long workshop process for that?*
JT: It was kind of drawn out. You know, we never had a formal, formal workshop. We did a glorified reading at the O'Neill Center. We did years and years of readings and invited gatherings and things like that. So it was always in the process, but it wasn't really until we did the Off Broadway production that we had an actual on-its-feet production.

KW: *Early on, did you expect* Avenue Q *to reach the heights that it did? Did you see something there?*
JT: Oh God, no! No, no, no, no. Every step of the journey was always a surprise and kind of "I can't believe that we're going to go there now and do that." I mean we hoped that we would maybe get a little Off Off Broadway run. We never thought we'd even be Off Broadway. We always called it "The Little Show That Could" because it was this little, teeny show out of nowhere that kept growing and growing.

KW: *Your roles as Princeton and Rod earned you a Tony nomination for Best Actor. Was that a big turning point in your career?*
JT: Oh absolutely, absolutely. I mean it changed everything. And that was another thing that was hoped for, but I didn't expect. And from an actor point of view, doing something so different that could've been looked at as less than…it was nice to be acknowledged for that work. So it was actually a huge compliment and a huge surprise at the same time.

KW: *For the show to make it to Broadway and then run for six years clearly it connected with audiences. What was it about it that connected so well?*

JT: There are the puppets, there are a lot of different things people love about it, but I think the thing that universally appeals to people is the search for who you are and the whole sense of finding your purpose.

And I think that you don't have to be twenty years old like Princeton to understand that. I think that everyone, even people later on in their lives, are still looking for what they're really supposed to be doing. And I think that journey is what people love.

KW: *It has such a big heart.*

JT: Yeah, exactly. Which I think isn't something people expected. In the very, very early days of the show that really wasn't the focus of it. It was much more about the puppets being bad. And I think that works for a little while, but then you need something to carry on beyond that. And I think that's the part people were shocked that they responded to and felt the most—the sympathy and the emotion for these characters.

KW: *And then after* Avenue Q *you went into* Beauty and the Beast *as Lumiere and then into* Shrek the Musical. *How much did getting those shows have to do with your notoriety for* Avenue Q? *Did that give you an edge or did you have to audition like most actors?*

JT: Well, I think every actor still has to prove himself, no matter how much he achieves. Everyone has this idea in their head and I certainly did when I was younger that, "Oh, you do a Broadway show and people know you're on Broadway and then you never have to worry about auditioning again." And that's just not the case. I mean you are always having to prove yourself.

I had to go through the audition process like anyone else would, but because they knew me, it was a lot easier than it would've been had I been an unknown performer.

KW: *What were your auditions like?*
JT: My friend had worked at the Las Vegas production of *Avenue Q,* and I mentioned to him in passing that Lumiere was a role I'd love to play some day. And so when it became available, because I think I was the eighth Lumiere, he thought of me and told Tom Schumacher, the head of Disney Theatrical. And Tom knew my work from *Avenue Q* and liked the idea of me playing the role, so all I had to do was come in and read through two of the scenes just to make sure that I had the right vibe for it. And then I got the call a week later that they wanted me to do it.

Shrek was a new show and its director, Jason [Moore], had been our director for *Avenue Q.* I guess he either recommended me to the team or had mentioned me as a possibility. I just had to go to the callbacks, meet with the creative team and sing through the songs and do the scenes and that was it.

So both were much easier processes than they would have been if they hadn't known my work. It was half making sure they knew I could do it, but also half trusting because of the work I'd done before what I would bring to it.

KW: *How do you prepare for auditions?*
JT: Most of the time now when I go in for something it's because people know my work. I usually just have to sing something from the show that I'm auditioning for.

It's funny. When I was younger, I used to worry so much about what I would sing and about making the right choice. But as I have gotten older, and luckily because of *Avenue Q,* I can go in and have more fun with things and be a little looser with it.

KW: *Has training played a significant role for you? Or has most of your training been on the job?*

JT: Most of it's been on the job. I definitely learn the most by watching and doing. So sometimes going to a piece of theatre and watching the actors and understanding what they're doing and how they're relating to an audience and how they're getting the audience on their side—those are big things. And sometimes just being on the job and doing it.

I had some great voice and acting teachers, but I think you can only teach someone up to a point all the technique and all the rules. And then you have to take it yourself, fly with it, and make it your own—or keep looking for somebody to tell you how.

This is one of the only businesses in the world where there are no rules. It's just being at the right place at the right time and making a choice that works for you. I find that the people who are most successful are the people who jump. They take the risk and hope that it pays off.

KW: *Can you give me an example or two of when you've jumped?*

JT: Well, I think number one would probably be moving to New York City. I mean that was a huge risk at eighteen. I had a full scholarship to the University of Maryland, but I had an opportunity in front of me with *Sesame Street*. Many people were saying, "Do it, this is a great opportunity," and many people were saying, "Play it safe." And you know, I knew that I would regret not taking the opportunity if I didn't.

The other example was when I left *Avenue Q*. It was a role that was very much identified with me. I had work. I had security. But I felt that I wanted to take the risk of leaving and leaving while I still loved the show, not when I started to resent it. There were a lot of people who said, "What are you doing? You have a hit show." I just knew that if I didn't jump and go for it maybe the other things I wanted to achieve, I wouldn't.

Sometimes it's just trusting your own instincts and making a decision for you, not because it's worked for someone else in the past but because it's what's going to be best for you.

KW: *I've heard it said about the acting profession that if you have a fall back plan, you'll fall back. Do you believe that?*
JT: Yeah, I think that's very true. I mean you have to have drive, you know. And I've met so many actors who are so very, very talented, and they just don't have that drive. You have to know that this is what you want to do. This is all you want to do. And you have to take the risk to do it. And I think when you put that kind of energy out there and you are throwing all your eggs in one basket, then you almost force everything to work for you. I know a lot of people who try to play it safe in this business and you can't.

KW: *And is passion a part of that, your passion for the art?*
JT: Oh yeah. I'm always fascinated by people who are in this business because they feel like they have to be or they're stuck. I mean if you don't wake up loving what you're doing what's the point of doing it? You know? Nothing drives me crazier than going to see a show and seeing someone who's clearly just going through the motions for the paycheck. And I think to myself, "How many actors are there out there who would give anything to be up there on the stage doing it?"

I've always been a performer who doesn't feel like you can give less than 100% on stage. I feel guilty if I do.

KW: *Was there a moment when you decided, "This is it; I'm going to be an actor and nothing else?"*

JT: You know what? I don't think I ever consciously made that decision. I was so lucky to always have opportunities. Because it's all I've ever done; it just always felt like it's what I should be doing.

I'm usually not a person who says "never" about anything. And I've been lucky because it's that attitude of, "Well, what about this, what about that?" that's allowed me to do a bunch of different things in this business, not just one thing.

I don't think I would be satisfied if I *just* acted, and I don't think I'd be satisfied if I *just* puppeteered, and I don't think I'd be satisfied if I *just* created. I think it's all those different things I like to do that add up to what makes me happy, that kind of variety.

KW: *You wrote the book for* ImaginOcean *which I thought was just a brilliant idea—*
JT: —Oh thank you!—

KW: *—a children's musical that ran Off Broadway at New World Stages. You wrote a similar show for a cruise company and then some New York theatre people saw it and wanted to produce it. Most people in your position would be actively pushing that to make that happen, but it seems that it sort of fell into your lap. There's a strong sense of serendipity here. Does that happen a lot for you?*
JT: It does actually. My stepfather, who's probably my biggest fan in the world, always gets mad at me when I use the words "lucky" or "blessed" because he feels like I work very hard, and I do. But I also think that there are a lot of people out there who work very hard who don't get a chance to pursue the things they love, to live their dreams. So I'm very aware that I'm lucky, and a lot of things have worked out for me.

KW: *Right.*
JT: …but it *was* serendipity. I saw *ImaginOcean* as this sweet little

show for a cruise line, a first experience with theatre for a lot of kids. One of my coproducers wanted to invite some industry people from New York to come see the workshop. And I was like, "Why? We're putting it on a cruise ship." And he said it could have a life outside of the ship. So I said, "Okay!" And it was kind of phenomenal to watch how people reacted to it. It was pure dumb luck that someone saw where it could go.

KW: *You said other people you know in the industry don't have that kind of luck and they also work hard. Why do you think you have it?*
JT: I think the biggest reason is, honestly, I bring something unique to the table. In the past twenty years, I can't think of anyone who was a puppeteer and an actor and known for both.

Broadway has lost personalities. The great Broadway performers like Carol Channing, Ethel Merman, George Hearn, Angela Lansbury were true personalities who all broke a mold and had something special about them. Not that I'm putting myself in that category, but if you look at my contemporaries, Kristin Chenoweth, Idina Menzel, Cheyenne Jackson, we've all done our own thing. And we're hard to categorize. We all have our little something that makes us stand out. So I think that's it. I think I stand out from the crowd a little bit.

KW: *I think you have an infectious energy which is very positive and connects with people.*
JT: Oh, thank you. You know, I've been accused of being annoyingly optimistic sometimes and part of it is because I really believe what you put out is what you get back. I also think that you decide, you tell the universe what you want to be doing.

It's funny. I remember when *The Secret* came out, that book that was on *Oprah* for a while. Everyone was talking about it. I had a friend who actually said to me, "You've been doing that for years!"

In this business where there is a lot of politics and backstabbing and bullshit, I think you have to keep a positive face on and move forward and just kind of believe that the best things will happen when they're supposed to.

KW: *What would you say are one or two of the smartest things you've done for your career?*
JT: I guess the smartest thing I have done is say "yes" to almost everything. I've had the experience, literally, where an intern of a show who I was very kind to, or at whose concert I volunteered to sing ten years earlier, was suddenly a huge producer who remembered me and brought me in for something. Or I've done an appearance on the *Today Show* and been really nice. So when they were looking for someone to come back they asked me.

KW: *Are there one or two things you would change?*
JT: Things I would change? Gosh. I mean there are lists. [*Laughs*] I wish in some ways I had taken more advantage of the kind of pseudo-celebrity fame on Broadway I had during *Avenue Q*. When I probably could have moved to LA and made a much bigger deal, I didn't.

But that's something I would change only because I would love to see what would have happened, not because I regret what *has* happened. I mean when I did *Johnny and the Sprites* a lot of people said, "What are you doing? Why are you doing a children's show? You should be moving to LA and pursuing movies and TV."

And the reality is that I could have done that, but it's not really what my heart said to do. So now, looking back, I'm so happy I didn't because if I had I wouldn't have had *ImaginOcean*, I wouldn't have had *Johnny and the Sprites*, I wouldn't have had a television show, I wouldn't have had an Emmy nomination.

KW: *Okay, last question. All of the statistics tell us that acting is an incredibly difficult profession and at any given time there are far more actors out of work than are working. However, you've defied those odds. You've enjoyed quite a bit of success in your career. How have you done it?*

JT: Oh God, if I really knew I'd be able to write a book and make a lot of money!

I think the main reason is I never fell for the words, "You have to." I constantly hear my friends say, "You can't sing that song at an audition," or "You have to do this or you won't be taken seriously." And I'm constantly saying, "Why?" I refuse to follow the "You have to" crowd.

I went in and sang songs that no one else would've ever thought to sing for an audition. Because I didn't sing sixteen bars of a song that every young guy in his twenties sang, I stood out.

KW: *Right.*

JT: Because I didn't hide my puppetry like some people told me to on my résumé, I stood out. And I think that when you embrace those things and you make those choices and you're not afraid to be different, then that's when things start to pay off.

So, if there is a secret, I think maybe that's it. I would be foolish to say that's exactly what it is. But that's my guess.

John Tartaglia Success Team Member

PENNY LUEDTKE

Ken Womble: *Penny, you're the owner of the Luedtke Agency in New York. Could you tell me a bit about your agency and the mediums you work in?*
Penny Luedtke: We're a New York based office that works in theatre, film, and television, and we also represent literary clients, so we have writers as well. Some of my clients are writer/director/producers. It's a small boutique shop.

KW: *What are you looking for in an actor that you want to sign?*
PL: Somebody who has a good attitude, who will work hard, has ambitions of being better every day, and gives back to the community while doing it.

KW: *That's nice.*
PL: It's important because otherwise when people get success if they don't think that way their head is screwed on a different way and they can get lost. Be a giving actor, be a giving director, writer, whatever. It's all about working together. You have to be a selfish person to do it, and if you don't have some sort of leveling in your life, you can really only be about yourself and it's difficult.

KW: *It's interesting because as soon as you said that I thought about how kind John seems and really friendly.*
PL: He is. You have to keep your eye on the prize, but you still have to be able to enjoy it and enjoy others while doing it.

KW: *Do you think that makes a difference in an actor's career as well as their life?*

PL: Yeah, I do. Nice guys don't always finish last, that's for sure. And I've seen an awful lot of instances of people who I would call—words you probably shouldn't print—who sabotage other people or who are always looking for their next green pasture. I've seen them get ahead farther than people who are nice, right? But what kind of career is it if it's hollow?

Being an actor is putting your acting first and having a life with it. But you have to be able to balance it.

KW: *When you first met John Tartaglia what was your impression of him?*
PL: I loved him from the minute I met him. He was adorable. He had incredibly wonderful energy—he still does. Just a completely open personality, accepting, and he's like a sponge wanting to learn and grow and constantly working, always working. I mean he was always doing something with his creativity. He wouldn't sit still.

KW: *John told me that the most successful people are people who jump, who take the risk.*
PL: That's right.

KW: *Do you have an example you can share from your experience with John about that?*
PL: Gosh, I mean there are a lot of them. He really worked as a puppeteer from a very young age, and he was in the first group of people developing *Avenue Q,* and he had to make a decision whether he was going to go to the Eugene O'Neill and be paid $500 maybe for the entire time or continue the season on *Sesame Street.* So, I mean if you look at what you get paid to be on *Sesame Street* as a performer on television versus a $500 stipend, what would most people do? He didn't. He went into *Avenue Q.*

The two of us sat and talked about it and said, "You can play it safe and be in *Sesame Street* for the rest of your life"—because people do—"or you can jump and take this new experience." We both thought it was a terrific show, and we thought it was worth taking the risk. You know, when you look at what performers have to do every day, weighing one choice against another, it's tough. You decide, "Okay, we'll pass on that one or we will do this one." And you never know if the one you passed on is going to be the next Broadway hit or not.

KW: Avenue Q *started Off Broadway, then moved to Broadway where John was nominated for a Best Actor Tony. Then the play won the Tony for Best Musical in 2004. It's quite a Cinderella story. What part did John play in the huge success of that show?*
PL: He did absolutely every single publicity opportunity that was suggested. He never slept. He was out selling the show whether it was on the street or at malls or whatever. I think that really helped define the show. Really helped get people in.

KW: *Was* Avenue Q *a turning point in John's career?*
PL: Oh, it was *the* turning point. I mean to anyone who gets to do a leading role on Broadway that's a turning point in their career. Period. But in a new work, I mean, it gets *the* most immediate press and if it's successful it continues.

KW: *What would you say are some of John's best qualities as a performer?*
PL: He's gracious and giving and caring and he's a doll and a dream to work with because of that. He's a team player. He's compelling and he's charismatic and he's fun and he's interesting. And even when he's doing a play that's dark material, it just hits you as be-

ing real. It's not "acting," it's instant. And to me that's the art of being an actor.

KW: *One of the things that strikes me is how well he seems to connect with audiences.*
PL: Oh, yeah. When he was doing *Avenue Q*, and still today, people would call and ask him to host birthday parties and pay enormous amounts of money to be the MC for the evening. He's "good in the room," you know. He makes people feel at home. He's a performer; he's an old-fashioned entertainer.

KW: *How long have you worked together?*
PL: I think since 1998 or '99.

KW: *That's a long time.*
PL: Yeah. Oftentimes they're much shorter than that. The standard trajectory in this industry is people hop around. Nobody's ever satisfied, always looking for greener pastures. But there are a group of people that don't do that, and I have clients that I've worked with from almost the day I opened my door in 1998.

KW: *John has turned to writing and producing in recent years, most notably* Johnny and the Sprites *for Playhouse Disney and* ImaginOcean, *a children's musical, Off Broadway. Not all actors have the ability or the desire to wear all these hats.*
PL: Right.

KW: *What does that say about John do you think?*
PL: That he's been true to his desires from the time he was a kid because he's always done this. I mean, if you talk to him about theme parks, he'll bring out his design for a theme park.

He has always been involved in the creative side of things. It's difficult because in this world you see people as doing one thing; you don't see what else they do. Like if they know John is an actor, that's how they know him. He's an actor. And if they know John as a puppeteer, he's a puppeteer. It was difficult from *Avenue Q* to get Johnny something without a puppet on his hand or without being children's television because of Disney. I mean, you really don't know until you give someone the opportunity to show you.

KW: *You just mentioned that he has been true to his desires since he was a kid. How important is that for an actor? Should actors follow their desires?*
PL: Yes. Because if you could do something else then do it. You'd be better off. If acting is what you have to do, then you have to do it.

KW: *In her book* Acting Q's *Bonnie Gillespie says that "Working performers seemed to have tapped into a sense of authenticity that most aspiring actors search for." Do you feel that's been true for John?*
PL: Oh, yeah. That's just being true to yourself. I mean that's what I see as authenticity.

KW: *How important a role has type played for John and does he have a clear idea of his type?*
PL: Yeah he does, but he's a little bit different than some other comic actors or best friend types because he has this huge history of puppetry and children's television that follow him around, or opens the door for him, depending on how you look at it.

He's been cast opposite type sometimes, and he's done well with it. He just did a play in LA called *The Temperamentals* which was completely opposite type, and he got great reviews.

KW: *How important a role has talent played for John in his career?*
PL: Oh, I think if you don't have talent you're not going to be in the game. I mean, we have this expression when we go see a show and there's someone who's just awful; you know, he or she is "a true triple threat: can't act, can't dance, can't sing." There are people who actually get away with it, but not a lot. I also think that talent's just a small part of it. It's what you do with it.

KW: *How important would you say that John's belief in himself has been in his career?*
PL: A thousand percent. A thousand percent. Seriously.

KW: *Did he have to believe in himself to make the jump from* Sesame Street *to* Avenue Q?
PL: Oh yeah. Absolutely. And in pitching the show to Disney [*Johnny and the Sprites*] he had to believe that he actually was coming up with ideas that the head of Disney Playhouse would want to listen to and being able to move forward and be an executive producer, having created the show and starred in it.

KW: *How would you describe him overall as a client?*
PL: Delightful and charming, and you know, I'm lucky that we work together. I feel very lucky.

KW: *He probably feels the same way about you.*
PL: Well, maybe. I don't know. But when you find the right fit with the agent or the manager, it's the right fit. It's not that there's not going to be bumps in the road somewhere, there always are, but you have to respect each other enough to be able to look out for each other and care for each other. He doesn't just treat me as an agent. You know, the whole thing that you hear about, "Oh my agent, I never get to talk to her." That just doesn't exist here.

KW: *Do you think that sort of synchronicity is helpful?*

PL: Oh sure. The thing is that I'm able to talk to Johnny about anything. If I think that he's missing something or slacking off on something, I tell him. And he'll tell me the same thing. If he thinks that he needs to do something and it's not happening, we'll talk about it. But that's because it's coming out of respect and love for each other, not out of, you know, "What have you done for me today?"

KW: *Exactly. All of the statistics tell us that acting is an incredibly difficult profession. At any given time there are far more actors out of work than are working. However, John has defied these odds, enjoying quite a bit of success in a short time. How has he done it?*

PL: I think he's kept his eye on the prize. Here's what I tell clients all the time, and I think this is what you have to do if you're going to continue to work: "As soon as you book that job, you look for the next one." I mean, never be content. It's great to have an opening night on Broadway, but then the next day you've got to go to the theatre and work again. It never stops. So, I think Johnny has always done that. He doesn't rest on his laurels.

KW: *Well, thanks so much for all your time Penny.*

PL: And thank you very much for taking such an interest in Johnny.

John Tartaglia Success Team Member

MICHAEL EINFELD

Ken Womble: *Michael, you're the owner of Michael Einfeld Management, a Los Angeles management company. Could you tell me a bit about what you do and the mediums you work in?*

Michael Einfeld: Well, I have people in both New York and Los Angeles. I do TV, film, and theatre.

KW: *You started out as an actor, a singer, and a dancer. How have those experiences influenced your work, especially with musical theatre actors?*

ME: I understand what the medium is. I understand what it takes to actually do it. I have good taste in talent. Sometimes people have a whole lot of things working for them, but there's one thing that's wrong. I can figure out what that is and help them fix it.

KW: *How closely do you work with actors to develop them?*

ME: Very closely. When I'm in New York, I go to classes five days a week with all my dance clients.

KW: *Really?*

ME: I mean I go to class for myself, but it's kind of a benefit because I can see where they are. And I've coached them on stuff. There are a lot of auditions now that are on tape, so I can look at the tape and see what's wrong and have them redo it before they send it on. I'm really involved.

KW: *What are you looking for in an actor that you want to sign?*

ME: Well, I spend time with people, so I want to find someone that I like. I don't want to work with a jerk. I mean it's just no fun. If you're going to spend that much time with someone, you'd better like them. It's a combination of things. It's talent, it's training, it's a look, it's charisma. I want someone who's going to listen to me. It's like, "If you're not going to listen to my advice, then maybe I'm not the right person for you."

Because you know what, this business is tough. And you can come up with any reason why you can't do something and it could be totally valid, but it doesn't matter. Someone else is going to figure out how to make it happen and they're going to get the job.

KW: *Let's talk about John Tartaglia who you represent. When you first met, what was your impression?*
ME: Well, I saw him in *Avenue Q* before I even met him and thought he was fantastic. And when I met him, he was just an absolute doll. I mean it's hard not to fall in love with him.

KW: *What was it about him on stage that you connected with?*
ME: I think his work is honest. He has an incredible charisma and he's funny, but you believe it. You don't feel like anything is being manufactured. He's so appealing and emotionally available.

KW: *What are some of his other qualities as a performer?*
ME: He's entertaining. But he'll surprise you. I've started putting him in stuff that's more serious. He's got a level of emotion that you would not expect.

KW: *He was a puppeteer and an actor on* Sesame Street. *What effect do you think that experience had on him as a performer?*
ME: Working on *Sesame Street* you certainly have to learn to work with other people. I think it's probably a show without ego because the puppet's really the star, not you.

KW: *How much of a turning point do you think* Avenue Q *was in John's career?*
ME: It was a *huge* turning point. He was nominated for the Tony! And it took him out of being a puppeteer into being an actor. And it gave him some recognizability.

KW: *Did that change his status, help him to get into some doors?*
ME: Absolutely. After you're nominated for a Tony, they have to at least find out what else you can do. I'm trying to transfer him into now doing adult material as an actor. He just did a movie called *Hotel Arthritis* [later renamed *Silent But Deadly*] where he's like Norman Bates from *Psycho* a little bit, *Scream* meets *Clue*. And he's the lead in that.

And he did a play out here called *The Temperamentals* which was done in New York Off Broadway. It's got some funny stuff in it, but it's also got some very serious stuff. It deals with some of the fights for gay rights back in the '40s and '50s.

KW: *And, as you know, in addition to acting he writes and produces:* Johnny and the Sprites *for Playhouse Disney and* ImaginOcean, *an Off Broadway musical. Not all actors have the ability or even the desire to wear all these hats. What do you think this says about him?*
ME: He can multi-task, he's multi-talented. You're right; some people do just one thing. He's an artist; he's a creative force. And that just takes many forms. He's also smart. You have to be smart to do all those things, too.

And the truth is producing sometimes takes him away from that. There are times when he's not available for acting gigs that would be good for his career because he's in the middle of producing things.

KW: *Do you think that's in any way detrimental to his acting career?*
ME: It just changes it. I mean you're creating things for yourself and you're producing, so it creates work.

You know, he's producing *ImaginOcean*; it's opening in different parts of the country and different parts of the world. You start to make choices, "If I take a role in this show, that means I'm unavailable for this production possibility; if I go with this production possibility, then I'm not available for pilot season." All those other things come into play.

KW: *Let's talk about auditions for a moment. What kind of feed-back do you get about John from casting directors and directors?*
ME: Most people love him.

KW: *Are there one or two things that he does right, that really impresses them?*
ME: I mean, again, he's so genuine as a person and likeable. That's the thing that's most popular about him.

KW: *That's not true for everyone. I think you have to have a certain amount of easy confidence about yourself to bring that into a room.*
ME: Of course!

KW: *You have also been a casting director.*
ME: Years ago.

KW: *So, putting on your casting director hat, is there anything else that you would say that helps him get so much work? He seems to be working all the time.*
ME: I think he has a fantastic manager!

KW: [Laughs] *Great answer.*
ME: [*Laughs*] I mean that really is part of it; it's all teamwork. It's not like he works for me or I work for him. It's all about everybody working together, deciding what it is we want and what we are going to do to get there.
Does that mean you turn certain things down in order to be available for other things? There's always got to be a balance of certain things you take because they make you money and certain

things you take because they advance your career and certain things you want to do as an artist. So it's mixing all those things together.

You know, I'm not any good as a manager if the person I represent isn't talented. I can get them into any room I want, but if they can't deliver, that's no good. And you can be extremely talented as an actor and if no one ever sees your work, that's not good either!

If I know something is right for him even though it's not how people have seen him before, I'll fight for it. And not everyone's willing to do that.

KW: *How important a role has type played for John?*
ME: You know, people think of him in a certain way and that's changing. People thought of him as the funny guy from *Avenue Q*, and I think with things like *The Temperamentals* people started looking at him differently. I had him go in to play the father on a TV show, and they didn't believe that he could play a father. And then he walked in the room, and they're like, "Oh yeah! We bought it." If you can get him in the room and he can show that to people, he totally changes their minds.

KW: *How important a role has talent played for John?*
ME: Oh, well I wouldn't say it's everything, but that's the end all be all. I mean you can be a nice guy, if you're not talented who cares? You know what I mean? Talent's going to win out in the end.

If you're talented and you're a jerk, you're still going to work sometimes. If you're talented and you're a nice guy, then you're going to work all the time because you deliver the goods, but you're also pleasant to be around so that makes it an easier situation.

KW: *That's a great quote. If you're talented and a nice guy you work all the time.*

ME: It's true. It's like Hugh Jackman works all the time. He's talented and he's a nice guy, and the same thing with Tom Hanks. I've met Tom Hanks. He's the sweetest guy in the whole world. Would he not work if he wasn't a nice guy? He'd still work; he's talented. But he wouldn't work nearly as much as he works now.

KW: *How important would you say that John's belief in himself has been?*
ME: Well I think it's very hard to get anywhere unless you believe in yourself. If you're not going to believe in yourself, how can you make anyone else believe in you?

KW: *How would you describe him overall as a client?*
ME: Oh my gosh. I mean he's fun to work with; sometimes hard to get a hold of. [*Laughs*] He's so busy; he's always got five things going on at once. I adore him as a person too. He's creative, and he's an absolute doll and a hard worker. He works his ass off.

If it's not coming to him, he's creating it. I mean he definitely creates his own destiny.

KW: *Fantastic. Here's the last question. All of the statistics tell us that acting is an incredibly difficult profession. At any given time there are far more actors out of work than are working. However, John has defied these odds. He's enjoyed quite a bit of success in a relatively short time. How has he done it?*
ME: He creates his own work. He writes things, he produces things, he's talented and he's a fun guy to work with. Everybody wants to work with Johnny because he's a doll. He sings, he acts, he can do comedy, he can do drama.

And he surrounds himself with good people. I think if you have a team that's working and you keep that together that's important. Johnny's worked with Penny [Luedtke] for a long, long time, and when *Avenue Q* won the Tony, of course every major agency was climbing after him. And he stayed with her because she understands him and knows what he's about and got him to where he is.

When you stick with those people that got you there to begin with…you know, we all fight for him.

KW: *And it sounds like you really want to.*
ME: He makes you want to because he's such a great guy.

What are the keys that have led John Tartaglia to a successful acting career?

He has always been an actor

Making theatre is what John Tartaglia does and has done all his life. Starting with one of his earliest professional jobs [that came to pass because he was ambitious enough to write a letter to *Sesame Street's* Jim Henson], John's complete immersion has kept him on a path with only one destination—a career in show business.

He believes in himself and jumps

Playing it safe isn't for John. Making the decision to jump has taken his career to new levels.

When he passed on a college scholarship in favor of a puppeteering job on *Sesame Street*, it led to a twelve year stint on the show. When he left the PBS classic to act in a workshop of a "little show that could," it led to Broadway stardom and a Tony Award nomination for *Avenue Q*. When he gave up the ongoing glow of *Avenue Q*, it led to producing opportunities and an Emmy Award nomination.

Each of these decisions reflects John's belief in himself, and his willingness to take risks.

He has a great team

Teamwork is crucial to the strong relationship John shares with his agent, Penny Luedtke, and his manager, Michael Einfeld. A sense of mutual trust and respect allows each party to be honest, even brutally so when necessary. John remained faithful to his reps when others wanted to sign him. Penny and Michael are equally devoted through their singular attention to John's career.

People love working with him

John knows that respect and kindness where given are returned. And because he naturally exudes those qualities he reaps their benefits through repeat television appearances and unexpected auditions. Michael perhaps best summed up John's attraction, "Everybody wants to work with John because he's a doll."

He never fell for "you have to"

John has created a career based on his own unique personality, not on a formula prescribed by others. From resisting the suggestions of well meaning friends, to choosing audition songs, "no one else would've ever thought to sing," to refusing to hide his puppetry skills on his résumé long before *Avenue Q* made puppets fashionable, John does things his way. And he believes it has made all the difference.

He creates his own luck

And finally there is the question of luck. John is the first to point to his amazing luck in show business. However, it seems to me John has *created* that luck through an unfailing commitment to his craft, talent, and drive.

As John said himself, "What you put out is what you get back."

ROBERT CLOHESSY

CHAPTER 8

I Want to Do What I Want to Do

ROBERT CLOHESSY

Robert Clohessy won a Screen Actors Guild Award for Best Ensemble in HBO's *Boardwalk Empire* and Best Actor awards in three film festivals for the feature film *Crimson Mask*. He was nominated for a Tony Award (Best Play Revival–Ensemble) for Broadway's *Twelve Angry Men*. He was also nominated for best supporting actor for his performance as Touchstone in *As You Like It* for the New Jersey Professional Theatres and for best actor in *Frankie and Johnny in the Claire de Lune* by the Northeast Professional Theatres.

Recently, he played Bradley Cooper's Chief in *The Place Beyond the Pines* and Leo DiCaprio's lawyer in *The Wolf of Wall Street*.

....

Ken Womble: *What made you decide to become an actor?*
Robert Clohessy: Why did I become an actor? Well, it wasn't anything I thought about growing up. It wasn't anything that was in my family. I went to three different high schools and the third high school was about twenty miles north of the Bronx—Rockland County.

I don't even know why I was in it, but I was in the senior play just for a goof or something. And I kind of wanted to play sports in college. And I got invited to play football at the Merchant Marine Academy on an official visit, and I went there for a weekend to visit the school—I had a friend that was playing football there. I said, "Ah man, I can't do this. This is not right." And so I ended up going to the local community college, Rockland Community.

243

And it just so happened that the same year Isaiah Sheffer, who started Symphony Space in New York City, also started the theatre arts program.

It just so happened that year they started a theatre arts program. So I went there for two years and then transferred to SUNY Purchase [State University of New York at Purchase] and had to start all over again because it was like a conservatory thing. You have got to start from the beginning, which was cool because I was just starting to act and my family income was low enough that I was eligible for the government to pay for all my schooling. I studied with Walt Witcover, who I loved. That's so important, because if you don't trust your teacher you're not going to take risks.

When I got out of Purchase in '81, I didn't know what I was going to do. It was more about trying to figure out how to make a living, so I could support myself. So I did all sorts of jobs—and some I won't mention on this tape machine. And I finally got this freaking funny job—an aerobics teacher in Italy, in Milano [*speaks in Italian*]—

KW: —*pretty good for an Irish guy*—

RC: —and I was teaching all these Italian girls aerobics. You know, my mom thought I was going over to be a prostitute. I guess I was to a certain extent a prostitute [*Ken laughs*], but I was a having a bunch of fun doing boxing and karate with them too because that was what I was into prior. And I ended up breaking my leg. Worse than that—I tore the ligaments.

So I had to come back to America and then I was back in the same place. I was four years out of Purchase, and I hadn't done anything.

So after my foot healed, I just started writing my own monologues. I said, "Oh man, I've got a ton of freaking stories to tell growing up in the Bronx and my family. Send out my picture and resume to wherever. I don't care. Just do my own thing."

And I got into the Williamstown Theatre Festival with Bonnie Monte, and she offered me this non-Equity thing. So I said, "Oh, freak it, why not? I'll do it." And here I was—at this point now I was twenty-eight years old, right? And I was making twenty-five dollars a week, and I had to break down a set and do all that shit. I said "Oh my God, I'm too old for this, right?"

And they put me in a little part in a play with Blythe Danner, *Undiscovered Country*. And we got friendly. And after that season at Williamstown, she contacted me to meet the musical directors, this husband/wife team of this new workshop they were doing Off Broadway. Her husband, Bruce Paltrow, the executive producer of *St. Elsewhere*, who I didn't know, was going to direct this workshop, right?

And you know, I'm not a musical theatre guy, but I could carry a tune, whatever. Anyway, I went in there and sang some Frank Sinatra song. It wasn't very good, but they hired me.

But a week before the workshop Hartford Stage called me up and asked me to audition for this new play about these construction workers that had racial issues. So I ended up getting cast in the lead, and they were going to make me Equity. I wasn't in any unions at that point. The agent, who I wasn't signed with, said "You've got to take this. They're going to make you union and you'll make union scale. This other one's not even going to do anything for you." And I just said, "You know what, I want to do what I want to do. I want to be in the musical with Blythe." And I lost that agent, I lost that job. I did the musical, and I wasn't very good in it.

But MTM [Mary Tyler Moore Productions] was producing the musical, and after it was over, they flew me out to LA to audition for a pilot. I didn't get it, but then they told me to go across the street. *Hill Street Blues* was looking for a new character on their show.

And I went across the street, auditioned and I got it.

KW: *Do you think that happened because you made a choice to stay with the musical because it felt right?*
RC: Oh, yeah—absolutely. Most people were leading me in one direction, and I waited and I saw things, and I said, "No, this is what I want to do." Subsequently, he [Bruce Paltrow] ended up paying me what I would have got paid at the theatre. I didn't get in the union, but I made the money and then I got *Hill Street Blues*.

KW: *What was the time frame from getting cast in the musical with Blythe Danner and being cast in* Hill Street Blues?
RC: Like six months.

KW: *And you played Officer Patrick Flaherty on* Hill Street Blues *for two seasons.*
RC: Right after I did *Hill Street* I still wasn't in Equity, so I went back to Williamstown as a non-Equity actor.

KW: *Oh, really?*
RC: And that was another thing people would say, "Why would you go non-Equity? You were just starring in a freaking TV show?" You know what, I liked it. I liked Nikos [Psacharopoulos, then artistic director of Williamstown Theatre Festival], I liked the whole experience there, and they were going to turn me Equity. So I went back as a non-Equity actor, and as a result of going back, I played some great parts that summer.

KW: *Was there a moment when you decided to be an actor and nothing else? Or did it just sort of happen to you as opposed to you making it happen?*

RC: I never really decided to be an actor Ken, I've got to tell you. Even after being on TV shows, I was always off thinking I was going to do something else. And it wasn't going to last. I didn't feel it having longevity. I never felt like I was a really good actor. I felt I had things to offer, but I never felt like, "Oh, I want to be a freaking star or I'm a great actor." I was just doing it for fun or for the experience, you know. I was more into being a part of a family situation. I like going back to the people that I like.

KW: *Do you still feel that way?*

RC: Yeah. That's why I really like working with Bonnie Monte at the New Jersey Shakespeare Festival. I mean, I really like her. I like being a part of it. You know, I feel like I'll do stuff with her until I am dead.

KW: *Did you ever train professionally?*

RC: Herbert Berghof came up and directed the last play we did at SUNY Purchase. And he offered for me to study with him free. So I went down there [to HB Studios in New York] right away and studied with him for the summer and ended up doing a couple of plays with him.

I remember two things he said to me: one, he used the word "destination." You're on stage and you have a destination. You go from here to there. But it's also hooked up with destiny which is kind of like a through line of action for the whole thing. I always thought that was a good word.

And the other thing he always used to say was [*in a playful voice*], "I *love* my problems. My problems are *my* problems. You have your own problems. I love my problems. I love talking about my problems. I love dealing with my problems. They're *my* problems."

I think for young actors the most important thing is managing their intellectual and emotional life. You know, coming to terms with themselves and that has to do with their own problems. It's really about becoming friends with your problems so that you can use them, but more importantly that you can live a happier life.

And that's a tricky thing, you know. Some actors are fortunate enough to have great parents who tutored them and cared for them, so when they hit nineteen, they had their shit together and they kind of have a direct course of action. But most people are troubled by a lot of stuff. And you have to find a way to manage those troubles, your problems, your emotional life so that you are able to one, live a good life, and two, use all that stuff in your work.

KW: *Do you still audition for things?*
RC: Everything.

KW: *So what are thinking about when you walk into the audition room? Is it more technical, or are you trying to be the character or are you just trying to relax? What's going on?*
RC: I think the most important thing is to be relaxed. Be in a place where you just don't freaking care. Then you can play "make believe."

What I do sometimes is pump myself up by starting a dialogue with myself, like a pre-dialogue to what the scene is about. I'm trying to use the situation in the audition process as something analogous to the situation that I'm in at the audition.

KW: *Right.*
RC: Do you know what I mean? So you have a relationship with the casting director. That's a real person. Do you know this per-

son? Have you seen this person before? So you're asking all these same questions about the auditioner that you would ask about the character. As a way of focusing your energy so that when the time comes you're right there with it.

How is this room and this space and the person you're talking to—how is it related to the room and the space and the person who you talk to in the scene? So you're trying to use that person more specifically.

KW: *So you are really focusing on the work. You're not thinking about externals, you're not thinking about the casting director or the reader or any of that stuff—except in service of the scene.*
RC: Yeah. There are a couple of good casting directors out there who actually were actors who are really good. Some of the casting directors who read with you suck, but most of them, you know, hire a reader. They bring in young actors and they're good. But they've gone through a lot of people, so you have to make it fresh and alive.

KW: *Is there anything you do at auditions that always works, where you think, "Oh I did that and I nailed it—and I booked the job." Is there any consistency there?*
RC: Well, only in the value of how much you care about the character you're playing. And if what you are investing in that character is something you care about within yourself. You always have to find it within you.

When I did *Across the Universe* and I went up against some real name people, I knew I was totally hooked to it. It had to do with father and son and that kind of stuff I love. And I just had it down and Julie Taymor saw I had it.

KW: *Yeah, you were really good in that.*

RC: It was nice stuff, right? It's about the emotional relationship within the scene. So you are not playing it, you are not acting it. It is something that you really do care about.

KW: *You said something that I thought was interesting. You said you are surprised when you get it and surprised when you don't get it. What did you mean by that?*

RC: Sometimes I rock it and I don't hear anything, and then sometimes I go in half-assed and I hear something, you know. When I left the audition for *Blue Bloods,* I was with a friend of mine. We were walking away and I was going, "Oh shit, I'm retiring. I just suck. Did you see me in there? Do you know how much I sucked?" He says, "Yeah, I sucked, too." "Let's get out of here—I'm going to shoot myself." And I got it.

And then there's other times when I leave and I go, "How did I not get it?"

I was auditioning with Steve Buscemi, right, who I worked with on *Boardwalk Empire*. When he's not working on *Boardwalk,* he directs. And I'm auditioning for Edie Falco's show; I'm playing this dad. It had all these elements I was so right for. I said, "Oh, shit, I can win a best guest star for this role." Do you know what I mean? I really worked on it. Steve is there, gives me a big hug. I do it. I knock it out. Just freaking call me up now and tell me I have it. But I didn't get it.

Do you know what it is? There are a lot of actors. There are a lot of talented people. So that's why I'm surprised when I don't get it and I'm surprised when I do get it.

And I really don't mind when I don't get it sometimes because if it's an actor that I like, and most actors I like, I don't really care ultimately, you know.

KW: *Do you think the fact that you don't really care has contributed to your success?*
RC: I guess it made me have the kind of career that I've had. Maybe if I cared more or was more determined…You know, when I worked with Kevin Spacey, I went, "This freaking guy, he wants it bad." I haven't met anybody who wanted it so desperately as Kevin Spacey. I thought, "This guy is going to make it. He wants it more than anything in the whole world." And I didn't feel that way.

KW: *In 1998 you moved from LA back to New York? Why did you make the move and how did it affect your career?*
RC: Well, you know, it was a combination of things. I had just starred in a pilot called *Whitey,* and they were so convinced it was going to get picked up, but it didn't get picked up. And my wife hated living in LA, and so we decided we would move back and start all over and start doing some plays.

When we moved back in '98, the first play I did was at Hartford Stage. So, it was funny I had turned that play down years ago and then the first play when I came back, *A Streetcar Named Desire,* was at Hartford Stage.

Anyway, right after Hartford I was suffering one of the really deadly acting diseases called "funzulow." I had to make money, right? And the following fall I get an offer to understudy *Death of a Salesman* that was coming to Broadway, the two boys, Hap and Biff. I went in and I read for casting and Arthur Miller and they hired me to be the understudy.

I went, "OK shit, I've never understudied, plus I'm a little scared. I've got to learn all of these freaking lines without any rehearsal. I don't think I can do it." Anyway, I accepted it because I needed the money, right? A week after I accepted it and was about to go into rehearsal—it was a Friday, and I go into rehearsal on Monday—Tom Fontana calls me up: "Hi, Bob." "Hi Tom." [*Pause*]

They don't call you up unless they have a job for you. "I wrote this new role for you on *Oz*." I went "Okay, when do I start?"

KW: *So you didn't end up understudying* Death of a Salesman *I take it.*
RC: I didn't end up understudying *Death of a Salesman* and the producer of the show said [*ominous voice*] "you will never work in this town again." I went "Geez, that's a cliché line." He was all pissed off. Ended up doing *Oz* for four seasons.

KW: *So Tom Fontana wrote the role [Officer Sean Murphy] for you. Did he tell you why?*
RC: He just said he's going to bring boxing in. Tom knew I was a fighter. I went, "Cool man. Right up my alley." You know Tom has helped me out before. I actually lived with Tom when I first went out to LA. I met him through Blythe and Bruce. And actually Bruce was the one who hired Tom for *St. Elsewhere*. And I had this great experience with him with *Oz*. It was a lot of fun.

KW: *I thought you did a great job on* Oz.
RC: Thanks. People have commented that they thought that I had done really a great job.

KW: *Did you think so?*
RC: I've had a lot of people come up and, you know, compliment me, even fellow actors who I worked with on the show like Chris Meloni. Last time I worked with Chris on *Law and Order: SVU* he said, "I revisited that show *Oz*, man, and you did some really good work on that show." I went, "Thanks, dude. Do you have some money?"

KW: *How do you think a director who has cast you several times would describe working with you?*
RC: Fun. You know I always try to have fun and make it playful. I don't get too intense about it, and I'm easy to work with.

KW: *You've portrayed an assortment of blue collar guys and law enforcement officers. Why do you think that you've been cast this way?*
RC: Well, I've got a big, fat head, so if I'm walking down 23rd Street and there's a hooker on the corner, she walks away. Why? She thinks that I'm a cop.

KW: *Really?*
RC: Yeah. The only time you really get to play something in TV or film outside of your physical and emotional type is if you become a star.

KW: *Bob, what would you say is your best quality as an actor?*
RC: What's my best quality as an actor? [*Long pause*] I don't know.

KW: *You don't have to be modest.*
RC: No, I think having fun, just trying to just make it fun and exciting. I try to be really specific. I guess my best quality is—well the thing I aim for the most—is to really understand what I'm doing and then put a twist on it somehow.

KW: *I think your work is very specific. It's as if it's coming out of your mouth—out of Bob Clohessy's mouth.*
RC: I want whatever comes out of my mouth to sound real. And so I try to set it up with all my acting skills to make it come out spontaneous and natural.

KW: *There is so much about the acting business that seems to be inconsistent and illogical, especially when it comes to creating a career. However, in your experience, are there also other things that are logical, that you can count on?*

RC: Yeah. You've got to take care of your body. You've got to look good for TV and film, but you don't have to be beautiful. If you're a terrific actor but you're slovenly, people are not going to pay attention. You've got to take care of your spirit. You can't freaking beat yourself up. That's a huge thing.

And the other thing is just try different things. You know, don't say, "I would never do this, I'd never do that."

KW: *Like, for example?*

RC: You know try Off Off Broadway, try a play in Brooklyn, try a musical, try all these different things because that's the only way you find out what you want and don't want.

KW: *Some people would look at your early career and say you had lots of momentum because you went from one show to another to another.*

RC: Well, that happens. Once you get your first part, then you're in the mix. You jumped a level; you jumped up. So now you're going to be considered for a whole bunch of things because you had that exposure.

KW: *Right.*

RC: And now more than ever you get a part in a TV show you have the exposure. So now you're on that next level; you're on the list. You see? That's the momentum that you're talking about. So then you jump to another show, you jump to another show until finally they realize that you being on a show is not going to make it a success and then they find a new person—a younger person.

KW: *So it sounds like you are talking about a sort of a tier system or class system in the business.*

RC: Oh wildly, yeah, and it all has to do with exposure and being on something, you know, and selling tickets. And it's not all up to you; there are other considerations: other actors, is it a good show, the time slot—so many factors that go in. But if it becomes a hit, then you're swimming. Then you're making some bucks.

I did a pilot called *Couples*—it was about three thirty-year-old couples, right? And it didn't get picked up. So the same people did a show about three twenty somethings the following year. You know what that was called? *Friends.*

KW: *So, you are giving me examples of good luck and maybe not such good luck.*

RC: Yeah, I mean they all turned out to be not good luck. I remember early on Julie Duffy was doing a new show, and they were interested in me playing the part, and I went to the network and the whole thing. Do you know who got the part? George Clooney. We all know where George is.

KW: *Yeah, he's doing pretty well. You've had a lot of good luck too it seems to me.*

RC: When Tom Fontana called me up, that was great luck.

KW: *Do you think that you create your luck?*

RC: Yeah, to a certain extent, sure. Being positive, being out there, trying different things. You have to try different things—that's big.

KW: *Early on, it seems to me, your willingness to do that musical instead of the play that was going to pay more made a huge difference in your career.*

RC: Oh, yeah. But prior to that after I came back from teaching aerobics and started writing my own monologues and decided I'm going to do my own stories was another thing that got me into Williamstown.

KW: *What would you say is the smartest thing that you've ever done for your career?*
RC: Not quitting.

KW: *Okay, last question. All of the statistics tell us that acting is an incredibly difficult profession. At any given time there are far more actors out of work than are working. However, you have defied these odds, enjoying quite a bit of success in a long career. How have you done it?*
RC: First, you have to love being around actors, which I do. Second, you have to create good working experiences, making lemonade out of lemons. Third, fuck the statistics, you've got to wish everyone well. Fourth, you have to be honest with yourself constantly, you've got to know you got the training and you feel enough confidence in your talent to have a career.

Lastly, and most importantly, you can't beat yourself up. You have to be really kind to yourself, finding love and joy in the whole painful process of becoming a working actor.

Robert Clohessy Success Team Member

BONNIE MONTE

Ken Womble: *Bonnie, you're the artistic director of the Shakespeare Theatre of New Jersey. Could you tell me a bit about your theatre and the types of plays that you produce?*

Bonnie Monte: It's the state's largest professional theatre company dedicated to Shakespeare and other classic authors. There are a couple of smaller companies that do Shakespeare now, but we remain the largest. We do anywhere from seven to eight major productions a year, and we have two touring companies, twelve different education programs. It's a very, very busy place.

KW: *And you have been there for twenty years, or just over now?*
BM: Yeah, I'm going into my twenty-second season.

KW: *How did you first meet Bob?*
BM: I was working at the Williamstown Theatre Festival, and he submitted his résumé and headshot for the non-equity company. And I brought him in, in part because he had "SUNY Purchase" on his résumé and that was a very good program at the time, I'm sure it still is, and in part because his headshot was very appealing.

It was one of those auditions that you just don't forget. He came in jeans and a t-shirt looking like Stanley Kowalski, spoke like Stanley Kowalski and I don't remember the pieces that he did, but the room was just electric.

KW: *He mentioned to me that he had started writing his own monologues.*
BM: Oh, that's right! He did one of his own pieces! [*Laughs*] I said what's it from? And he said, "Oh, I wrote that." And I was like, "Oh my God, this guy is totally…" what's the word, well I'm sure I said something like, "This guy has balls." I mean he just had no shame about him. And I remember thinking, "Wow! That was awesome!"

He understood intuitively, and still does, the art of telling a story, whether that's through a two-minute monologue or through a two-hour play. Those people make us listen. He has this great

257

ability to speak the truth; whatever comes out of his mouth as an actor sounds like the truth. I don't see the acting, which is really one of the main things we look for when we're looking at new people.

And so I brought him back in for a callback for our artistic director, Nikos Psacharopoulos. And Nikos could be very cruel and very judgmental and to some extent snobby about training on occasion. And he fell in love with Bob instantaneously.

KW: *So he was seeing some of the same things you were it sounds like?*
BM: Absolutely. And so we hired Bob to be a member of the non-Equity company, and he spent a number of years with us up in Williamstown.

I directed him in a bunch of stuff. We did some John Patrick Shanley, we did *Danny and the Deep Blue Sea,* and he eventually landed a wonderful role of the young boxer in Harold Pinter's *The Homecoming.* That was certainly one of his crowning achievements. And then I directed him in *A Streetcar Named Desire.*

KW: *Right. As Mitch.*
BM: As Mitch, yeah.

KW: *What was that experience like?*
BM: Well it was fantastic. I mean, it was an extraordinary production, and it was an extraordinary cast. I was frustrated only in… it brought up some memories for me when I had cast the show years ago for a Broadway production. And I had campaigned very, very hard for Bob at the time to play Stanley Kowalski. He was the right age, and he would have knocked people's socks off. And they didn't want him because he wasn't famous enough.

KW: *Oh my goodness.*

BM: And it was very, very upsetting to me because that's the role he should have played back then. And so it was very fulfilling to get to do the play with him and to have him play Mitch and to have him do it so—he was a brilliant, brilliant Mitch.

KW: *Bob told me about being cast in a musical at Williamstown, directed by Bruce Paltrow, but then getting an offer to do another show that an agent he was freelancing with had gotten him. That show would have made him Equity. Are you familiar with that?*

BM: Yeah, *Lucky Lucy*, that was all part of the Williamstown stuff.

KW: *He told me he decided to stay in the musical, not knowing that Bruce Paltrow was producing* St. Elsewhere *at the time, because he wanted to. However, he lost the agent he was freelancing with and he didn't get into Equity. What does that say about him? That he decided to stay with something that didn't, at the time didn't seem as promising as the other option?*

BM: Well it says volumes, and it's what separates Bob from most people. He follows his heart and his instincts.

And the moral of the story is it paid off great because Bruce Paltrow was probably one of the most powerful men in Hollywood television at the time and took care of Bob in a lot of ways. And Bruce's wife, Blythe Danner, became very fond of Bob and that decision was a very smart one whether he knew it or not at the time.

It is what continues to make him a very smart guy, a very beloved guy, and it sets him apart. It makes him an artist as opposed to just an actor.

KW: *I don't know if he thinks of himself as an artist.*

BM: I don't think he does, and he should because he is. He's a great artist.

KW: *I'm sure he would love to hear that because he doesn't toot his own horn very much. We had a long interview, and I had to kind of push him to tell me...*
BM: Oh, he's very modest, yes.

KW: *What is he like to work with?*
BM: With Bob there's a joy in doing the work. I mean nobody, unless you're you know, Brad Pitt, is getting paid enough to be miserable. It's a tough life for directors, it's a tough life for actors, it's a tough life for anybody involved in the theatre, and he's fun and he's funny.

You know, I worked with him on and off for years including a kind of high-profile project at the Manhattan Theatre Club. He could goof around like crazy, but the minute we started that rehearsal there was an extraordinary level of professionalism and skill.

I was thrilled to see how his skill set had developed over the years. And all of that kind of raw talent that I saw when he was a young, young man was there, but it had been completely fine tuned by many years of experience.

KW: *How would you describe Bob's career to date?*
BM: I think that Bob has attained what I would kind of call an ideal actor's life. He's done some big films and he's done some big roles in film. He's done a lot of television, some of it crappy and some of it fantastic. And the fact that he was part of that ensemble that won the SAG Award for *Boardwalk Empire*—it's a truly wonderful project to have been a part of and a wonderful achievement.

He makes a good enough living that he can go off and do theatre; he's appeared on Broadway, he's appeared in many regional theatres, he's appeared Off Broadway.

I mean he has an extraordinarily well rounded and varied career. He's got film, television and theatre projects happening, many times simultaneously. He never stops working. He's a very lucky actor.

KW: *What part, if it's played a role, has type been for Bob? And does he have a clear idea of his type?*
BM: No, because if you look at all the stuff he's done, they're all very different things. I mean I'm sure there are some people who look at him and see a particular type. But you'd have to ask those people what that is. I don't see him like that.

He's quite able to change his physicality in some extraordinary ways. So you may see him one day doing something where he looks like a big lumbering, kind of clumsy bear and the next he's in *Pal Joey* spinning around scenery and looking pretty debonair. He can be physically scary and imposing, and he can just be a big teddy bear. I mean he really is like a chameleon and I think that's just extraordinary.

KW: *What would you say are some of his best qualities as a per-former?*
BM: His ability to speak nothing but the truth when he's on stage. And this kind of natural charisma that he has in telling a story. He understands comic timing brilliantly, and he understands dramatic timing brilliantly. He knows how to manipulate—and I use that word in the best sense—his audience so that they're following his story in the right way.

He is so courageous. I mean that's something that does hold a lot of actors back from being great. He doesn't care how he looks; there's no protective system. He's absolutely willing to be vulner-able, clownish, to look ridiculous, to be brutal. He is absolutely willing to do anything if it represents humanity. And that kind of fearlessness, I think, is one of his great qualities.

KW: *We talked about* St. Elsewhere *being a turning point for Bob. Are there other turning points that you're familiar with in his career?*
BM: That whole *St. Elsewhere* thing lead also to his introduction to Tom Fontana.

Only by getting to an old enough age can you look back and go, "Wow! Who knew it would be a turning point?" But it was because through that connection I met this other connection and through that connection I got that television show. He has followed his stepping stones. He has stepped on the right stepping stones all along his path.

To come to Williamstown as a young man, he didn't have to do that. I mean he probably could've skipped the whole theatre thing and gone right to playing tough guy roles on TV. And he didn't do it. He went and got himself involved with a group of artists versus just business people. And that, to me, was one of the greatest, smartest things he ever did.

KW: *How lucky do you think Bob has been and how important has luck been for him in his career?*
BM: Well listen, everybody in the theatre has bad luck and good luck.

KW: *Ah.*
BM: Because it's the nature of the business. You can't possibly get everything you want role-wise or project-wise. So I don't call that bad luck necessarily. I call it the things that happen because there's an equal measure of good luck things. So it is what it is. I mean luck does sometimes make us lose out on things, yes. You know, you're not in the right place at the right time or whatever.

But for the most part I don't think that luck really has a whole lot do with anything.

I think what it's more about is perseverance, hard work, talent, ethical professionalism, it's a whole bunch of things. And the little bit of luck is being lucky enough to continue to do it despite the things that are happening in your life. I know so many actors who have had to give it up before they should have or before they wanted to because the demands of family or economics didn't allow them to keep going. Bob had just enough money coming in at the right times in his life, so that he never had to give it up. And I think that's where the luck comes in more than anything.

But in terms of everything else that's come his way he's earned it. And in terms of things that haven't come his way, then yeah, perhaps it's a tinge of bad luck, but I don't even know if it's bad luck. It's just, it wasn't meant to be for some reason.

KW: *Bob has been a busy, working actor for about twenty-five years now and it's quite an achievement. What has kept him going for so long?*
BM: I think he loves it! I think he has fun. And I think that even the jobs that he doesn't love they pay him money.

And then his family keeps him going. I mean he adores his boys and his wife. Bob just has this *joie de vivre,* and I think that he is a very lucky man—there I bring the word "luck" in again— because he has found a profession that he truly does love.

KW: *How important a role has talent played for him?*
BM: The biggest role. That's the biggest factor in his success, I think. He's a very talented guy.

KW: *How important has his belief in himself been for Bob?*
BM: All I can tell you is that having worked with thousands of actors I've never seen Bob get self-indulgently insecure. So I think

that his belief in himself is pretty deep, and he's happy with himself from an intellectual, spiritual, emotional and physical point of view.

In the many conversations that Bob and I have had over the years, I've never had to talk him out of quitting acting, unlike many other of my colleagues. There's a kind of wonderful down-to-earth craftsman approach to Bob and his work, and I think that's given him a very sound base.

KW: *How would you describe him overall as an actor and a person?*
BM: He's this incredible artist, a talented man, a secure man, professional, dedicated, fun, funny, sometimes he's crazy.

But what he also is…he's a brave man. And not just in his choices and not just when he gets up on a stage, but because he is not afraid to buck certain things in the business that other people are afraid of. If he needs to stick up for somebody, he will, even if it means losing a job. His level of ethics and his kind of sublime morality as a man is just tremendous.

KW: *And that's pretty impressive because there's always something to lose.*
BM: Exactly. And I'm just in awe and admiration of that.

KW: *Last question. All of the statistics tell us that acting is an incredibly difficult profession. At any given time there are far more actors out of work than are working. However, Bob has defied these odds, enjoying quite a bit of success in a long career. How has he done it?*
BM: It's not any one factor. It's a huge combination of perseverance and hard work and talent and skill and right-minded behavior and courage and truthfulness. All of the things that make anybody successful in whatever endeavor they choose to pursue.

KW: *Excellent. Anything else you'd like to add?*
BM: Nope. I think you got it all.

KW: *Okay.*
BM: I'm delighted that you're giving him some attention because he deserves it more than most actors in the world. He's just a sublime guy.

KW: *Well you should be his agent.* [Laughs]
BM: I know. [*Laughs*] Don't worry, I tell people that all the time. I'm his kind of secret publicist. He doesn't even know it.

Robert Clohessy Success Team Member

WALT WITCOVER

Ken Womble: *Walt, I've heard your name mentioned a number of times as a wonderful acting coach. So, you come with quite a pedigree.*
Walt Witcover: Thank you.

KW: *You've taught some very successful actors, and you trained with the legendary Lee Strasberg.*
WW: Yes.

KW: *How did that training influence your own teaching?*
WW: When I came to New York, I came to Strasberg. And then I became more of a director, and I came with him to the Actor's Studio. I did the Actor's Studio version of *La traviata* in 1968, an experiment in theatrical opera. I gave them the first two acts, Strasberg was very impressed, and finally finished it in 1969, which

lead to my starting with my laboratory theatre, Master-works Laboratory Theatre, which we had forty years.

KW: *You were Bob Clohessy's acting professor at the State University of New York at Purchase in the late 1970s and early '80s.*
WW: Right.

KW: *Do you recall some of your first impressions of him?*
WW: Always very strong, very positive. I remember Bob playing in *Yellow Jack*, remember that Sydney Howard play about the conquest of yellow fever in the 1890s? Bob was one of the young officers, and he made a very commanding appearance as he broke through the walls and he marched into the audience.

We had a very good four-year class of training. By the time they got through, they knew what they were doing pretty well. And yes, it was very clear that Bob had what it takes.

KW: *Bob and I met on a tour of* The Taming of the Shrew. *Bob played Petruccio and my impression of him was that he was very natural, truthful, and funny.*
WW: Natural, truthful and funny, three good words. He has a natural reality that audiences relate to.

KW: *What was he like to teach?*
WW: As an actor he was continually adventurous in what he chose to do.

KW: *By adventurous do you mean he would take actor risks?*
WW: Yes. That's right. He recently did Bottom [at The Shakespeare Festival of New Jersey], and he has a wonderful affinity for connecting with real people in a Shakespearian way. He makes them come alive, you know.

KW: *In your long career you've taught and directed some wonderful actors, F. Murray Abraham, Jane Alexander, Jerry Stiller, John Leguizamo to name a few. What are some of the qualities that they share as actors?*

WW: They bring a very personal reality to the stage. When you see them, you know they're there. You mentioned Leguizamo and Jane Alexander. They always make something very personal, and they make an impression that you know they're not like someone else. I guess that's what we call a star thing, right? Star category.

KW: *Do you see any of those same qualities in Bob?*

WW: You pick him out. You recognize that's a person who is alive at this moment. He takes that character, and he turns it inside out. So you never forget him.

KW: *When I asked Bob how he thought a director who had cast him multiple times would describe working with him he thought for a second and answered, "I always try to have fun and make it playful." Do you think this sense of playfulness has made a difference in his career?*

WW: I think everybody enjoys working with Bob. He makes the experience very enjoyable.

KW: *Do you believe that his own natural talent has contributed to his success?*

WW: Yes. Yes, of course.

KW: *What about his belief in himself? Is that important?*

WW: I think it has to be, especially for a leading actor.

KW: *How important a role do you believe that type or being typecast has played for Bob?*

WW: I think of Bob as a guy who can do anything. He brings himself to each character. He makes it seem like the part is written for him.

What are the keys that have led Robert Clohessy to a successful acting career?

He auditions very well

An actor's livelihood is dependent on booking roles, and Bob books constantly. In a recent year he appeared in five feature films and recurred on two television series. How does he do it? He gives dynamic auditions that showcase a powerful set of skills: an innate sense of truth, a lack of self-consciousness, and an ability to use his own personal experience.

When Bob auditioned for *Across the Universe*, he used his relationship with his own teenage sons as emotional fuel for his character. Julie Taymor was impressed, and Bob's portrayal of a regretful, absent father is, in my opinion, some of the best work in this fine film.

He follows his heart, even when it's risky

Bob isn't only courageous in his acting choices but in his life. When he was cast in the workshop of a new musical and then offered a lead role in a full-fledged Equity production, Bob had a choice to make: fulfill his obligation to the workshop or do the Equity production.

Acting in the Equity production could have been a breakthrough event—a leading role at a major regional theatre and the opportunity to join Actors Equity Association. Also, Bob booked the job through his talent agent. Acquiring an agent is tough, so most actors want to keep that relationship strong.

However, getting his Equity card and keeping the agent wasn't as important to Bob as fulfilling his *commitment* to the musical workshop. So, he turned down the play and lost his agent.

When Bob's decision led to an audition for Bruce Paltrow, which led, six months later, to being cast on *Hill Street Blues*, it must have seemed clear that Bob made the right decision.

However, it's important to note that *Bob didn't know those events would lead to the television series at the time.* In fact, he didn't even know who Bruce Paltrow was.

Bob took a risk and followed his heart—and it led him to a big start in show business.

He knows his type

Bob has played lots of cops in his career, from his breakthrough role as Officer Patrick Flaherty on NBC's *Hill Street Blues*, to Sgt. Gormley, Donnie Wahlberg's boss, on CBS's *Blue Bloods,* to Chief Weirzbowski, Bradley Cooper's boss, in *The Place Beyond the Pines.* And for good reason: he was brought up the son of a cop, is a husky 6'2" and was a Golden Gloves boxer and college athlete.

Bonnie Monte sees Bob as an actor of range, able to change his physicality to fit an array of stage roles like the lumbering Mitch in *A Streetcar Named Desire* and the overly confident Bottom in *A Midsummer Night's Dream.* And there has indeed been variety in many of Bob's on camera roles: good guys, like attorneys and prison guards and bad guys, like underworld thugs.

However, actors who play these roles tend to be large and dexterous—like Bob. So, if there is consistency regarding Bob's type it may be his ability to portray characters with a *strong physical presence.*

He puts art over business

Bob's roots are in the theatre, and his decision to come to Williamstown early on to work with artists, Bonnie believes, was a wise one.

When after twelve years in Los Angeles he decided to move back to New York and the theatre, Bob was again respecting the art within. He was also saying goodbye to the biggest TV market in the world. For an actor who makes his living on TV that was a *risk*.

Yet the risk paid off. Bob soon made his Broadway debut in a Tony nominated revival of *Twelve Angry Men* and has continued to work regularly on television and in feature films.

Starting his career in Williamstown—as an artist—did indeed turn out to be a smart move.

He has perseverance

As is true for most actors, Bob's career has had its share of bad luck, like rewritten series that became hits for other actors. Yet, it seems good luck has played an equal, perhaps greater part in Bob's career resulting in leading roles in over half a dozen TV series, Tony nominated Broadway shows and numerous film performances. And Bonnie believes that Bob's success has more to do with "perseverance, hard work, talent, ethical professionalism," than luck.

After more than two decades Bob is still at it, and in my opinion, doing some of his finest work. When I asked him the smartest thing he had done for his career, Bob replied, "Not quitting."

He has talent

Clearly, Bob's talent impresses and delights Bonnie Monte and Walt Witcover. Walt even believes Bob has star quality. Just like his former students John Leguizamo and Jane Alexander, "You never forget him."

Describing his work as truthful, charismatic and personal, Bonnie stressed Bob's ability to tell his story "in the right way," an important quality because actors are communicators. Through their stories audiences are entertained, touched, sometimes enlightened, things that Robert Clohessy has been doing for years.

JOSE LLANA

CHAPTER 9

Focus on Your Career and Have Perspective

JOSE LLANA

Jose Llana was born in the Philippines and raised near Washington D.C. Jose made his Broadway debut as Lun Tha in the 1996 revival of *The King and I* (opposite Lou Diamond Phillips and Donna Murphy). He would go on to play Angel in *Rent,* Wang Ta in *Flower Drum Song* (opposite Lea Salonga) and originate the roles of Jessie-Lee in *Streetcorner Symphony,* Chip Tolentino in *The 25th Annual Putnam County Spelling Bee* (Drama Desk Award) and El Gato in *Wonderland.*

Off Broadway appearances include: President Marcos in David Byrne's *Here Lies Love* (dir. Alex Timbers), Gabey in *On the Town* (dir. George C. Wolfe), Adam Guettel's *Saturn Returns* (dir. Tina Landau), all at the Public Theatre and Adam in *Falling For Eve* (York Theatre). Regional appearances include: *Oliver!* (Bill Sikes, Papermill Playhouse), Cameron Mackintosh's *Martin Guerre* (Guillaume, Guthrie Theater), *Ballad of Little Jo* (Steppenwolf Theater, Jefferson Nomination–Best Supporting Actor) and *Candide* (The Prince Theater, Barrymore Nomination–Best Actor).

TV/film appearances include HBO's *Sex and the City* opposite Margaret Cho and *Hitch* opposite Will Smith. Numerous cast albums and a best-selling solo album under the *VIVA Philippines* label. Jose is a constant advocate for Broadway Cares/Equity Fights AIDS and Broadway Impact for Marriage Equality.

....

Ken Womble: *You were born in the Philippines.*

Jose Llana: I was born there, but I moved to the States when I was three years old. I grew up in a suburb of D.C., in northern Virginia. A very typical, suburban upbringing, you know, football games on the weekends and things like that. My sister and I both went to a math and science accelerated high school. She went to MIT to be an engineer, and I became the artist in the family. So, two very different paths but from the same spawn.

KW: *Did going to a math and science magnet high school influence the character you played on Broadway in* The 25th Annual Putnam County Spelling Bee, *Chip Tolentino?*

JL: [*Laughs*] Very much so. Chip Tolentino, the Boy Scout character, was pretty much lifted from a photo of me at ten years old that I showed my director.

KW: *Really?*

JL: I was in my Webelos costume. And actually, when we started the show Off Broadway at Second Stage and we were creating our characters, I named my character Chip Tolentino. Tolentino is a family name on my mother's side. And he was originally supposed to be an athlete, and so we tried a lot of football jerseys and lot of basketball jerseys, and I ended up just looking kind of thuggish. And one day I brought in a picture—James Lapine and Bill Finn asked everyone to bring in pictures of ourselves at the age that we were playing, ten to fourteen years old—and I brought in a picture of me in a Boy Scout uniform when I was ten and he says, "Well, there's your costume."

KW: *That's interesting because seeing your more recent work you strike me as very much a leading man—and you played this very character role.*

274

JL: I'm very fortunate because I'm an ethnic actor, and I think I tend to hop that line back and forth between leading man roles and character roles. I find it a joy and I take full advantage of that ability because in the Asian-American-Latino world I am a leading man. I'm tall and my voice dictates that and my first couple of shows in New York that's what I was cast as. When I do shows where I'm the only ethnic person in the company, I tend to be the character; I'm the best friend, I'm the villain.

And so I think *Spelling Bee* was one of the first opportunities that casting directors were able to see that I could do comedy in New York, and I think that's where I'm most comfortable.

Sometimes flexing your leading man muscles are fun, but it doesn't tend to be as interesting as the character roles. Leading man roles are a lot more work and not as much of a payoff to be truthfully honest.

KW: *After high school you moved to New York and attended the Manhattan School of Music. Were you were going more toward classical work? If so, was there something that changed your trajectory toward musical theatre?*
JL: I actually intended to go into musical theatre. In high school I was introduced to a lot of touring companies that came through D.C. at the National Theater and at the Kennedy Center, and I fell in love with *Les Mis* and *Oklahoma!* and *The Sound of Music*. I knew I wanted to focus on singing.

I got accepted to Tisch, the NYU program, and to Manhattan School of Music. I chose Manhattan School because I was an impatient seventeen-year-old who just wanted to live and breathe music. I realized very quickly that I was not going to stay there more than a year because that focus, entirely on classical and opera, was not where I was the most excited. And so I moved to the Royal Academy of Music in London for my sophomore year.

But it was during my freshman year in school that I started auditioning for shows. It was spring break, I was working in the administration office, and I had just booked my first professional summer job, *The King and I*, at the Mill Mountain Playhouse in Virginia. And at the audition someone said, "You're going to go to the Broadway audition." And I'm like, "I didn't even realize there was one."

KW: *So you were not a member of Actors' Equity yet, but you went to an EPA, an Equity Principal Audition?*
JL: The buzz around Broadway is that they will see non-Equity people at the end of the day. You go and you wait all day and the monitor can see that you've been waiting all day. They'll go into the room and say, "Hey, this kid's been here all day. Can you at least hear him sing?" And that's what I expected to do. And what happened…was around noon someone didn't show up for their time slot and I just raised my hand and walked in the door.

And they called me back all summer and the rest is history. To this day I haven't found that person to thank them for flaking on their audition.

You know, I had lot of balls. I was seventeen, eighteen then. The courage that I had to tell my parents I was not going to pursue an engineering degree and go pursue music, that was one of the hardest conversations I've ever had with my parents.

And I think any parent out there who has a kid who wants to pursue a career in performing, you have to allow that kid to show that kind of courage. You can't make it easy for them. My parents made it very hard for me to go against their wishes and pursue it. And if the kid doesn't have that kind of drive and that kind of passion and that kind of courage, then I worry that they're not going to have the courage to walk into that audition room and tell someone, "You need to hear me sing."

And I was very lucky that *The King and I* happened when I was eighteen years old. You know, that was my break, that was my opportunity. But there was a lot of preparation to get to that opportunity and every teacher and performer will tell you the only way to get success is if you combine preparation with luck and opportunity. So if one of those three things aren't there, it's not going to happen.

KW: *Was it luck in the sense that you happened to find out about the audition? Is that what you mean by luck?*
JL: They were looking for a teenager, bass/baritone who looked like he was from Siam. So there I was eighteen years old, Filipino-Asian looking. I was completely deer in headlights, and there was an aspect of who I was at eighteen that was perfect for that part at that moment in time.

And that's luck, random. And the fact that it happened to be exactly when I was graduating high school and coming to New York—that show happened at the right time for me.

And a lot of people saw me in that, and they were able to cast me in other shows because of it. I mean it wasn't luck that I went to the audition, that was gumption, that was courage. And also finding out about the audition; that's not luck, that's research. You know. Luck was that the show was happening in the first place.

KW: *Also, it seems to me there were a lot of things that weren't just luck. It seems that in a sense you made that happen for yourself.*
JL: Exactly, because the opportunities are out there, you just have to go look for them. I wonder in awe at some people in their mid-twenties who say they want to be an actor, and they've been in New York for five years, and I ask them basic questions like, "Have you picked up a *Backstage* magazine? Do you know how to find the auditions?" And they're like, "What? What's that?" There are so

many resources for actors out there to find out what to do to find a job in this city and sometimes lazy actors just want something to happen for them.

If you talk to the most successful performers out there, they're the ones who go find the opportunities and make it happen for themselves. A lot of times, especially when actors get agents, they get lazy and sit at home and wait for their agent to call them. And a lot of times an agent is waiting for *you* to find the opportunity and say, "Get me an audition for this show."

KW: *Can you give me other examples of how you've found the opportunities for yourself?*
JL: I make sure every day I check Playbill.com and Variety.com. You've got to make sure that you're on top of what's coming in. When you read online that some director is prepping a workshop of an adaptation of this show and you know the show or you know the book and there's a character that you might want to play then, the first thing I do is e-mail my agent and say, "Hey, what's the buzz on this show? Keep an eye out for it. I'm going to look for the casting director. Make sure that my name is in the mix." So I have myself and I have my agent making sure that the first opportunity that show is auditioning I get myself in the door.

KW: *Right. So you're not depending on your agent, you're working cooperatively with your agent.*
JL: Of course.

KW: *Who is your agent?*
JL: I've been with Paradigm for a long time now. I've been very lucky to have a good relationship with them.

KW: *How do you prepare for auditions?*

JL: That's a good question. I love auditioning. It's very stressful but it's also exciting and I feel lucky that when I'm stressed and nervous I do some of my best singing and performing.

When my agent calls me and says, "You have an audition on this day, for these directors, for this music, for this show," I pick a song that I think is appropriate for the audition, or they'll give me a song to learn and I'll hire a coach. I have two or three coaches in the city who are not only accompanists and piano players, but they're also acting coaches. I'll learn the song with them and then work through it and make some acting choices. Memorize it, that's a really important part.

I think where a lot of young actors misstep is their preparation for auditions. I think you have to treat the audition like a performance. A lot of young actors make the mistake of under rehearsing.

KW: *Could you give me an example of a recent audition where you feel like you nailed it?*

JL: Several years ago they were auditioning for the tenth anniversary of *Les Mis* and that was my dream show. I wanted to get into *Les Mis* so badly and they kept calling me back and calling me back and calling me back and I didn't get the job and I was so disappointed. Tara Rubin, who was the casting director, saw me at a benefit and pulled me aside and said, "I can't tell you why, but if you book anything long term in the next couple of months please let my office know." And I had no idea what she was talking about and I forgot about it.

And a year later everyone's auditioning for *Martin Guerre*, which was another show Cameron Mackintosh produced, along with *Les Mis* and *Miss Saigon*, and I booked one of the lead roles. I was the villain Guillaume.

And at the first rehearsal, David Caddick, who was the musical supervisor of all of Cameron Mackintosh's shows, says "You know, we basically cast you from your *Les Mis* callback.

KW: *Really?*
JL: Yeah, and I said, "That's really fascinating." He's like, "Yeah, when you were auditioning for *Les Mis* on Broadway we were already casting *Martin Guerre* in London and we knew that you were perfect for this part, but we weren't doing it on Broadway for another two years." And I thought back to my disappointment of not getting *Les Mis* two years prior, but I booked a job! [*Laughs*]

You have to remember that out of some of the biggest disappointments you could still get something. You will always get something out of a good audition. Whether or not you book the job you're auditioning for on that particular day, if you do a good audition for that director and for those composers and for that musical director it will always help you down the road because everyone works on different projects after that show.

KW: *Knowing that something might happen later down the road really kind of reframes it in a healthy way, it seems to me.*
JL: I think every good performer needs to have the mentality that sometimes you're the best square peg on the planet and they're just looking for a round peg. You know, no matter how much you try to fit into it it's not going to happen. Down the road there's going to be a show looking for that exact square peg just for you. And you have to think that or else you're going to go home and cry yourself to sleep every night. And some people do.

KW: *After* The King and I *you went into several other musicals on Broadway in fairly quick succession. Was there a sense of momentum from* The King and I *that helped you get those shows?*

JL: I think so. I always say that *The King and I* was my big break. But *On the Town* in Central Park at the Delacorte Theater was what helped my career.

KW: *How?*
JL: When I was doing *The King and I*, I auditioned for *On the Town*, the Central Park version, and George Wolfe decided to cast me as the Gabey character.

KW: *Right. Gene Kelly played that in the movie.*
JL: The Gene Kelly role, yeah. And I think that was the first time that the Broadway community said, "Hey, there's that kid from *The King and I*. Oh, we can see him in parts other than Asian shows." And I think it was really important I did that and that started a lot of momentum for me.

[After] *The King and I*, I went straight into *On the Town* and then I did *Street Corner Symphony*, which was short-lived but a lot of fun, and then I went into *Rent* right after that. So, for three years I was not unemployed for very long in between those jobs.

But when *On the Town* went to Broadway, George Wolfe decided to recast my part with somebody else. I was twenty-one years old. I was demolished! I thought, "I'm done, no one's ever going to hire me, this is so embarrassing, this is terrible."

And you know I look back at that and I thank God that happened. Because it woke me up. It kind of burst my ego and my bubble where my twenty-one year old self thought, "Oh, this is easy, I can just go for any job and I'll get it. I'm always going to be in a Broadway show."

And I finally realized not everything's going to come easily. You could even have a job and have it taken away from you. My notices Off Broadway were mixed to good and I'm proud of the work I did in the part, but you've just got to move on and say, "You know, they wanted to recast it with some new energy."

That was a significant speed bump in the early momentum of my career that made me grow up a little bit. I think that helped me form a thicker skin, and I had a little bit better perspective, which is what you need.

KW: *When you auditioned for the role of El Gato in the Broadway musical* Wonderland, *you said you "went in all guns blazing and created this ridiculous, over-the-top character." I love "all guns blazing," because that seems to indicate you're taking big risks. Do you always go into auditions that way?*

JL: Yes, you have to.

KW: *You have to?*

JL: I think you either go big or go home. Any director who is worth working with will tell you, "Go for it and if it's too much I'll pull you back," because unless I give you a lot, you can never know what I have to offer. The worst thing is watching an actor make safe choices and boring choices because it's not exciting. There's nothing there.

And it's also the character of El Gato. I was given the freedom because the description of the character in itself was ridiculous. They described El Gato as this lothario, this ridiculously Latin, silly cat. And I knew the casting director, Dave Clemmons, and I was comfortable going in there.

I was planning to go out of town and I had delayed my train ticket a day to make this audition and I was kind of impatient. I just wanted to get out the door so I could get on a train and go to Boston to visit my sister. So I was like, "Hey, let's do this." And I think I probably didn't even want the job but it was like, "If I get it, I get it, if I don't, I don't." And I invented this silly, ridiculous kind of Puss 'n Boots. You know, I tried to mock the Antonio Banderas accent and rolled every "r" I could. And there was a little bit of my father in there and my father's a bit of a comedian and I just made him this ridiculously over ethnic goofball. And I thought, "Okay, if it's too much, it's too much and he'll tell me to pull it back." And I had them in stitches.

And I walked out of the room and that afternoon I get a call from my agent on the train and he's like, "What did you do in that room?" And I'm like, "Oh God, was it a lot?" And he's like, "Well, yeah. Apparently it was hilarious. They called me on their first possible break to tell me that, 'You're one of the first offers out and to not change a thing.'"

KW: *Wow.*
JL: I'm like "Okay, there you go!"

KW: *What you said about getting ready to board the train, do you think you had more fun because you took the pressure off yourself?*
JL: That's exactly right. Whenever I want a job so badly, I put so much pressure on myself and I prepare for so long. You know, you psyche yourself out and you walk into the room with such stress and even the most seasoned actors—I won't name names obviously, but some of my heroes in the performing world, some people I consider friends who are Tony winners—even they psyche themselves out.

Luckily I've worked long enough where I will probably know at least one person in the room: either the casting director, or the assistant director, or the assistant musical director, or maybe the pianist. And just having that familiar face will sort of calm your nerves.

I think every performer should jump at the opportunity to be either a monitor or an assistant or an intern, to be in the room and sit behind the table for an audition because it will completely open your eyes to the sense that it's true that they just want you to do good. They want you to walk into the room relaxed and do your best job.

I think a lot of performers, especially young performers, go into the room thinking, "Oh they're going to hate me." And it's the complete opposite of the truth. I've been a reader for some auditions and the more time you spend behind the table and see that environment, it makes going into an audition less stressful.

KW: *Was there a moment when you decided not to fall back, to be an actor and nothing else?*
JL: You know, there was a moment probably my senior year in high school where I told myself, "I need to go for it." And I tell young kids today if there's any profession that you think that you would be content and happy making a living from, do that. Because if you think that you will find contentment and happiness from that, then you will never give your all to performing because you'll always have one foot somewhere else. I think there's a real beauty in people putting their all in their art. And I think you have to make that decision young.

That said, when I turned thirty, I was doing *Spelling Bee* with Sarah Saltzberg, a cast member and also one of the writers of the show; she spent most of her twenties starting a real estate company up in Harlem. And it's become very successful and she kind of recruited me while we were doing *Spelling Bee* to become a real estate broker, and I started showing apartments up in Harlem with her. I got my real estate license and I did that for about three years, made a pretty decent living from it.

And the weird thing is, as much as I was liking the money, it was kind of sapping my soul a little bit. Some of my friends caught wind that I was doing it and so a lot of people thought I had quit performing. It was something I was doing with that extra time during the day and I thought, "You know, if I can go make a thousand dollars showing an apartment I'll do it."

I made a specific choice to stop doing it because I began liking the money too much. And it started sapping my energy away. And I didn't like that people began to know me as a real estate broker. Just like performing, to be the best broker I could be I had to really focus my energy on it and I didn't want to do that.

I think to be a working actor takes a lot of devotion and time, and when you have free time, it's best to fill that free time with things that are going to make you a better performer.

My partner sometimes marvels at the time I spend in preparing for benefits that I do around town that I get paid nothing for. He understands why I do it, but he marvels at the sweat and stress that I go through just to learn a song to sing once in a concert to raise money for some charity that he's never heard of.

But it's all to keep my name out there, to let people know what I do. I just sang in a concert last night; there could be a director in the audience that says, "Wow, Jose Llana. I never realized it, but he could be great in my next show."

KW: *Right. But also by doing that you're giving back, I mean you're doing a tremendous thing for people.*
JL: Exactly. You know, the amazing thing about Broadway Cares [Broadway Cares/Equity Fights AIDS] is they give us a platform to perform and be able to use our performance not only to benefit us but to benefit a charity, which is such an amazing thing to be able to do, donate our skills so that we can raise money for this amazing organization.

KW: *What would you consider your best quality as an actor?*
JL: Oh gosh, that's a loaded question. I've been branded versatile from a lot of different directors. I can do the leading man stuff, I can do the comedy stuff, I'm a decent dancer. So I think I'm the wild card for a lot of casting directors in the city. I tend to be placed on lists. There'll be ten guys going for a part and then they'll just throw me in the mix: "You know, the character description is nothing like Jose, but let's see what he does with that." And that to me is exciting. I'm always game to try something different and to sort of stretch myself.

But I think on stage—and a lot of my improv background and what I did in *Spelling Bee* has helped me—I can honestly say I am fearless and I am not afraid to fail and not afraid to look foolish. And I think the only way to achieve something interesting and brilliant is if you sometimes look foolish getting there.

KW: *What would you say are one or two of the smartest things you've done for your career? And if you could go back and change one or two things in your career, what would they be?*
JL: Wow.

KW: *Loaded.*
JL: Loaded, right? Let's see. I moved to New York. You know, there are amazing theatre communities in Chicago and in D.C., but if you want to really be where the theatre performing is you've got to move to New York. I think, as my impatient teenager self knew, I would've suffocated living someplace else.

If I had to change anything, I would've taken more dance classes as a kid. And I would've not stopped taking piano classes. You know, to this day I wish I played the piano better. I wish I danced a little bit better. I can still take dance classes now and I can still learn to play the piano now if I had the gumption to do so. But I think there's a window of opportunity when you're young to pick up those skills. And these days there are so many parts out there that involve playing the piano.

KW: *Okay. Last question. The statistics tell us that acting is an incredibly difficulty profession. Many more actors at any given time are out of work than are working. However, you have defied these odds working in six Broadway shows and enjoying quite a bit of success in your career. How have you done it?*

JL: I am passionate and I love it. I love auditioning, I love theatre, I love being a part of the community. And I think it has to be said that I have a really strong support system. I have a loving partner of eight years who is both my biggest cheerleader and my biggest reality check. He reminds me that I'm one of the lucky people in the world who gets to love what I do and make a living from it. It's an industry that is meant to just be joyful. He reminds me to keep perspective, that there are wars going on in the world, that there are bigger things in the world that are happening. Like when I don't get that job, woe is me, I'm not on the street and I'm not homeless, I'm not sick.

I think to keep that kind of perspective is what I hopefully instill in my students. I bring a newspaper to my audition class and say, "You know, you've got to pick this up and read it once in a while because if you only live in your theatre world, then you're going to be in a dark hole." Keep alive interests outside of theatre. You know, I love cooking, I love to travel with my family. Not only will it make you a healthier, more interesting person it will actually help you become a better actor.

I've had the opportunity to have six Broadway shows and a couple of touring companies and this and that. I think I'm the luckiest person because I've been able to support myself doing it and make some really amazing friends.

One of my first mentors was Lou Diamond Phillips in *The King and I*. And Lou knew every cast member by the third or fourth day of rehearsal and there were fifty people in that cast. He knew every doorman, he knew every stagehand, he knew every wardrobe person by their name. We had a lot in common; he started doing theatre when he was nineteen in Texas before *La Bamba*. I always asked for his advice and he pulled me aside and told me, "You know, Jose, whether you're a success or not, from job to job what people will remember is how you treat them and the relationships you form." And that's something I take with me every, every, every show.

I look back at my jobs and I look at the friendships that I made and how I became a better person from knowing those people. And I think that's what's allowed me to look at the next year and go, "Hmm, I wonder what I'm going to do? I wonder what people I'm going to meet this year to make myself a better person, to make myself a better performer?"

Jose Llana Success Team Member

STEVEN LUTVAK

Ken Womble: *Steven, you are a composer, a music coach and a singer based in New York. Could you tell me a bit about what you do?*

Steven Lutvak: When I want to be poetic about my life's work, I say that my work is about song. It's about writing songs, singing songs, helping people write songs, helping people choose songs, helping them perform them and helping them interpret lyrics. And I've supported myself for thirty some odd years now as a vocal coach, helping actors prepare for auditions.

KW: *Could you tell me a bit about your current musical,* A Gentleman's Guide to Love and Murder, *for which you wrote the music and cowrote the lyrics?*

SL: I cowrote the show with Robert L. Freedman, who wrote the book, and Robert and I wrote the lyrics together. It's been an extremely gratifying collaboration. We had an interesting road to getting this show on, to say the least. On the positive side we were lucky enough to be invited to be developed at the Sundance Theatre Lab, and we also had a reading early on at the Huntington Theatre in Boston. Additionally, we won the Kleban and the Fred Ebb awards for songs from this show, both of which were very important validation on the way to making this happen.

On the not-so-positive side, there were many…stumbling blocks on the road to getting this show up. To put it mildly. Too many to go into here, but I'll give you two examples.

We found a champion in one of Broadway's most important producers. We showed the show to him, and he was ready to come on board. We were thrilled, of course, because this was one of the greats, and we had a meeting scheduled to get together with him on Monday to begin to work out details. And he died the Thursday before. Seriously.

At another point, we were defendants in a lawsuit where we were sued for copyright infringement. Robert and I decided to fight the suit, and ultimately the case against us was dismissed in its entirety. That's a very few words for what was, ultimately, a very difficult thing to get through. It was one year, one month, one week, and one day from the time we were sued 'til the judge ruled in our favor. I'm told that's not very long for this sort of thing, but it felt many times longer than it actually was, I can assure you.

Of course, it was much more complicated than all of that, but we want to be speaking about Jose, right? In any case, the good news is that we opened at Hartford Stage last fall (2012), in a coproduction with the Old Globe in San Diego, where we played last spring, and we just opened on Broadway—oh, it's about two months ago now—and I'm very, very happy to say the show is doing really well. I feel very gratified and very, very grateful. We're very lucky. And come to think of it, Jose Llana was there on opening night!

The show is really delicious. It's the story of a man who discovers that he stands in line to inherit a great title and fortune—we're in England in 1909—and decides that he's going to kill all the family members that stand in the way of him inheriting. And all of the family members that he kills are played by the brilliant Jefferson Mays. And it is a comedy, by the way. It'd better be!

KW: *Wow. That is a great story. Congratulations.*
SL: Thank you, thank you and thank you.

KW: *How did you first meet Jose?*
SL: It was actually through my work as a vocal coach.

KW: *What was your impression of him?*
SL: I don't remember how he came to me, but as I recall he already had been to the open call for *The King and I* and he was being called back for Lun Tha. And my impression of him was he was very young, very beautiful and very, very talented. He just had it written all over him.

Can I wax a little rhapsodic right now?

KW: *Yeah, please.*
SL: I do a series of cabaret concerts on Long Island in one of the Guggenheim mansions, and I call singers that I've loved working with. And I don't even remember when it was that I called Jose for this, but the thing that always astonishes me about him is that he's

completely capable of living in whatever genre you put him. So that he can sing "I Have Dreamed" from *The King and I* as beautifully as he sings Adam Guettel's "Hero and Leander" as beautifully as he sings "Just Once," the old James Ingram pop song. He can sing in any musical style without sacrificing the integrity of what is required. It's one of the amazing things about him.

And he actually did a reading and a recording of a show of mine some years ago, and I was trying to figure out who could possibly play this, and I smote my forehead and went, "Oh my God, it's Jose, of course it's Jose." He was so easy and fun to work with.

Somebody said to me years ago, "If you want to have a career in the theatre there are three things you have to do and in this order: number one, don't be late; number two, be nice to work with; and number three, be good at your job." And it's so true. Jose is wonderfully optimistic and has a delightfully positive energy.

When I hired him for this cabaret performance, we also had him do his big song "My Unfortunate Erection" from *Spelling Bee*. He wondered if that would be too much for this crowd and I said, "Oh, no, no, no, no, no." I mean, part of it is because he's so lovable, that this rather older stage crowd was not unhappy watching Jose sing about his erection. It's a testament to his genuine likability that he can get away with that.

KW: *It's interesting—you're talking about his ability to sing all types of songs. Jose and I also talked about the range of the characters he's played; from a leading character like Lun Tha in* The King and I *to character roles, like El Gato in* Wonderland. *And of course you just mentioned his role as Chip Tolentino in* Spelling Bee. *Do you find in your work with Broadway actors and singers that it's common for an actor to have that kind of range?*

SL: Oh no, not at all. I mean, you can't have a conversation about this without discussing Jose's ethnicity which, I'm sure, has in many ways served him well and in other ways has not. He's Filipino. And so there are roles that he can't play. Although we live in a world where those barriers are blessedly changing that's still a part of the story, there's no question. But his versatility is profound.

You know, he just opened in *Here Lies Love* [at New York's Public Theatre] playing Marcos himself. Has he played [other] bad guys?

KW: *You know, I don't think so.*
SL: I don't think so either. He works all the time. I mean, there is no other Jose Llana. There's no other Asian-American man working in the musical theatre as regularly as he; maybe there's Jason Tam, but I think Jose was a little bit of a trailblazer.

KW: *When Jose and I were talking about* Wonderland *he mentioned making big choices in his audition for the role of the cat, El Gato. He said, "I think you either go big or go home." Clearly that worked for* Wonderland *since he was cast. How do you think that mentality has worked in other ways for Jose in his career, if it has?*
SL: I mean clearly it has because he has sustained a career for a long time now starting from a ridiculously young age. I rarely encourage anybody to make big choices. I encourage people to make *specific* choices, and I would say, bold choices. Big can be dangerous for some people, but because Jose's sense of reality is very grounded in his work, he can make big choices.

One of the things that I always tell my clients is part of the reason to make specific choices—this is the teacher in me speaking now—is certainly so that we can see how deeply you can burrow into material, but also so that you're not in the room auditioning. You're actually in the room singing to your boyfriend's mother who's just told you blah, blah, blah, and you're singing to express blah, blah, blah because this is the situation that's happening. Anything to make it not an audition.

KW: *Do you believe actors should, when they go into an audition, treat it like a performance?*
SL Oh, absolutely. I mean it is a performance in as much as you could always go deeper. And should, whenever possible.

KW: *Jose also talked about how important his work ethic has been especially since we're talking about him preparing for auditions. I don't know if you've had an experience with him where you saw his work ethic in use?*
SL: I mean right back to the beginning, Lun Tha, we really, really worked that material. It was clear that they were interested; it was down between him and the guy who ended up understudying for him.

I mean, it's funny even to talk about it because I find the work ethic and Jose are sort of inseparable in a way because I think of him as such a hard worker. He brings so many skills to the table. He's a real musician to his bones. And that's years of preparation.

KW: *What would you say was the most important turning point in Jose's career?*
SL: He's twenty years younger than I and watching his coming out process was just beautiful to me, and certainly informed his work.

KW: *Do you think that helped him become a more dynamic performer, or more confident?*
SL: Oh absolutely. I mean we as artists, we are our instrument. And the more honest and open one can be about all aspects of oneself, I think that affects the work deeply. How could it not?

KW: *What would you say are some of Jose's best qualities as a performer?*

SL: His emotional availability, top of the line, his extraordinary vocal technique, and as I said before, his ability to sing beautifully in any number of styles.

KW: *What kind of feedback have you heard about Jose's auditions? Are there one or two things that he consistently does right?*

SL: That's an interesting question. I think he's so profoundly himself. You know, what you see is what you get. I don't think there's a lot of artifice about Jose in the world in any way. And I think that just translates thrillingly.

KW: *That leads me to the next question which you've kind of already answered, but I'm going to ask it anyway. In her book* Acting Qs *writer Bonnie Gillespie says that "working performers seem to have tapped into a sense of authenticity that most aspiring actors search for." Do you feel that's been true for Jose?*

SL: Oh, absolutely. I mean that's the thing about Jose. I have one friend who is a Tony Award-winning actress in musicals and hates, hates, hates the notion of any kind of cabaret performing. I've tried to bring her into that setting. Part of the reason Jose is so good at it is because he's just himself. Not to say that she's not, but she is a different kind of performer. You know, Jose walks onstage and there it is. There he is.

KW: *You see him in totality.*

SL: And always authentic.

KW: *How important a role has type played for Jose? We talked about his range, but has type or lack of type, been a good thing for him? And does he have a clear idea of his type?*

SL: Oh absolutely. Look, he's a very good-looking, six foot tall Asian-American who sings like a motherfucker. [*Laughs*] There are not a lot of people around about whom one can say that sentence.

KW: *Yeah, I believe that's true! How important a role has talent played for Jose?*
SL: Oh, it's all one and the same. I mean, he's exquisitely talented.

KW: *How important would you say his belief in himself has been and have you had a personal experience with him that illustrates that belief?*
SL: I mean, it's sort of a cyclical thing. You can't do it without a belief in yourself and yet we're always looking for a belief in ourselves. I've always had the feeling that Jose was raised really well, that his family was very loving so that he was always able to be confident without being over-preening.

I'm also a great believer that for many actors that confidence actually masks a terrible lack of confidence. I don't think that's so with Jose.

KW: *You mean those performers are able to sort of turn it on when they need to?*
SL: Oh yeah, turn it on when they need to and get past it. You know, they're able to sort of step over their genuine lack of confidence in themselves.

KW: *How would you describe Jose overall, as an actor and as a friend?*
SL: I know I keep saying this, but what you see is what you get. I think that part of Jose's charm is his easy directness. And it's all completely real. And as a friend, you know, he's just there and present.

As somebody who has also taught for a million years, Jose is brilliantly talented. And I use that word advisedly. And he's also lucky that the gifts he has add up in the right way.

But it's not always so for people. I remember once this couple came to coach with me. They just moved to New York and he was really good looking and she was not so good looking. But she had four hundred times more talent than he. And I thought, "He's going to be working in ten minutes and she's not, she will work years from now and their marriage is not going to last." And all of that, all of that is exactly what happened.

All the parts of the package, if you want to call the actor the package, add up to something that's going to be successful. And that's because actors are commodities. We hate to think of it that way but they are commodities. And Jose had the discipline to take all of those God-given gifts and make them work for him.

KW: *Last question. All of the statistics tell us that acting is an incredibly difficult profession. At any given time there are far more actors out of work than are working. However, Jose has defied those odds, enjoying quite a bit of success. In addition to all the other ways you've told me, how has he done it?*
SL: He's genuinely a loving person.

KW: *He does seem really humble and conscientious.*
SL: Yes, yes he is. And you know there's the difference between aggressive and assertive. Jose never has felt in any way aggressive. Assertive, yes.

KW: *And he mentioned doing benefits quite often to keep his name and his face out there, but also to help others. I thought how wonderful that is to do all that work to give back. Nice thing.*

SL: Yes. And he's often sung a particular song of mine at benefits, which I'm always grateful for.

KW: *Which one is that?*
SL: A song called "Museums." When I perform it it's clearly my story and I'm sort of boring into my audience. He's much more expansive. It's a bigger story when he sings it.

Jose Llana Success Team Member

JOAN LADER

Ken Womble: *Joan, thank you so much for talking with me.*
Joan Lader: My pleasure.

KW: *As a voice coach based in New York, you work with some of the finest singers on Broadway. Could you give me an example or two of how you work with actors who are doing eight shows a week on Broadway and really using their voices extensively?*
JL: I use a very holistic approach with every singer. It's not only the very small area of the neck that needs to be exercised. Every performer should have a checklist of do's and don'ts. This does not involve the sound, but rather information on vocal hygiene. For example, hydration, medications, dietary concerns, etc. Posture and breath management are evaluated and recommendations are made. Areas of tension, maladaptive behaviors are addressed and students are then referred to osteopaths, massage therapists, chiropractors, Pilates instructors, Feldenkrais practitioners, Alexander teachers, etc. Vocal evaluation and lessons should include vocalises that address breath, tone, focus and support.

KW: *Do they generally respond? I mean, do they create those new habits?*

JL: Usually, yes, because they want to keep their job.

KW: *Patti LuPone called you "the singing teacher in New York City," and you've coached Broadway and film stars like Miss LuPone, Sutton Foster, Hugh Jackman and Anne Hathaway. Clearly you're great at what you do. Could you just give me a couple of different approaches, ways that you would work with actors?*

JL: The one-to-one relationship is what's most important. You know, many people have the same information and the reason one teacher is better than another has to do with communication. You have to listen, really listen! Some people respond to a lot of information in terms of anatomy and physiology. Others don't. And so you have to find ways to make them feel it. Some people may have to move their arms, jump around or loosen their necks. There are people that you just have to show things to and they imitate you. At times students are angry or upset, and you have to be able to reach them in order for them to work.

KW: *You met Jose Llana in 1995 when he auditioned for the role of Lun Tha in the Broadway revival of* The King and I. *How did you meet?*

JL: He was sent to me. The conductor said, "I'm not sure, he's very young, that he can do this because they hired opera singers against him." And he sang for me. I thought it was a nice voice, but I was afraid of the top. They wanted an answer right away and I said, "Well, I'm not sure that he can do it." And they said, "Okay, thank you very much."

The producers came back to me several weeks later and said, "Look, we still really like him. Would you consider working with him for three months and then we will re-audition him." And I said sure.

So we worked, and he absolutely took my breath away. He was such a musician and caught on so quickly. It was one of the most stunning voices I had ever worked with. The rest is history; he got the part.

KW: *What was your first impression of him, in addition to his singing?*
JL: He was a very sweet boy, eager to learn, extremely good looking and had an innate musicality.

KW: *Jose said that you were "a mentor and a guiding force" in his career. And, clearly, he's gotten great value out of your work together. Over the years what changes and improvements have you seen in his voice and his performance style?*
JL: I think he's become a much stronger actor for one thing. But vocally he's matured. His voice is fuller and richer and his musicianship is superior. You should listen to the recording of him—I just heard this on Sirius radio and I hadn't heard it in so long—from *Flower Drum Song* of "You Are Beautiful." It is stunning.

KW: *As you know, Jose also appeared in a number of other Broadway shows, among them* Rent, Street Corner Symphony, *a long run in* The 25th Annual Putnam County Spelling Bee *and* Wonderland. *Did you work with him on the auditions for those shows?*
JL: We worked on material from the shows before auditions for, I think, each one of them. And, you know, once you're called back, you have to sing from the show. He is always so prepared and it was just a question of was he the exact type they were looking for. I never worried about him vocally. Jose has such an amazing ear. He can actually hear a piece of music once or twice and get it.

KW: *He said* The King and I *was his big break. However,* On the Town, *which he did in Central Park, was what helped him with his career because he played the Gene Kelly role from the movie and for the first time people saw him in a different way.*

JL: The mold was broken when they cast Jose...they were color blind.

KW: *Did that sort of open him up to other opportunities as far as casting? More range?*

JL: I think so. Then he did *Rent*, which was totally different as well. And things have changed in the theatre, you know. Thank goodness. People are not so narrow minded.

KW: *Jose talked about how important his work ethic has been for him, especially in preparing for auditions. Have you had an experience with him where you saw this work ethic in use?*

JL: Well, certainly the way he prepares a book. He makes sure that he has music that represents different periods of Broadway musicals so that there's some variety. He has pop music, country music, traditional music theatre as well as new composers' music ready to go. He's prepared to sing in many vocal styles. In other words, he's prepared.

KW: *What would you say are some of Jose's best qualities as a performer?*

JL: His musicality, his incredibly unique voice and his commitment to the work.

KW: *What would you say are one or two things that he consistently does right as a performer, as a professional actor?*

JL: He is willing to explore!

KW: *In her book* Acting Q's, *Bonnie Gillespie says that working performers seem to have tapped into a sense of authenticity that most aspiring actors search for. Do you see that in Jose?*
JL: Without a doubt.

KW: *How important a role, if any, would you say that type has played for Jose and does he have a clear idea of his type?*
JL: Well, he's done things that go from romantic lead to character parts. And it's changed as he's gotten older. So, I don't know that there is a specific type because it's really varied.

KW: *How important a role has talent played for him?*
JL: It's major, it's major. But talent alone isn't enough. You have to develop that talent and if you don't do everything to develop it then somebody else will be around the corner. However, you have to start with that.

KW: *How important would you say that his belief in himself has been for Jose?*
JL: I think it's very important. When you don't believe in yourself you hide. And things don't come out the way you want them to. It certainly affects your voice since your voice is definitely a barometer for your emotions.

KW: *It sounds like you're saying that becomes part of the job—believing in yourself.*
JL: Yeah.

KW: *How would you describe him overall as an actor?*
JL: Well, I've watched him grow as an actor. I think he was primarily a singer and there was some degree of indicating, but he's really learned to get inside a character and view the world as if

it's happening for the first time through the eyes of this character. I've watched him do that and that's really very exciting.

KW: *Last question. All of the statistics tell us that acting is an incredibly difficult profession. At any given time there are far more actors out of work than are working. However, Jose has defied those odds and enjoyed quite a bit of success. In addition to all the things you've told me, how do you believe he's done it?*
JL: That's a very difficult question to answer. Jose is a true professional. He continues to study and grow and is able to *survive* the disappointments and the ups and downs of work in the theatre.

KW: *Anything else you'd like to add?*
JL: His talent and perseverance have served him well.

What are the keys that have led Jose Llana to a successful acting career?

He has courage

Making a decision to become an actor and to have a career in the theatre can be daunting. It means making a commitment to a profession with far more applicants than jobs. It requires courage.

As a young man, Jose Llana's parents had high expectations of him becoming an engineer. Yet Jose had another plan and he summoned the courage to face them and declare his intention of becoming an actor.

And it seems that Jose has used his parents' challenge to his own benefit, as a metaphor for his career. He knows that if he can face them he can face any situation the acting profession throws at him.

He works hard and finds opportunities

Jose does everything possible to get into auditions for any role he's right for by reading the trade papers online and working proactively with his agent.

Joan Lader mentioned how impressed she is with the way Jose prepares his book for musical auditions and with his commitment to the work. Steven Lutvak adds that, "the work ethic and Jose are sort of inseparable."

He is talented

When I asked Joan and Steven about Jose's talent, they used superlatives such as "stunning" and "brilliantly talented." And because he is, as Steven calls him, "a real musician to his bones," Jose's work continues to grow.

He uses luck to his advantage

Jose was certainly at the right place at the right time when the 1996 revival of *The King and I* was being mounted on Broadway. With his youthful, handsome looks, Filipino ethnicity and beautiful voice Jose was perfect for the role of Lun Tha.

He was lucky to be a musical theatre actor in New York in the 1990s when racial barriers were beginning to come down in the theatre, winning the role of Gabey, a character traditionally played by a white male, in *On the Town* in Central Park. He feels lucky to have a good relationship with his agents at Paradigm and also lucky to do his best auditions when he's "stressed and nervous." And finally, Jose calls himself lucky because he's been able to make a living in the theatre.

Jose said "the only way to get success is if you combine preparation with luck and opportunity," and throughout his career Jose has done just that.

Auditioning is his job—and he loves it

Jose is willing to do more than most actors in his audition preparation, including spending money on vocal and acting coaches—investments that don't always get him the job, but seem to always yield positive results.

He has reframed his experience of auditions, turning them from the negative experiences many actors endure to exhilarating *opportunities* for work. When he auditioned for El Gato, a "ridiculously Latin, silly cat," in *Wonderland*, that sense of exhilaration freed him to make huge acting choices and won him the role.

And because of his thorough preparation Jose's auditions become performances. His willingness to totally commit has created other job prospects, as when his dynamic *Les Misérables* audition later led to his being cast in *Martin Guerre*. Jose knows that when he gives a great audition for one role he's also showcasing his ability to play other roles.

He is a unique type

As a Filipino-American actor Jose has faced challenges in casting, yet it seems more often than not he has turned his ethnicity into a positive factor. From the young lover Lun Tha in *The King and I*, to the drag queen Angel Schunard in *Rent*, to the corrupt Filipino president Ferdinand Marcos in *Here Lies Love*, Jose has defied convention by playing a wide range of both leading and character roles.

And, as Steven points, out, in every role he's completely authentic.

Clearly he has the talent to make those leaps of character. Steven said Jose's versatility is unusual and "profound" in the Broadway community of actors, adding that "there is no other Jose Llana."

He perseveres and has perspective

For even a successful actor like Jose a career in show business is inevitably a roller coaster of exhilarating highs followed by humbling lows. Yet, as a young actor Jose had only experienced the highs—a string of Broadway shows he thought would never end.

Then *On the Town* moved to Broadway and Jose wasn't asked to reprise his role. All of a sudden his roller coaster had come to a screeching halt. This was a tough pill to swallow, but what Jose found out, "not everything's going to come easily," was more important than his momentary setback. And instead of being defeated he persevered to become a mainstay of New York theatre.

He had also turned a negative into a positive and learned perspective. And when Jose forgets to have perspective his partner reminds him that whatever hardships he endures as an actor pale in comparison to the "bigger things in the world that are happening."

RICHARD PORTNOW

CHAPTER 10

Understand the Business and Pitch Positive

RICHARD PORTNOW

A veteran of stage, film, and television, Richard recently starred opposite Anthony Hopkins and Helen Mirren in the Fox Searchlight film *Hitchcock* and has appeared in the feature films *Perfect Stranger, Law Abiding Citizen,* and *The Spirit* among others.

Richard has been privileged to work with some of the best directors working in film today. They include Barry Levinson, the Coen Brothers, David Fincher, Woody Allen, Sydney Pollack, James Foley, Jim Jarmusch, Heywood Gould, Cameron Crowe and Sidney Lumet.

His latest guest star roles on television have included *CSI NY, The Mentalist, Hawaii Five-0, Franklin & Bash, Nip/Tuck, Cold Case, Boston Legal* and *Dirt.* He was a recurring guest star on the NBC series *Outlaw* starring Jimmy Smits and played attorney Hal "Mel" Melvoin on the Emmy winning HBO series *The Sopranos.*

Richard began his professional career at the famed Café La Mama in New York City. He starred on Broadway in *The House of Blue Leaves, A Month of Sundays,* and in the original cast of *Moonchildren* at the prestigious Royal Court Theatre in London. His most recent stage appearance was in Woody Allen's *Writer's Block.* The play was directed by Mr. Allen at The Atlantic Theater Company in New York.

Ken Womble: *Richard, I've seen your work for many years and I'm a fan.*
Richard Portnow: Thank you.

KW: *In so many things,* The Sopranos, Father of the Bride, Sister Act, Good Morning, Vietnam. *I really enjoy the specific character choices you bring to every role. Could you tell me a little bit about your preparation?*
RP: Sure. Actually the concept of choice was instilled in me by the teacher who did me the most good, Michael Howard. He talked about choice; when you are general, it is unexciting, but when you are specific, when you have made a choice, whether it's the right choice or not, at least there is something specific to watch and to embrace and you can run with it and let it lead you in many different directions. So when I'm breaking down a script, I try to go within the lines and figure out what choices I would make as I'm embracing the character's traits.

KW: *I actually studied with Michael too.*
RP: Did you really?

KW: *Yeah, I was there '85 to '87.*
RP: Oh I had already left by then. We just missed one another. I was with him in the earlier part of the decade.

Terrific teacher. You know he taught the Meisner technique which is based in sensory awareness. And he said one day during the coffee cup exercise, "You try to smell it … it's not there. If you saw the coffee cup in front of you'd be insane. You're imagining. It's not there. So you try to smell it. If you can't smell it, you try to taste it. And if you can't taste it, you try to see it. You tap on the side of it so you can hear it."

And then he said to us, "And if none of that works, fuck it! The exercise doesn't work for you! Move on!" That was the best advice I ever got because you can get stuck and that's the last thing you want to do.

So in my work I use anything and everything. Anything I can put my hands on, wrap my mind around, I will use, even if I reference previous performances because it's always going to be filtered through me. It will be my point of view.

One of the things you want to do, especially in the audition room, is win. And if you have to reference someone else's performance, do it! I use whatever I need to use in order to illuminate the scene and the human condition that is inherent in the scene.

KW: *I love that expression, "You want to win." So what caused your first spark of interest in becoming a performer?*
RP: Oh, that's a good question and a good answer. I was not burning to be an actor. I was in Brooklyn College, and I was flunking out. At that time the conflict in Vietnam was starting to escalate. Back then if a guy of draft age was able to walk, they would send him overseas. And I didn't want to go.

However, when you were in college back then you were deferred. They couldn't take you. And a friend of mine said, "Well dude, you can't flunk out. They'll send you to Nam." And I said, "What do I do?" He said, "Take acting. You take the course, you get an A. *Guaranteed*…because they want to encourage you, they want to build your confidence. And there are no papers to write, no books to read, no tests to take, always pretty girls in the class." It sounded like a great deal to me. So I said, "Terrific. Where do I sign?" And that's how I got involved.

I did not shine in college. The faculty seemed to infer, "What are YOU doing here?" But the minute I got out of college something clicked. I guess I found something in myself and I scored immediately.

KW: *What happened that made you score immediately?*
RP: I really don't know what it was that I found in myself. I can't put my finger on it. But my sister had told me about the Café La MaMa and I tried to get in there in 1966 and they wouldn't give me the time of day. And then the head of the drama department directed a little play there and asked his class who's interested in doing three lines? And my hand shot up!

And I showed up early for rehearsal one day and Ron Link and Tom Eyen were casting their extravaganza, *Give My Regards to Off Off Broadway* and I walked in. I was nineteen-years-old, I had a full head of hair, I was thin and cute and they said, "What are you doing here?" And I said, "I'm here to rehearse!" And they said, "We're casting our new play, would you like to try out?" And I did and they cast me and that started the ball rolling.

I think, perhaps, what I found was that all I had to do was be myself, and that's all we can ever be. We can only be ourselves within the given circumstances of the play. I am playing a character, but I'm always Richard Portnow. I'm embracing the givens for the character and coloring them with my point of view. For instance, I might be called upon to play a character awaiting execution. I need to ask myself, "How would I respond to that set of circumstances?" By using the magical "as if" and by taking into account the time period of the piece, the place, the story line, etc.

I was very green and just took it for granted that I knew what I was doing and it worked out. I had them fooled and I've still got them fooled!

KW: *[Laughing]*

RP: One of these days they're going to find out that I'm a charlatan and that's going to be it.

KW: *Since then, of course, Café La Mama has become internationally renowned.*

RP: Ellen [Stewart] is gone now, but when my parents would come to see the plays, because I did many plays for her, she would say to my mother, "You're his real mother, but I'm his other mother." She was very supportive and we liked each other a lot.

Judy Abbot, George Abbot's daughter, was the head of new talent [at the William Morris Agency]. I got an interview with her through a friend and she said, "Well, you haven't done anything. But something in your eyes tells me you've got what it takes." And she signed me up, and right out of the gate I scored a huge play and was flown over to London to do the original production of *Moonchildren* by Michael Weller. I created the part that Steven Elliot eventually did on Broadway.

And after that I quit acting for seven years and knocked around the world. I had learned how to tend bar, and I let that skill take me to London where I ran two different night clubs and tended bar in Rome and in Amsterdam as well.

KW: *Do you think that experience made you grow up a bit when you went back into the business?*

RP: Yeah, I learned about people. And, you know, learning about people is crucial to being able to illuminate people on stage or in front of the camera.

But when I came back, I expected the world and the world was not served up and I became disillusioned. The shiny patina of youth had dimmed somewhat and it wasn't as easy, you know. By then I was thirty, thirty-one years old and it was a different ballgame. It took me ten years to break through and my forties were my most productive years.

KW: *What was your first break in New York?*
RP: I was doing regional theatre and I went to an open cattle call for the Berkshire Theatre Festival and it was run by a woman named Josephine Abady. And we struck a chord of rapport together. I was not cast. But we liked each other, something clicked.

And then she started casting me regionally and directed me in *The Dresser* at the Cincinnati Playhouse in the Park, *A Grand Romance* at the Long Wharf and *Tally's Folly* at the Merrimack Repertory Theatre. And then she cast me for a season at the Berkshire Theatre Festival. And the Berkshire Theatre Festival had stars in the leads and real comers in the supporting roles. And it was interesting because when they gave out the cast list, next to each actor's name is their agent and all these comers had hot agents at the time. But when you looked across the page from my name there was no agent because I didn't have one. I couldn't even get a bad agent. No one wanted me. I had a commercial agent and I did commercials, but I had loftier dreams.

The leading lady of the first play that I was in was a wonderful actress by the name of Anne Twomey. We became friends. We liked to talk. And she asked me one night, "Who's your agent?" And I said, "I don't have one." She said, "Why not?" And I told her that nobody wanted me. She said, "Well that's ridiculous, you're terrific!" And she said her agent from Writers and Artists would be coming, "If he doesn't, I'll fire him. I'll introduce you and he will give you an interview."

When the Berkshire season ended, I returned to New York and called Anne's agent, Jonathan Sand, may he rest in peace, a wonderful guy, a terrific agent. Writers and Artists was a powerful agency at the time, and I had not done anything but regional theatre. I hadn't done any movies or TV shows or Broadway, hadn't even done Off Broadway.

And I just pitched positive. I never mentioned anything that I had not done. I never said, "Well I haven't done any TV yet." I never said, "I don't have a reel." No. I pitched positive. "A, B, C, always be closing," *Glengarry Glen Ross*. And I was closing from the minute I walked in; I'd discovered how to market myself. I realized I'm a suit. I wear suits. I'm always well shaved, well groomed and hard. I'm an urban guy and I have an edge. I am, if I may be so bold, a tough guy. And I told him this. I defined myself for him. I said, "The only reason I'm not doing movies, playing this type of part is because you are not my agent. You get me in the room, I'm going to knock the ball out of the park. We're going to make nothing but money."

And he said, "Well, I got to say I couldn't tell much about you as an actor from the play that I saw you in because you had thick glasses, a moustache and a French accent and were onstage for two minutes."

KW: *It would be tough to discern a tough guy out of that.*
RP: "But from the way you present yourself here in this room, today, in front of me, I'm inclined to believe everything you say. And if the rest of the agents do, you're on."

And they did and they signed me and then I didn't get a job for a year! [*Laughing*] I must've had fifty auditions, didn't score. Why? Because I was nervous.

And I imagined what must have happened up at the agency after ten or eleven months of failed auditions was that the assistant who took my call most likely said, "Jonathan, it's Richard Portnow," and she would probably roll her eyes and he would say, "Tell him I'll get back to him." You know, I wasn't exciting. I hadn't scored.

So I went into an audition for a TV show called *The Equalizer* and I had, by then, just fucking given up. I thought, "Well, I'm not going to get this either. So I'll just go in and have fun." Relaxation. And *bang* I scored that and then I got job after job after job, including studio films and TV shows and Broadway.

And you know, I owe it all to Josie Abady, all to her. She passed on. And I think about her every day, and she was the shining light in my life and career. She was my best friend and she was just a wonderful, supportive director, producer, friend. Without her I might still be tending bar.

KW: *That is a great story and it says so much about the power of relationships.*
RP: Oh yeah. And that's one of the things that I would suggest to any actor. Be nice to everyone, especially in Hollywood, because you never know who you're insulting. The next day you might be sitting across the desk from them and they have the power to put you in *CSI*. But you have offended them the previous night by being nasty. *Always* be nice. It's really important.

KW: *You were based in New York until 1987. Was your plan to stay in New York and be a stage actor?*
RP: My plan was to stay in New York. I was on Broadway, I was also doing studio feature films, and I was doing television shows. I grew up in New York, it's all I ever knew, I was happy there… and I didn't know how to drive. So California was not a plan. I was already making it, if you will, in New York and I had no intention of coming out to Hollywood. None.

KW: *So what changed that?*
RP: I did a film for Barry Levinson called *Good Morning, Vietnam* and we shot in Thailand—and that was the second one I had done

in a row for Barry—the first was *Tin Men*. And I became friendly with his producer, Mark Johnson.

And Mark asked me towards the end of the shoot what I was doing when we wrapped and I said, "Well, I'm going home." He said, "Have you ever been to LA?" I said, "No, never been." And he said, "Your plane has to land in LA to get back to New York and it's a first class open return ticket. Why don't you stay at my house and see if you like the town?" And I said, "Well, that sounds good."

So I did that and then on my second day in Los Angeles I called the agency that represented me at the time and told them I was in town. I had never met the LA office. They said, "Why don't you come up?" And I did. And the agent that I sat down with said, "Would you want to go on any auditions? Everybody wants to meet you." And I said, "What do you mean, 'everybody wants to meet me?'" because this is the very beginning of my career as far as having broken through into the mainstream. He said, "While you were in Thailand a lot of your movies were released and TV shows were broadcast and you've arrived with a loaded gun." And I said, "Well yeah, sure I'd like to meet people, but I don't know how to drive." He said, "Learn fast because you're meeting over at Universal with Cameron Crowe tomorrow." That was for *Say Anything*.

As far as I was concerned I was just passing through. Consequently, I brought no need into the room with me when I met producers and auditioned for directors because I was not in Hollywood to make it. As far as I was concerned I had already made it. I wasn't bringing in any desperation, "Oh, I've got to get this part," and that's very attractive to producers.

I have been on the other side of the desk. I have coproducer two films. And when someone walks in who doesn't need the job, they're not at all nervous or bringing anything into the room except positive energy—it's *very* attractive.

And I nailed a dozen jobs in a row, literally. Twelve in a row.

KW: *You said you brought no need or desperation into the room because you'd already made it in New York. That's an incredible lesson for actors.*
RP: Oh yeah.

KW: *Have you been able to sort of maintain that sense when you go into auditions now?*
RP: Well now, at this point, I'm a known actor in the business. Anyone that I'm going in to meet knows who I am.

I just finished co-starring with Anthony Hopkins and Helen Mirren in *Hitchcock*. I have four scenes with Anthony Hopkins and one with Helen Mirren. It was a very heady experience, you know, it was a dream cast: Anthony Hopkins, Helen Mirren, Scarlett Johansson, Jessica Biel.

I really wanted that film. And I set out to get it. Sometimes when I really want it I do much more work than when it's a part that I've done twenty times already. You know, if I'm going to go into NBC to try out for a mob boss I've done that part over and over and over. So it's not going to be that exciting. But this project was different. It was something I had never done before. And while I wanted it as much as I've ever wanted any part, I left the need outside.

KW: *That's a great quote.*
RP: Well, I can talk for a long time about auditions. I used to teach a seminar about what you need in addition to talent in order to function effectively in our business. It has nothing to do with acting technique. I've learned over forty years through trial and error. You know, don't make the mistakes I made.

Everybody should want to win that part. And, you know, there are lots of good actors out there, *lots* of good actors. Why don't some of them get the part? They don't know how to do the audition process effectively—which means more than just the acting.

KW: *What are a couple of other pieces of advice you'd give about auditioning?*

RP: Think of your audition as a rehearsal. When you go into a rehearsal you're as free as a bird. So think about the audition as a rehearsal for a job you've already got and that will empower you. You'll walk in with the confidence that you walk into rehearsals with.

Another piece of advice is never put the sides down. Memorize them. Know them inside out. But never put them down. Once you put the sides down, it's no longer an audition. They are seeing the performance, and they think that's as good as it's going to get. You act as if you have to read some of it. So you look down at the paper even though you know the line. And they are then seeing a reading, an audition, not a finished performance.

KW: *It sounds like you're saying bring in a performance, but let them think it's not a performance.*

RP: Exactly. They want to see what's going to be on the screen. They don't want to see an actor trying to find it in front of them. They want to see the performance.

So, you're bringing in your best work. You never get a second chance to make a good first impression. You don't want to screw up in a casting room. Ever. It can hurt you in more ways than one.

KW: *How do you handle nerves?*

RP: You trust the material and your preparation. It's important to be a little nervous, that's necessary to keep you on your toes. But being too nervous you can be overwhelmed and that will undermine the work. So when I was just breaking through, I was nervous but I would trust the work. And that would help enormously.

When you're auditioning for a pilot, my advice would be to not discuss the money with your agent. Because the way things work is you have three tryouts for a TV pilot. The first time you're in front of the producers. If you get past that, then you do the same thing for the company that's going to be producing the project. And then you have the network tryout. And that's when all of the important executives from NBC watch you.

Before you do that, your deal is in place. Because if they want you and the deal's not in place then you can say, "Okay, I want a hundred thousand an episode," and they're screwed because they've already offered you the part. Knowing in advance (because at this point you've discussed it with your agent) that you can walk out of that room with $50,000 a week can undermine the work.

So my advice is trust your agent, that they're going to get you the best possible deal and don't ask about the money.

KW: *It sounds like you really trust your team.*
RP: Yeah I do. They're very good. I've been with Buchwald [Don Buchwald & Associates] for sixteen years. I don't jump around, and I wouldn't advise any actor to jump around.

KW: *When you book a role are there things that you hear from your agent or from the director, things they liked about your work?*
RP: Well, no, you don't really get much feedback. What I get now is we're so happy that you're doing it. When I got *Hitchcock* the producer said, "We're just so happy that you're doing this for us. We really wanted you." And that's nice to hear.

Back in the day when I first started working I would ask them, "Why did you cast me?" And I remember I got a commercial for Finesse Shampoo and there were all these models, these perfect looking people with good hair and perfect noses and me, bald, sweating profusely. And I asked the producer—his name was

François—I said, "Why did you cast me?" He said [*with French accent*], "I like your style man, you got style."

So, you have to embrace your own personal style. And I think it's important to dress for the part. You're not going to wear jeans and a tee shirt if you're going in for a stockbroker. Put a suit on. You know, show up looking like a million bucks.

When I interview with people, sometimes I refuse to read. I say, "I'll meet, I won't read." I walk in looking like I make more than they do. They want to smell success walking in that room, man. They want it. They want someone that, "Jesus, this guy, he could probably produce the movie out of his own pocket."

KW: *How important is confidence when you walk in the room?*
RP: That's the name of the game. It is *all* about confidence. They do not want to see a shrinking violet in front of them. They don't want to see an actor who's got problems. They're making up their minds as you are walking in the room. You want to walk in owning the room.

That's one of the things I told my actors, "Own it. Own the room, own the audition. It's your time. Walk in brimming with confidence."

KW: *In your long career you've played many different character roles. How important has type been for you and has that been more positive or negative?*
RP: Okay. This is what I tell my students, "If you can—not everyone can—but if you can, type yourself. When you sit down in front of an agent for an interview, he's going to ask you, 'So, who are you? How do you see yourself?'"

If you went to Harvard and were brought up in Connecticut but you look like a hillbilly, you've got to look in the mirror and say, "What do I look like?" If you look like a hillbilly, you just jump into that accent and tell that agent [*with southern accent*], "I play hillbillies." And he will say, "Right, hold on a second," and he'll call *Lonesome Dove, Part 2* and say, "I've got this kid over here, I'm sending him right over." And you'll get the part.

And my strategy was exactly that. Not to play hillbillies, but when I sat down in front of Jonathan Sand, I took a very objective look at myself and I realized what I looked like and what I could do, how I could function effectively in this business. I knew back then that I don't kiss the girl. That is not how the business sees me and never would. I knew that I don't wear a sweater. I'm a suit. I knew that I'm not rural. I'm urban. This is the way I looked. Not what I was capable of acting.

I mean, I could act like a southerner, I could act like a college professor. But that's not what I looked like. So I typed myself. I walked in, I said to them, "I play wise guys. I got the look, I got the voice, I got the instrument, and I certainly have the experience. You get me in the room. We'll be doing *Gangster Chronicles* next week."

And my strategy was that I knew I would work in that role. And I knew that I would do the same part over and over for a while.

But in so doing I would stop tending bar, I'd start making real money and I would establish credibility as an actor who works in front of the camera. And a few years down the line I would be able to expand my horizons in terms of the parts I played and that's *exactly* the way it worked out.

You want to tend bar or you want to work in front of the camera? Get over it. Get in. Start working. Play into your strengths.

I was lucky. I got a mug. And I got a voice. And they just were given to me. If you look like everyman, that can also help you. I mean look at Paul Guilfoyle. You know who he is?

KW: *Yeah.*

RP: Okay, he looks like everyman. In the crowd he disappears. But looking like everyman he gets parts like everyman, and constantly.

KW: *Edward Norton sort of has that everyman look.*

RP: Absolutely. And he plays anything. I mean from *American History X* to *Primal Fear* to *Fight Club*, the guy plays anything and everything. He's also very, very talented.

Also, it's always good to be able to say something like, "I'm a young Robert Loggia." If a studio executive said well, "Who are you?" I'd say, "I'm a young Robert Loggia. I'm tougher and I'm sexier, but basically I'm a young Robert Loggia."

So if they ask you something, say, "I'm a darker James Franco, I'm a tougher Tom Cruise, I'm a softer Jennifer Lopez."

If you can equate yourself with someone then they know what to do with you, how to pitch you. They're waiting for you to tell them, the same way people that are holding your audition are waiting for the right person to walk in and illuminate the character in a way that they don't know.

KW: *Right, exactly. And in film and television the roles are new; no one's every played them before, as opposed to theatre.*

RP: That's right.

KW: *Richard, I've heard it said about the acting profession that if you have a fallback plan you'll fall back. Do you believe that?*

RP: Well I....

KW: *Have you ever thought about it?*

RP: No, I've never really thought about that. I never had a fallback plan, ever. I knew how to tend bar and that was my survival job. But you know I never thought about quitting acting, but then as it turned out, I did quit for seven years. But when I came back after the seven year hiatus, for a decade all I could get were commercials and I did a lot of background work as an extra and I continued to tend bar.

And by the time I was approaching my late 30s, I saw friends that I knew who were not in the business buying co-ops and fancy cars and I thought, "Man, I'm making $25,000 a year here with these commercials, I'm not making a lot of money, this isn't what I expected. But, you know, it's better than tarring a roof."

There does seem to be a bit of truth in that catch phrase, "If you have a fallback plan, you're going to fall back."

KW: *Richard, what would you say is your best quality as an actor?*
RP: Confidence. From confidence comes relaxation. If you're confident, if you know what you're doing, then you can relax into it. And through that relaxation you get the best work. All good work comes from a relaxed instrument and confidence will give you that relaxation. I'm a very confident guy.

KW: *I couldn't tell that!* [Laughing]
    I watched your reel and I thought the placement of the last scene, which is from The Sopranos *was perfect when you said—*
RP: —"You're worth every penny."

KW: *Yeah.*
RP: That was intentional.

KW: *It sounds like that's what you believe.*
RP: Well, yeah, I do. I think they're lucky to have me.

KW: *What part has momentum and timing played in your career?*
RP: I think it's been all important. Momentum, there's nothing like it. Sometimes it does dry up, you know, it's a capricious business. Every actor has ups and downs and the momentum stops. But when it's there—and it's there for me right now—I want it to continue.

And timing is also very, very important. But you can't do anything about timing. You can't mold it or shape it, it's just there. You know. I arrived in LA at the right time. I just arrived at the right time.

KW: *Yeah, it sounds like it was the perfect time for you.*
RP: Yeah, but you know timing is similar to luck. I was lucky to show up in the summer of 1987. If I had come out to LA in the summer of 1990, things might have been very different.

KW: *How important is your belief in yourself to your success?*
RP: It's all important.

KW: *All important.*
RP: Oh yeah. You know, creative visualization also helps. Seeing yourself in front of the camera, seeing yourself sitting at home and getting that call.

Belief in yourself is key. If you don't believe in yourself, no one else is going to believe in you. You can't second guess yourself or doubt yourself. It's very, very important.

KW: *What part would you say talent has played in your success?*
RP: It's played a gigantic part. If you're not that talented, you can still do well because of your looks. Usually those are the really beautiful people. Eventually those careers dry up because the looks do.

A character guy's got to be talented, you know. You have to be able to deliver and deliver something that they're not expecting, like, "Whoa, I never thought about that possibility." So talent is key.

KW: *Yeah, I hear that over and over. But I think some people who want to be professional actors don't perceive that sometimes. They see actors who they think are not that talented working. And I say, "No. They're the small group. The big group is the really talented ones."*

RP: Exactly. It's the small group that is in front of the camera because the camera loves them. They're physically beautiful and they might be very charming in the room. I know actors that can just charm the pants off studio executives, but they're terrible actors.

KW: *What are one or two of the best pieces of advice that you've ever been given about your career?*

RP: That's a tough one. I haven't really been given too much advice. You know, I've arrived here basically on my own. I was blessed with a friendship that helped me along the way.

Well, one piece of advice I could give is be nice. Word gets around…"Oh, he's difficult."

Barry Levinson, perfect example. He's casting *Tin Men*, all right? And he's getting down to the wire and he needs a particular role filled. And they're thinking "Well, maybe this particular actor is right." So they fly him in from New York to Baltimore because they were already in Baltimore doing prep. And the guy goes in and, I don't know what he did in the room, but I guess he acted like a bit of a dick because when he left Barry said, "I don't want that guy on my set." You know? He probably wasn't so nice or was maybe dismissive with an assistant.

So always be gracious. And when you're on the set be gracious. They like people that are fun to be around. Have a sense of humor about stuff. If you have an attitude they feel it, they don't like it and it will haunt you.

KW: *What would you say are a couple of the smartest things you've done for your career?*
RP: Marked myself. Understood what I looked like and I mean *really* understood. I'm incredibly handsome and sexy [*laughs*], but the industry doesn't see me that way and I got it, I understood that. So it's really being objective about what you visually present.

And I'm a firm believer in prepare, prepare, prepare. *Know* your material backwards and forwards. If you're trying out for a one scene part, but have the time to read the whole script, read the whole script. Why? Because the director might say, "You know, that was great, but I don't want an older guy…take a look at this part."

Do as much research as you can. Dress appropriately for the part. And now that we have the Internet you can research *any* director. So know a lot about the key players on the project: the director, the writer, and a couple of the producers. That's your homework. So that you can talk intelligently and you can say, "You know in the film *Pick-up Sticks* that scene with Melanie Griffith, man! What inspired you to do that?" You know? People love to talk about themselves! So get them talking about themselves and they'll think you're their best friend.

KW: *If you could go back and change one career decision what would it be?*
RP: It would have been to abstain from commercials and pursue film more aggressively. The look I affected when I did commercials was very, very different. There was nothing hard about me. I was a nice, ethnic boy. I would not have done that. I would have held out. And I would have tried to immediately define myself as

a film actor, as a serious, legitimate actor. I would've tried to be courageous enough to continue tending bar until I got a movie.

KW: *Okay, last question. All of the statistics tell us that acting is an incredibly difficult profession. At any given time there are far more actors out of work than are working. However, you've defied those odds, enjoying quite a bit of success in your career. In addition to all the many things you've told me today, how have you done it?*
RP: Gifts of money, sex and drugs.

KW: *Perfect! Thanks!*
RP: [*Laughs*] How have I done it? I've been persistent and I've made it my business to understand the business end of show business. And that's been key to my success, understanding that it is a *business*. It's not personal. Understanding that there are many variables that go into a casting decision and even though you might be the best actor in the room for that part you might be too tall, or not tall enough, or too fat, or not fat enough, or too bald or not bald enough. There are so many variables that go into it that you have no control over.

You have to embrace the positive energy of leaving a great audition and a great impression in that room, which is what I've always done. I've left rooms and felt, "Man, I could not have done that any better," and didn't get the part. But I can still derive positivity from having done an audition like that.

Because I know that when they think of Richard Portnow, even though I didn't get that part, they're going to think, "Boy that fucking guy was great. He was wrong for the part, but he was *great*."

Often I think that talent is there or it's not, you know, it's God given. Technique? That you can learn. Craft? You can learn. Business? You *must* learn.

KW: *That's a great quote. It was inspiring talking with you Richard.*
RP: Oh good, I'm glad. I like to inspire people.

Richard Portnow Success Team Member

RICHARD GABAI

Ken Womble: *Richard, you're an independent film and TV director, writer and producer. Could you tell me a bit more about your career?*
Richard Gabai: I was an actor as a kid, and then I got my degree in journalism from USC. In my senior year I started acting professionally and I had an agent and I found myself getting work, but I realized that I wasn't the type of person that had the desire to do the networking and pavement pounding that you really do need to do to have a successful acting career.

And I also realized that I had interests on the other side of the camera as well. So, I raised $40,000 and made a little independent movie called *Assault of the Party Nerds* that we shot in five days and ended up selling all over the world. So, I spent the next several years acting, but always directing like one movie a year. I had a lot of fun being an actor/director in those days.

I starred in a bunch of Roger Corman movies. I got a good amount of work, but it was fun…it was monster movies, you know, all kinds of crazy things.

The same directors would keep hiring me because they always knew I was going to be professional, I was going to know the lines, I wasn't going to be a pain in the butt, I would be okay with the lunch, and would hopefully bring something special to the role.

I slowly became less interested in worrying about my hair and whether or not I shaved that day and I got more and more interested in the filmmaking process. And I'm a songwriter, so I would often use my own music in the movies and that allowed me to segue into doing what I do most now, which is direct and produce.

I've always thought of the business very pragmatically. I try to make a film that either is sold or I know will sell and I think that's key for an actor as well.

I think that's one of the things that makes Richard Portnow brilliant beyond his talent; he understands that it's the movie business, it's not the movie hobby and it's not the movie "my parents didn't love me enough so I want to be an actor." It's the movie business.

I made a film called *The Bike Squad* which actually won a pretty prestigious award called the Genesis Award, which goes to movies that have animals in them. And that kind of got me on a streak of making some family films. And now I've been making these thrillers that we've been selling to A&E that air on Lifetime.

And that's when I first got the chance to work with Richard—on a film I made a couple years ago that was called *One Eighty*, but has been released on television under the title *Imaginary Friend*.

KW: *When you first met what was your impression of Richard?*
RG: My first impression of him was that he was approachable, sincere, and we just happened to have a good amount in common. I'm originally a New Yorker and he's a New Yorker and he was just completely unpretentious, not at all full of himself.

And let me tell you how we met. One of the producers on *Imaginary Friend* said, "You know, Richard's a friend of ours and he'd do a role for us."

And I've been a big fan of his since *Tin Men* and *Radio Days*, and I said, "The only role left is this apartment manager. It's a scene with Ethan Embry and it's a moment, but I mean it's a couple of lines. I'd be embarrassed to offer it to him." They said, "Well, we'll talk to him about it." They asked him. And he took the role!

And then he came to set and we instantly hit it off. We had a lot of common friends and common values. And he killed the scene. I mean he made nothing into something, you know? And he ended up coming to my holiday party, we had a good time and I said, "The second I read something that has your name on it, I'm sending it to you, something of substance." And that's when I got this project, *In the Dark*, and there's this detective character and I sent him the script and I said this thing is *you*. And we couldn't afford his rate, but the material was interesting enough to him and he took the job and he just hit this thing out of the park.

KW: *What does that say about him that he was willing to take the small role at first?*
RG: In my opinion it shows that he's extremely smart. He likes to go to work, he likes to do his job, but there is no ego involved. I mean, thank God he has an ego, but it's all about the work. And he's funny as all get out.

KW: *Yeah, he gave me a couple of funny lines…irreverent also.*
RG: Yeah, but I think it just shows that he really understands the business. I mean his set etiquette is without peer. He is a consummate professional.

You know, if his call is 7, at 6:20 you turn around and there he is sipping his coffee, "Good morning, Rich, how you doin' buddy?" You know? And that gives a director a comfortable feeling. Because there's a little piece of us that's always going to wonder if someone's going to show up. So that would go back to the advice to actors. If your call time is 7:30, show up at 7:00!

KW: *What would you say are some of his best qualities as a performer?*

RG: Well, the mechanics of acting to him are second nature. And you can't overstate the importance of mastering the mechanics of acting, the basics of not looking at your feet to hit marks and not looking at the camera and knowing your lines.

When people see him, they believe him and they're interested in him. And I don't know what that quality is, but when he speaks you pay attention.

He's like a classic film actor. He's so accessible you like him; there's something about him that you identify with. And you can't bottle that, you know?

KW: *He told me his best quality was confidence. How important, in your experience, is confidence for an actor?*

RG: It's extremely important. And being able to walk the line between confidence and arrogance, which Richard does so elegantly, is really a great trait. When Richard Portnow says he'll accept a role in one of my films I am done. I am done thinking about that role until I say, "Action." We're going to work on it on the set, we're going to tweak a performance, but I am not worried about it at all. And it's not just that he's got the confidence—he can bring it.

KW: *Well, do you find that for some actors you are a bit worried?*

RG: Oh, absolutely! Like you have a real emotional scene to get through and maybe they didn't even audition. They were hired by some other producer. And you don't know that they're going to be able to bring it. So you're nervous to get the scene. Just because somebody can nail something in an audition…they've never done it on a set. You never know until that day, that moment, if you're going to get it.

KW: *Richard has been a busy, working actor for over twenty-five years—quite an achievement in a very tough business. What do you see in him as a person and as a performer that's kept him going so long?*

RG: Well, he's an incredible optimist. You know, he's definitely the "silver lining" kind of guy. It's hard not to be upbeat around Richard. So, I think that that's a big plus. He has an amazing love for the craft.

I have the same feeling when I'm at work. I mean, it's so hard to get movies made and especially in the independent world. But when I'm at work I'm stoked, you know? And I'm always excited about the next movie I'm going to make.

I'm lucky enough to be shooting an airplane thriller and we're going to be on these airplane sets and it's just a childlike quality. It's a mature, childlike quality that Richard has.

KW: *That's interesting—a mature, childlike quality—two opposites coming together.*

RG: Yeah. Well, you know, if I was smart I'd have a real job. Of course you run into actors that are just plain children. I mean a lot of them are wonderful performers and good people, but Richard gets it.

He knows the position that I'm in. I've been a producer on a studio movie, I know what that's like, and I've also worked on $40,000 movies. And he's been in the biggest studio films and he's done the smallest independent. He knows what's at stake.

He also appreciates, like I do, how privileged we are. The fact that I actually make a living in this business is amazing to me. And I think he appreciates it as well.

KW: *Bonnie Gillespie says in her book,* Acting Q's, *that, "Working performers seem to have tapped into a sense of authenticity that most aspiring actors search for." Do you feel that's been true for Richard?*

RG: Yeah, that's a great quote. There's certainly no question about his authenticity. That absolutely applies to him.

KW: *How important a role has type played for Richard and does he have a clear idea of his type?*
RG: I think he has a look, but I don't think he's a type.

He could play a bumbling, mumbling imbecile type of guy and he could play the most sharp-shooting, sophisticated SOB you'd ever want to know. So, I wouldn't type Richard. I mean he's got a mug on him that the camera loves.

KW: *Yeah, he's got a great voice too.*
RG: He's got an *amazing* voice. In the trailer to *In the Dark* there's only one shot of him, but it's so poignant and his voice trails on. And when he delivers a line it goes kind of inside your body. And it's not just because he has a deep voice, it's because it has that authenticity. He's there, man. He's for real.

KW: *How important a role has talent played for Richard?*
RG: Wow. You've got to have that. I mean he has talent. If he didn't have talent, he wouldn't have the career that he has. Even though he's the nicest guy in the world, even though he's the most persistent guy, even though he's the most optimistic guy, at the end of the day, it's talent. I mean he didn't get that huge role in *Hitchcock* because he's nice.

KW: *Have you had a personal experience with him that illustrates his confidence, his will power, his belief in himself?*
RG: Yeah. I called him after I saw *Hitchcock* and I said, "Man, you absolutely lit up the screen and you nailed it!" And he kind of agreed with me. [*Laughs heartily*]

KW: [Laughs]
RG: … in the sweetest of ways, you know?

KW: *Right. Well, that's pretty much what he told me, too. And I didn't take it as arrogance at all. I took it as truth.*
RG: And let me tell you, it is the truth!

KW: *How would you describe him overall as an actor and a person?*
RG: I would describe him as a good friend and a very versatile and extremely confident actor.

KW: *Okay, last question. All of the statistics tell us that acting is an incredibly difficult profession. At any given time there are far more actors out of work than are working. However, Richard Portnow has defied these odds, enjoying quite a bit of success. How has he done it?*
RG: He nurtured God-given talent, he had the personality and the stick-to-it-iveness to ride it through.

It's all the things we've spoken about. And saying far more actors are out of work than are working is the understatement of the decade. I think there's ninety-five percent unemployment in the Screen Actor's Guild at any given moment. And the interesting statement about that statistic is that it's kind of that same five percent that keeps working.

I mean it does change as people get older and retire or pass on and the new kid comes up. But it's a microscopic percent that's working and an even smaller percent that actually make their living at it.

So Richard deserves a huge round of applause, and there's nobody I know that deserves it more.

Richard Portnow Success Team Member

MICHAEL GREENWALD

Ken Womble: *Michael, you are Vice President of Talent at Don Buchwald & Associates in Los Angeles. Could you tell me a bit about your company and the mediums you work in?*
Michael Greenwald: We're a bicoastal talent agency representing writers, directors, producers and actors in film and television.

KW: *What are you looking for in an actor that you want to sign?*
MG: Somebody who we believe is a pure talent. You know, we look at thespians from the actor perspective. We look also for actors that are triple threats...actors/writer/director/producers or actor/director/writers. But I think it's really about finding talent that has a broad range and very believable in their craft.

KW: *You represent Richard Portnow. How long have you known him and what was your first impression when you met?*
MG: I have worked representing Richard Portnow for sixteen years. When I saw Richard's work on screen, I saw he had an incredible ability and range, both in comedy and drama. And then meeting him in person I thought he was a very charming actor.

KW: *One of the things Richard told me in our interview was right out of college, and I quote, he "knocked around the world for a while," actually for seven years. And he said he learned a lot about people and how, "learning about people is crucial to be able to illuminate people on stage or in front of the camera." How important is that quality for an actor and how important has it been for Richard?*
MG: I think it's incredibly important. I think that performers need to grasp the roles that they're portraying from real life experi-

ences. They have to watch the way people behave and the actions of people to create these very real, lifelike characters on screen.

KW: *Richard also talked about some of the audition techniques he uses and I know he doesn't audition a lot these days. But when he does what do you hear that he does well, and maybe things that other actors* don't *do as well?*

MG: He always gives 110%, he's always off book, he creates his own character. He doesn't play it exactly always the way it's written on the page. He always creates something quite unique and has his own perspective and take.

And I think that's what is very interesting in the rooms in front of these very high level directors, whether it's a director like James Foley or Jim Jarmusch or some of the great directors Richard's worked for, including David Fincher and Norman Jewison, Sydney Pollack and Ivan Reitman. You have to bring a character to life, and I think what Richard does in those rooms is really move people.

I would probably say the only person that he's never gotten to audition in front of, but obviously created an impression, was when he did *Radio Days* for Woody Allen.

KW: *So he did the film but he didn't audition?*

MG: It's just a meeting in the back of a hotel room and they have a five or seven minute conversation and Woody Allen asks a bunch of questions and you answer them and he studies your character and he makes a decision whether he thinks you're visually right and the right fit for his perspective on the great films that he makes.

KW: *Wow, very interesting.*

MG: As well as watching their work on camera.

KW: *Richard also told me an actor wants to win, his word, in the audition room, and how important it is to walk into the room relaxed and not needing the job; although, of course, you want the job. How important do you believe those qualities are for an actor?*
MG: I think you have to walk into the room with a positive attitude and confidence. You're walking into a room and you're trying to give them a reason to not say "no." I think there are certain factors that come into play that you can't always really change, whether it's your height, whether it's your skin color, whether it's your look, for what they really want for a character.

But as a smart performer you absolutely want to walk into a room feeling like this is your job. And I think that Richard's always taken that sort of approach.

KW: *He also said that as an actor, "You have to embrace your own personal style." How important is that for an actor and how important has it been for Richard?*
MG: I think that the casting community wants to box performers into a particular type. And the actor's responsibility as a performer and a thespian is to create lots of different characters, surprise them.

And I think that Richard is quite capable of doing that when you look at the body of work that he's done over the years, from *Radio Days* all the way to *Good Morning, Vietnam*, to movies like *Barton Fink*, *Seven* and *Private Parts*, all the way up to the most recent films that he's done like *Hitchcock* and *Oldboy* for Spike Lee.

KW: *What would you say are some of his other best qualities as a performer?*
MG: I think that Richard knows how to charm people and make people feel good. You know, we'd like to believe that every role he goes up for he gets, but I think at the end of the day he always

walks away with a respect that they will think of him not only for the role that he auditioned for, but other potential upcoming films and television projects.

KW: *Richard also said that it's important to understand the business end of show business. How important is that for an actor and how does he approach the business end?*
MG: I think it's vital but, first and foremost is to master the craft. There has to be some kind of business savvy, but I think that's where agents like myself come into play. They can rely on the agents to help them with creating these opportunities, giving them career advice along the way, making decisions and negotiating on their behalf.

KW: *How important a role has talent played for Richard?*
MG: He's talented. The man's talented. To be able to go up in front of these top directors, and I probably left out several like Barry Levinson, Cameron Crowe, Joel Coen, you have to be able to walk in the room and convince them that you are that character. You are that person. Or, you have a take on the character you created on your own, which I think Richard does very well.

KW: *How would you describe him overall as an actor and as a person?*
MG: Like I said, he's very warm. He's extremely talented. He's very gracious and he has a very wide range as a performer, and I think that's where his success comes from. I think that he's extremely well-trained.

KW: *All of the statistics tell us that acting is an incredibly difficult profession. At any given time there are far more actors out of work than are working. However, Richard has defied these odds, enjoying* *quite a bit of success and a long career. In addition to all the other things you've told me, how has he done it?*

MG: How has Richard done it? He's done it because he's got an incredible agent.

KW: [Laughs] *Good answer.*

MG: I think we're a team, you know, I think that's really what it comes down to. We're a creative team.

There was a cartoon that I saw many years ago, probably in *The New Yorker*, and the guy standing there was saying, "I need to find a better agent." And the agent's response was, "Yeah, well, I need to find a better performer."

They have to have the talent and the ability. We have to have the savvy and the insight and the creativity of getting him in the rooms.

What are the keys that have led Richard Portnow to a successful acting career?

He has always approached acting as a business

Richard Portnow loves acting. However, his first foray into the craft was only to satisfy his curiosity—and to avoid the draft. So, unlike many actors, he started as an outsider.

And that point of view—standing on the outside looking in—helped him understand that acting is a business first and an art form second. He knows that he's a salesman promoting a product, himself: "I've made it my business to understand the business end of show business. And that's been *key* to my success."

He pitches positive

In his first interview with an agent Richard "pitched positive." He looked incredibly stylish and *spoke the language of the agent* when he told Jonathan Sand of Writers and Artists Agency, "We're going to make nothing but money."

Even though no other agent would sign him on as a client, because Richard was so convincing, Jonathan Sand did.

He has mastered the mental aspect of auditions

A year after promising Sand to make him a pile of cash Richard hadn't landed a single acting job because he had been carrying his nerves into auditions with him. Finally, deciding that he had nothing to lose, he started to just have fun. And that decision proved incredibly valuable. He *relaxed and took the edge off of auditions*—and started booking "job after job after job."

When Richard arrived in LA, "with a loaded gun," after filming two major movies in a row, he felt successful and confident. In his mind (and in reality) he was already a winner. The perfect storm of being the new guy in town, confidence, talent and relaxation was irresistible to directors and they cast him in *twelve jobs in a row*. (If this isn't a record, I'd be surprised.)

He is always confident

Richard calls confidence his best quality. It's also his most effective quality because it wins him jobs: "That's the name of the game. It is *all* about confidence."

How could it not be when decision makers must trust the actor with their very important and often very expensive movie or TV show?

Yet, Richard's confidence never goes too far. Richard Gabai respects his ability to walk "the line between confidence and arrogance."

He embraces his type and his own personal style

Early on, Richard had a problem not uncommon for young actors: he wanted to play a variety of roles (and knew he was capable of it), yet also knew that casting a wide net wouldn't get him what he wanted—work as an actor.

So he made the decision to *embrace his type.*

In auditions he knew what he should and shouldn't do ("I don't kiss the girl."), what he should wear ("I'm a suit.") and where he belonged ("I'm not rural. I'm urban.").

Embracing his type catapulted Richard from bartender/actor to working actor. And he eventually started getting cast in a variety of roles because he had been willing to give up something to get something else.

He is nice and gracious—and it always pays off

Directors like to work with actors who don't bring unwanted attitudes or baggage onto a set and Richard embodies this. When he agreed to play a very small role in a film directed by Richard Gabai, he "killed the scene" and was a joy to work with. That gesture of humility and giving led Gabai to cast him again in a much larger role. And it seems the relationship will continue on and on.

He is a true professional

Richard has made it his business to know everything he needs to know, in order to do everything he needs to do as an actor.

He prepares intensely for auditions by reading the entire script, memorizing his lines and researching not only his character, but all the key players on the film or TV show.

Gabai calls his set etiquette "without peer" and relates how Richard arrives early and has mastered "the mechanics of acting" that are so very important for acting in front of a camera. Gabai also has trust in Richard's performances and knows that when he shows up on a set, "I am done…I'm not worried about a thing… he can bring it."

He is talented

Film and television seems to favor very attractive people. Sometimes looks seem to be as important as talent. Not so for character actors like Richard. They must bring their finely tuned acting skills to every role.

Richard Portnow has been a very successful actor for more than twenty-five years, working with some of the finest directors in show business on some of their finest films. There are many reasons for his success, but the biggest one is that he is immensely talented.

CHAPTER 11

The Master Keys

We have explored the journeys of ten working actors and talked with their success teams. We have found that each actor's career is unique with keys specific to him or her, keys that set each actor apart.

Now we will examine the keys that all or most of these actors share—the master keys to their success.

1. They have a powerful work ethic

"Hard work pays off" is almost a cliché; it seems required for success in just about any profession. And because show business is so very competitive, one would think every actor would be inspired to work hard.

Yet agents and managers repeatedly mentioned actors who don't do the work required, who don't memorize audition scenes, or return phone calls or put in a forty-hour work week.

So, why don't they work hard?

In a profession as elusive as acting, it's often difficult to gauge one's progress. And when actors can't see their work paying off, their inspiration is sometimes diminished. They hold back.

And sometimes fear holds them back.

These actors have moved past their fear. They understand deeply that hard work equals results. Their agents and managers all agreed, saying that a powerful work ethic is not only important, but key to their actors' success. And that work isn't random; it's *focused* and *consistent*.

How do they work hard?

✓ Jose Llana scours the trade papers looking for roles and people he knows who are connected with upcoming musicals;

✓ Eric Ladin watches countless hours of television to understand the various dramatic styles in shows he auditions for;

✓ John Tartaglia creates his own work through writing and producing;

✓ James Earl networks by performing in musical and improv shows;

✓ Tony Yazbeck uses his excellent web site to market himself, creating a powerful impression of an actor who works often, plays a variety of roles and has style.

2. They have talent

To portray a fictional character truthfully requires talent. Yet sometimes its value seems to be diminished when the most talented actor isn't cast.

Why isn't the most talented actor always cast? Often because, as several interviewees pointed out, the most talented actor isn't the most "right" actor for a given role. He or she is too old, too young, too dark, too tall and so on.

And there are sometimes other things that trump talent.

- ✓ *Lack of star power:* When Bonnie Monte fought for Robert Clohessy to play the lead in a Broadway revival of *A Streetcar Named Desire,* "they didn't want him because he wasn't famous enough";

- ✓ *Multiple decision makers:* Richard Gabai sometimes works with actors he didn't cast: "maybe they didn't even audition. They were hired by some other producer";

- ✓ *Sales to foreign markets, favors to friends:* Ross Dinerstein said that even though, "...talent is the most important thing. There are always other factors that come into casting decisions—foreign value and studio decisions and political things and friends of friends";

- ✓ *Circumstances out of an actor's control:* Eric Ladin said, "Maybe the producer broke up with a blonde boyfriend and you walk in and you're blonde and they're like, 'I'm not having it. He looks like my ex-boyfriend.'"

Even with all these obstacles, our success team members overwhelmingly agreed that talent is extremely important, perhaps most important, to their actor's success.

- ✓ Richard Gabai on Richard Portnow: "At the end of the day, it's talent. I mean he didn't get that huge role in *Hitchcock* because he's nice";

- ✓ Bonnie Monte on Robert Clohessy: "That's the biggest factor in his success";

✓ Richard Schmenner on Tony Yazbeck: "Oh, 100%";

✓ Ross Dinerstein on Eric Ladin: "I think talent is the most important thing";

✓ Marcia Milgrom Dodge on Gary Beach: "It's everything";

✓ Matt Floyd on James Earl: "Everything. I mean if he wasn't talented he wouldn't have gotten where he is";

✓ Michael Einfeld on John Tartaglia: "You can be a nice guy, if you're not talented who cares? …Talent's going to win out in the end."

3. They make the right decisions at critical moments

All of these actors have made strategic decisions at critical moments, big choices that led to big results, even breakthroughs in their careers.

✓ Gary Beach swallowed his pride and paid his own way to New York to do a workshop of a new musical; his decision made him a Tony winner and a Broadway star;

✓ Robert Clohessy followed his heart and kept his word when he turned down a lucrative job to take another, less lucrative job; his decision led to his first television series;

✓ Debra Monk couldn't buy an acting job so she wrote and performed in her own show; her decision led to her Broadway debut and Tony nominations;

✓ Richard Portnow "got it" early on when he realized that treating acting as a business would yield results; his decision led him to an enormously successful career as a character actor;

✓ Krysta Rodriguez humbled herself and accepted yet another ensemble role, trusting that something good would come out of it; it did when it led to a break-through performance on Broadway;

✓ Eric Ladin attended college in Los Angeles, so he could start his career while still in school; when he graduated with a SAG card, a manager and an agent, his decision gave him a huge jump on other young actors;

✓ Jose Llana courageously faced his parents to tell them he had chosen acting as his profession; his decision led to nonstop work on Broadway for years.

4. They have confidence

Practically everyone I interviewed agreed that confidence is important to an actor's success. And although these actors are real people with real problems, when it comes to their work they have confidence.

Why is confidence so important for an actor?

✓ Meg Mortimer said Krysta Rodriguez's confidence led her to book the first television pilot she tested for;

✓ Tracy Steinsapir believes Eric Ladin's confidence got him through a year in which he didn't land a single acting job and was dropped by his agents: "You have to believe in yourself because you're getting so much rejection. It's the only way";

✓ Richard Portnow said that in auditions, "That's the name of the game. It is *all* about confidence…Own the room, own the audition. It's your time. Walk in brimming with confidence";

✓ James Earl calls confidence "the main secret to acting."

5. They take risks

Risk is hard for most people. It requires a leap into the unknown and often a willingness to give up one thing to have another.

However, most of the actors in this book have taken risks. They were willing to take them, I believe, because their deep need for an acting career was more important than their fear of the risks not panning out.

They faced their fears and then—to paraphrase John Tartaglia—*jumped*.

✓ Debra Monk flew to Kentucky at her own expense, and without an agent submission, to audition for a major regional theatre company; her risk paid off big with role after role at that theatre, a New York agent and straight plays on Broadway;

✓ Tony Yazbeck gave up the security of steady employment in Broadway ensembles to move into principal roles; his risk led him to critically acclaimed roles in Broadway musicals;

✓ James Earl had the courage to break away from his tough upbringing and the smarts to teach himself to act; his risk got him out of trouble and into an acting career;

✓ Eric Ladin turned down an offered role on a series to screen test for another series; his risk won him the role he wanted and launched his career in high quality television;

✓ John Tartaglia quit a steady and lucrative puppeteering job on a high profile television show for an unpaid workshop; his risk paved the way for his Broadway debut and a Tony nomination.

6. They've mastered the skill of auditioning

Almost every actor has to audition to be cast and auditions are not always the most pleasant experiences. Yet, until someone comes up with a better system, auditioning will remain the go-to method for getting work as an actor.

It is absolutely mandatory that actors become outstanding auditioners. As Eric Ladin said, performing in the role is the easy part, "the hard part is busting your ass and trying to get the gig."

And outstanding auditions require thorough preparation. For many actors part of that preparation is trying to fulfill the director's vision of the role.

Yet, working actors know the value of bringing *their own vision of the role* to the audition.

Great auditions require craft preparation, mental preparation and social preparation.

Craft preparation includes reading the entire script, memorizing the scene and analyzing it. Based on that analysis, good actors make unique, even risky choices—they stand out:

✓ Making his character in *Wonderland* a "ridiculously over ethnic goofball" landed Jose Llana a leading role on Broadway;

✓ Singing more than the script required of a funny song to make it even funnier got Debra Monk a recurring role on *White Collar*.

Craft preparation also means working harder than other actors:

✓ Tony Yazbeck challenges himself to prepare more thoroughly than anyone: "I try to make it so that there's no excuse I didn't get it, other than the fact that it's out of my hands";

✓ Eric Ladin said, "I never want to be the guy that's not prepared";

✓ Jose Llana prepares so extensively for auditions that Steven Lutvack believes "the work ethic and Jose are sort of inseparable."

Mental preparation helps actors relax and go into a creative "zone," so they can do their best work with ease and confidence and execute the choices they decided on in their craft preparation:

✓ Robert Clohessy needs to be in a mental state "where you just don't freaking care," and uses the circumstances in the audition room and the actual relationship with the casting director to create a more grounded reality for his character;

✓ James Earl relaxes by breathing deeply before stepping into the audition room so "when you go in there you can control what you're doing";

✓ Eric Ladin is so confident and loose when he walks into an audition room that he can be enthusiastic about wanting the job, yet never conveys any neediness;

✓ Richard Portnow uses all his actor training, filtered through his own point of view, to "win" in every audition.

Social preparation, which is especially important for film and television auditions, includes the ability to *create rapport* with the auditors. The agents and managers I spoke with emphasized how important it was for directors, producers and writers to feel comfortable with actors because, if cast, they'll be spending many long days together.

✓ Eric Ladin and James Earl are superb in "working a room"; their humor and genuine interest in everyone there, their reps agree, have been key to booking job after job.

Finally, these actors know that every time they audition it's not just for one role, it's for all the future roles that director or casting director will see them for.

7. They know and play their essential qualities

All the actors I interviewed understand who they are and how others see them. They know and play their essential qualities. Every time they walk into an audition room they walk in with authenticity. They may not always get the role, but they always make an impression.

- ✓ Richard Portnow knows he's "a suit," who is much more urban than rural;

- ✓ James Earl is a physically imposing actor with a sensitive side, and is also very funny;

- ✓ Krysta Rodriguez has used her natural quality to create her "own brand in the middle";

- ✓ Robert Clohessy has mastered playing characters with a strong physical presence, like cops and underworld thugs;

- ✓ Eric Ladin has played a range of characters, yet most have a prominent dark side.

8. They have a great business/success team

To create a career in acting it takes a team. All ten actors in this book have an agent and some have managers.

Good agents and managers have valuable relationships in the industry that get their actors into audition rooms, the show business background and legal expertise required to negotiate favorable contracts, and the experience to provide actors with wise counsel.

These professionals have played profound roles in their actors' careers:

- ✓ Tony Yazbeck's manager and a veteran casting director helped him advance from ensemble to leading roles on Broadway;

- ✓ Krysta Rodriguez's manager helped her reach new levels—a breakthrough series regular role on television and her name above the title on Broadway;

- ✓ James Earl's agent and managers love working with him and collaborate seamlessly with one another;

- ✓ John Tartaglia and Eric Ladin have long time relationships with their teams, based on mutual trust and respect.

A strong business/success team also creates *synergy*. Two or three people sharing a common goal are much more powerful than only one.

9. They have perseverance

Nobody likes rejection. Yet actors face it on a regular basis. Over and over the actors in this book told me about roles they missed out on and disappointments they encountered. Yet,

- ✓ Just like a prize fighter, every time Debra Monk has been knocked down she has gotten back up; her perseverance got her into graduate school, and the training she received there laid the groundwork for a stellar career;

✓ When she was rejected by her high school musical theatre department, Krysta Rodriguez tried again and was
accepted; when she couldn't get an audition for *Spring
Awakening*, she persevered and the show ignited her
career;

✓ When his run of Broadway shows came to a screeching
halt, Jose Llana was "demolished," yet the sense of perspective he learned helped him to persevere and become
a mainstay of New York theatre.

The difference between successful and unsuccessful actors
is not in the rejection itself, but in the way each *responds* to the
rejection. Most actors respond by eventually quitting. Successful
actors just keep going. They learn from their mistakes and grow
from their rejections. They persevere.

10. They "make it happen for themselves"

Jose Llana made the above statement about successful performers,
and it's true for all the actors in this book. They are self-starters,
entrepreneurs who know that ultimately *they* are responsible for
the success or failure of their careers. They follow their own unique
path trusting their own choices. Although those choices may not
be right for someone else, they are exactly right for them.

Almost every one of them made a decision, either consciously
or unconsciously, to be an actor and then followed it up with a
series of other decisions that narrowed their career possibilities
to just one profession.

This laser beam focus on acting has been a major key to their
success.

✓ James Earl: "It's only Plan A…you have to figure out how you're going to do that…for me it's just straight determination, being determined to do whatever, by any means necessary";

✓ Krysta Rodriguez: "There was no kind of question 'I want to be a veterinarian or an astronaut.' It was like 'this is it'";

✓ Tony Yazbeck: "I might as well have been four-years-old when I knew this was all I wanted to do";

✓ Gary Beach: "I just had to make it work out";

✓ Jose Llana: "my senior year in high school…I told myself 'I need to go for it'";

✓ Eric Ladin: "I always knew that I wanted to do this… and I was going to be successful at this."

CHAPTER 12

Take the First Step

You've read the book—thank you—and thought about the keys. Now what?

Get to work! Here are three important and accessible keys you can put into action now.

1. Find and play your essential qualities

The ability to define yourself is one of the most powerful marketing tools you have as an actor.

Where do you start?

➤ Ask friends to describe how they see you. Have them use one word descriptions like upbeat, positive, inspiring; or mysterious, quirky, strange. Ask at least five people you know and write down their answers for future reference. You'll probably start to see similarities in their descriptions;

➤ Look for patterns in roles you've played. Are you always the bad guy, the perky one, the best friend? You've probably been cast in those roles because directors see the qualities of those "types" in you;

➤ Become aware of the emotions you relate to most. Are you comfortable with anger? Or are you mellow and rarely get stressed out? It's important to know the feelings that seem natural to you, for they are the ones that others (e.g., audiences) see emanating from you;

➢ Identify prototypes.

Richard Portnow described perfectly how actors can use prototypes when he said, "If you can equate yourself with someone, then they know what to do with you, how to pitch you. They're waiting for you to tell them."

2. Start creating a great business/success team

You may already have an agent or manager—great. As we've discussed, they are mandatory for an acting career.

However, if you don't have one *yet* go ahead and start building your business/success team now with a different makeup. Your group could include:

➢ members of a theatre company that you're in;

➢ a group that reads new plays or screenplays;

➢ a support group with other actors and industry professionals; or

➢ one or two friends with goals like yours.

As your career grows your team will change and grow. However, the important thing is to always have a team. People with mutual needs who come together and help each other create something very powerful.

3. Master the skill of auditioning

As actors and success team members said over and over learning how to audition well is essential for success in acting. And for actors just starting out the lack of this skill is often an Achilles' heel. Here's what I suggest:

> ➤ Read, re-read and absorb Michael Shurtleff's twelve guideposts from *Audition*; then start using them in your auditions;

> ➤ Enroll in the best audition class you can find;

> ➤ Discover as many audition techniques as possible through books (several excellent ones are listed in "Recommended Reading") and through actor training web sites, videos and blogs;

> ➤ If you are just starting out, audition for anything and everything you can. I would recommend going out for every role you feel you have a shot at, as extreme as it may seem, just for the experience;

> ➤ As you start to feel more confident in auditions, and start playing your essential qualities, begin to audition for only the roles you are right for.

The ten actors in this book have looked inside, made decisions and taken action to create successful careers.

I hope their journeys serve as inspiration for your own.

Recommended Reading

Here are some excellent books on the acting business and auditioning that I highly recommend.

Brandon, Mark. *Winning Auditions: 101 Strategies for Actors*. New York: Limelight, 2005.

Callan, K. *How to Sell Yourself as an Actor: from New York to Los Angeles (and everywhere in between!)*. Studio City: Sweden; 6th edition, 2008.

Gillespie, Bonnie and Blake Robbins. *Acting Q's: Conversations with Working Actors*. Hollywood: Cricket Feet, 2005.

Henry, Mari Lyn, and Lynne Rogers. *How to Be a Working Actor: The Insider's Guide to Finding Jobs in Theater, Film & Television*. New York: Back Stage Books; 5th edition, 2007.

Kerr, Judy. *Acting Is Everything: An Actor's Guidebook for a Successful Career in Los Angeles*. September; 11th edition, 2006.

Lyndon, Amy. *The Lyndon Technique: The 15 Guideline Map To Booking Handbook*. Los Angeles: I Am Enough, 2009.

Martinez, Tony. *An Agent Tells All*. Hit Team, 2005.

Merlin, Joanna. *Auditioning: An Actor-Friendly Guide*. New York: Vintage, 2001.

O'Neill, Brian. *Acting As a Business: Strategies For Success*. New York: Vintage; 4th Rev edition, 2009.

Pugatch, Jason. *Acting Is a Job: Real Life Lessons about the Acting Business*. New York: Allworth Press, 2006.

Shurtleff, Michael. *Audition: Everything an Actor Needs to Know to Get the Part*. New York: Bantam, 1979.

Tichler, Rosemarie, and Barry Jay Kaplan. *Actors at Work*. Faber & Faber, 2007.

About the Author

Photograph: David Grapes

KEN WOMBLE is an Associate Professor of Theatre at the University of Northern Colorado. As a New York and Los Angeles actor for over fifteen years he appeared in two Off Broadway premieres and was the voice of a BBC radio announcer in *Freud's Last Session* at New World Stages. He recurred on *Guiding Light* and three other soaps.

Ken continues to act regionally in such productions *The 39 Steps*, *Private Lives*, *God of Carnage* and *Picnic* (regional award Best Actor) at Colorado's Little Theatre of the Rockies. He is a member of Actors Equity and SAG/AFTRA.

He frequently directs, including *The Odd Couple* (*Female version*) at Colorado's Little Theatre of the Rockies, and award winning productions of *The Three Sisters* and *Dancing at Lughnasa*. For television Ken directed the situation comedy pilot *Under the Desk*.

Ken was commissioned by the University of Northern Colorado to write and direct the first-ever documentary film on novelist James Michener, *James A. Michener, An Epic Life*. His adaptations of *A Midsummer Night's Dream* and two other classics have been produced throughout the U.S.

He coaches actors for film, television and Broadway, and conducts audition and film acting workshops at numerous venues. Please visit his web site, kenwomble.com, for upcoming workshops.

Ken lives in the foothills of the Rocky Mountains with his wife Sandy.